JOURNEY FROM THE GALLOWS

Historical Evolution of the Penal Philosophies and Practices in the Nation's Capital

Mary Hostetler Oakey

Edited by

Belinda Swanson

UNIVERSITY PRESS OF AMERICA

Lanham • New York • London

Copyright © 1988 by

University Press of America,® Inc.

4720 Boston Way
Lanham, MD 20706

3 Henrietta Street
London WC2E 8LU England

All rights reserved

Printed in the United States of America

British Cataloging in Publication Information Available

Library of Congress Cataloging-in-Publication Data

Oakey, Mary Hostetler, 1919- .
Journey from the gallows : historical evolution of the penal philosophies and practices in the Nation's Capital / by Mary Hostetler Oakey : edited by Belinda Swanson.
p. cm.
Includes bibliographies and index.
1. Criminal justice, Administraion of—District of Columbia—History. 2. Corrections—District of Columbia—History. 3. Prisons—District of Columbia—History. I. Swanson, Belinda. II. Title.
364.6'09753—dc19 HV9955.D6015 1988 87-29423 CIP

ISBN 0-8191-6723-1 (alk. paper)

All University Press of America books are produced on acid-free paper which exceeds the minimum standards set by the National Historical Publications and Records Commission.

TO: Harry, Linda, Dianne, Warren, Jon, Kisha and Kindra

364.09753
O11
88-1563

TABLE OF CONTENTS

PART IV

APPENDICES

PREFACE

This book provides a comprehensive history of the District of Columbia's penal system from its beginning in 1800 to 1982. In that span of 182 years, three major correctional philosophies were practiced in the District. They were: the Penitentiary Movement, the Experimental Industrial Farm Movement, and the Rehabilitation Movement. In presenting the material in this book, I have attempted to show the evolution of those three theories as they were set to actual practice in the District of Columbia penal system.

The writing of this book could not have been possible without the assistance and support of many people. I am indebted to the District of Columbia Department of Corrections for granting me access to documents and records vital to researching the material. My deepest appreciation to the following employees of the Department, both present and retired, who granted interviews or shared bits of information from personal experience that helped to provide details which are not in written form: Irma Clifton, Joan Peed, Mildred Burdette, Calvin Scott, Dr. Donald L. Clark, Mary Frances and Ernest Petitt, William and Mary Ann Leatherland, Jack and Bess Garrott, Marcel Pfalsgraf, Kermit Weakly, Joseph Seaman, Paul Preston, John Preston, James Freeman, Ron Harbin, Thomas Sard, Anthony Del Popolo, Dr. William Carr, LeRoy Anderson, Michael Hagstad, Robert Delmore, Lorie Lewis, and Gordon Beach.

I also wish to express my appreciation to the employees of the following Federal agencies whose help was invaluable to me: Mrs. Harriet Grier, Armed Forces Medical Museum; Herbert Collins of the Smithsonian Institution; and Susan Lemke and Tina Lavato of the National War College, Fort McNair, Washington, D.C.

Special acknowledgement is given to F.E. Peters, an inmate confined in the D.C. Jail in the 1950s, who compiled information entitled "A Short History of The Washington Jails" from old records and registers on file in the Jail at that time. His effort is a valuable contribution to the history of the D.C. Jails, since some of the records he used were later destroyed or lost during the move from the old D.C. Jail to the new Detention Center in 1976.

I especially appreciate the assistance of Pat Stokes who typed the manuscript, and Bob Oakey for his assistance with the photography.

M.H.O

INTRODUCTION

ORIGIN OF THE CRIMINAL JUSTICE SYSTEM IN THE DISTRICT OF COLUMBIA

Since it was organized almost two hundred years ago, the Criminal Justice System of the District of Columbia has undergone many changes and alterations in both the practice of criminal law and the detention of offenders. This book attempts to encompass those changes and to provide an accurate chronicle of the development of the District's Correctional System. It is hoped that the sometimes lengthy quotes contained herein will serve to give the reader a sense of the times which compelled their recording.

The District of Columbia was created by the First Congress and became a Federal District in 1800. Situated on a piece of land ten miles square, it was composed of a portion of Maryland and a portion of Virginia. Section Two of the Organic Act of 1801 formed the District into two counties. The portion ceded by Maryland was known as Washington County, and included the municipality of Georgetown, and the newly developed City of Washington, or the "Federal City" as it was sometimes called then. The portion ceded by Virginia was known as Alexandria County and included the Town of Alexandria.

Both Federal and local officials were faced with the task of establishing a form of government that would meet the needs of the District as well as those of the Nation's Capital; a situation that created a blending of the two governments that has continued through the years. In the beginning, many problems were encountered, especially pertaining to trial law and the detention of prisoners. The difficulty arose in part as a result of the unique way in which the District of Columbia was created, and in part because of the haste with which the First Congress established the laws that would govern the Nation's Capital. In Section One of the Organic Act of 1801, the Congress declared that the laws of the State of Maryland and the laws of the State of Virginia "as they now exist, shall be and continue in force in that part of the District of Columbia, which was ceded by said State to the United States."[1]

Without considering the far-reaching consequences of its action, the Congress inflicted upon the newly formed District a situation in which two counties under the some legislative jurisdiction would be governed by two systems of law. In effect, when court convened in Alexandria County, it was governed by Virginia laws, and when it was held in Washington County, by Maryland laws. In addition, a circuit court was established with general jurisdiction both civil and criminal to hold sessions alternately in each county. The corporate rights of the Towns of Alexandria and Georgetown, however, were left intact, except for matters relating to judicial powers.

An even greater problem was created by the fact that as late as 1800, a large portion of the laws of both Maryland and Virginia had remained unchanged since Colonial days in America. These were the primative laws and cruel modes of punishing criminals brought to this country by colonists from England and other European countries.

> ...In Alexandria County alone, the law punished thirty crimes with death, while in Washington County, there were fourteen capital crimes. Among the capital crimes were burglary to the extent of $4; breaking out of prison by a person charged with felony; a slave preparing or giving medicine with bad intent; maliciously burning any house; breaking or entering a storehouse or tobacco house or stealing to the value of five shillings. On the Virginia side of the river, it was said that the life of a man is valued at $4, while on the Maryland side, the price is but five shillings.[2]

As late as the year 1817, a sentence of branding was executed. "In that year during a term of the circuit court held in the capitol, a man convicted of bigamy was branded with the letter T on the hand in open court."[3] The whipping-post, was continued in use until a law of March 3, 1831 modernized the criminal laws, and imprisonment, at least for free persons, was substituted.

The cruelty and indifference towards the value of human life that prevailed during the Colonial era had declined, and the citizens as well as the judges and juries of the District of Columbia resented the retention on the statute books of laws of an earlier age. So abhorrent were such outdated modes of punishment that the Intelligencer, a local newspaper, characterized them as "barbarous, at least a century too old for the refinement of the present age."[4]

An indication of the citizenry's attitude toward the old laws is exemplified in court records reflecting the outcome of jury trials. Though corporal and capital punishments for offenses such as larceny and housebreaking existed on the statute books through the first third of the 19th Century, juries would often find defendants guilty of lesser offenses in order to avoid imposing such penalties. Additionally, judges used their discretionary powers and tried and sentenced defendants under codes exacting lesser penalties (where the statutes of two separate jurisdictions applied). For instance, in some cases punishment under United States law was less severe than under codes existing in the local jurisdiction. "For the first fifty years of the circuit court but three sentences of hanging were carried out, although they were imposed in a number of cases, but was set aside by executive clemency, in most cases because the penalty was excessive."[5]

The beginning of the 19th Century marked a trend toward a more humane type of punishment for criminals, popularly known as the "Penitentiary Movement." This new concept was seen by both the courts and the citizenry as a solution in dealing with the outmoded laws in force in the District of Columbia at that time. A penitentiary would provide the courts with the alternative of imposing prison terms for offenders convicted of lesser crimes, thus avoiding the use of such archaic forms of sentencing as branding, whipping, and hanging, which were legal modes of punishment in the District until 1831. Therefore, from the summer of 1814, when the lotteries were authorized to raise funds for constructing public buildings, until 1826, when the Penitentiary Act was passed by Congress, a continuous effort was made by the City Council to erect such an institution.

It was not until 1816 that Congress made an effort to remedy the situation created by saddling the District with a mass of outmoded laws. In that year, Congress gave Judge W. Cranch the authority to codify the laws of the District. Two years later, November 19, 1818, Judge Cranch signed the preface of his proposed code indicating that the revision had been completed. "This code was obviously designed for enactment by Congress, but no official action was taken with respect to it."[6]

The task of compiling the mass of old laws, many of which were written in antiquated English and redundant verbiage, into a Code for the District was attempted on at least four or five additional occasions throughout the 19th Century. Each was formally submitted to Congress for approval but simply ignored or voted down by the citizenry. The retrocession of Alexandria County to Virginia in 1846 provided some relief, since after that date the District was only concerned with Maryland laws.

It was not until November, 1895, when the Washington Board of Trade extended an invitation to Mr. Justice Walter S. Cox of the Supreme Court of the District of Columbia to undertake the preparation of a code based on the existing Code of Maryland that a code was finally approved. Judge Cox, with the aid of a committee from the District Bar Association, spent between four or five years preparing the Code.

> The committee served without compensation over a period of nearly three months, during which time they were excused by the court from all trial work in order that they might give their entire attention to the subject. The cost of stenographic services, printing, etc., was paid by voluntary contributions by members of the committee and of the Bar.
>
> * * *
>
> The proposed code was introduced in the House of Representatives on March 21, 1900, by the Honorable John J. Jenkins of Wisconsin. It was reported to the House on April 14, 1900, and passed on May 28, 1900. It was reported in the Senate on December 15, 1900 by Senator Prichard, and passed by that body on March 2, 1901. It was approved by the President on March 3, 1901.[7]

Approval of the Code prepared by Judge Cox and the Bar Committee brought to an end a century of frustration in the courts, precipitated by the careless haste of the First Congress in giving the District of Columbia its laws.

Since its organization in 1800, the District of Columbia has experienced several changes in its form of government. A brief overview of those changes appears in Appendix A.

SOURCES

[1.] Organic Act of 1801, District of Columbia Code Annotated, 1973 ed. (U.S. Government Printing Office, 1973), p. XXXV.

[2.] Bryan, Wilhelmus Bogard, A History of the National Capital, Vol. II (New York: The MacMillan Company, 1914), p. 84.

[3.] Ibid., p. 83.

[4.] Ibid., pp. 83-84.

[5.] Ibid., p. 85.

[6.] Historical, District of Columbia Code Annotated, 1973 ed. (U.S. Government Printing Office), p. XVII.

[7.] Ibid., p. XXII.

PART I
(1800-1909)

CHAPTER 1

EARLY JAILS OF THE DISTRICT OF COLUMBIA

Only one small jail existed within the boundaries of the District of Columbia when it was organized. The jail was located within the corporate limits of Georgetown. The newly built City of Washington and the County of Alexandria had no facilities for confining prisoners. The population of the District at that time was made up of 14,093 persons, consisting of 10,266 Whites, 783 free Negroes, and 3,244 slaves. With the arrival of Federal workers and others to the new capital of the nation, the population began to grow. It soon became necessary to provide facilities for confinement of offenders of the law.

Section Seven of the Organic Act of 1801 provided for a U.S. Marshal for the District of Columbia, who would have custody of the jails within its two counties, and who would be responsible for the safekeeping of prisoners committed to the jails. The marshal possessed the same powers and performed the same duties as the other U.S. Marshals.

Georgetown was a well established municipality with a population of 2,993 citizens when it became a part of the District of Columbia. Having been incorporated by a Maryland Act of 1789, it continued to maintain its own form of local government until its annexation to the City of Washington, nearly a century later, in 1898. The Georgetown Jail was located on "...the side where the Market house was built, ...where the town constables confined those they had arrested."[1] Since the jail was in operation at the time the District of Columbia was organized, it is often cited as being the District's first jail. It should be noted, however, that while it was the first jail, it operated independently and only offenders who were arrested within the corporate limits of the town were confined in Georgetown Jail. The Department of Corrections as we know it today has its roots in the first jail established in the City of Washington.

At the time Alexandria became a part of the District of Columbia, it was a prosperous port town with a population of almost 5,000 people, and a promising future in the export trade that some observers thought would someday rival that of the City of Baltimore. Known for its fine homes and grand social functions, Alexandria was said to be one of the most beautiful towns in Virginia. In fact, one old story has it that for a brief period of time Alexandria was being considered for the honor of becoming the Nation's Capital. The story goes that "...the patriot Washington was twitted with the advantages that would accrue to him, with such vast holdings of land so near the new Capital."[2] The tale goes further to say "...Washington waxed very angry and replied that never, if he could help it, should a public building be put south of the Potomac."[3]

Before becoming a part of the District of Columbia, offenders in the Town of Alexandria and the surrounding land that made up Alexandria County, were confined in the Fairfax County Jail. After the land became a part of the District, it was necessary for the Federal Government to rent a private house in the Town of Alexandria to serve as a jail until a more suitable facility could be built. The jail, which rented for the sum of $150 a year, was located on Market Square, and served that purpose until the early 1830s.

According to a letter written by Simon Summers in 1814 to the Honorable Joseph Lewis, Member of Congress, plans to build a jail in Alexandria were being discussed. He wrote "...respecting the building of a new jail in Alexandria which I wish to call your attention to. When the Courthouse and Jail in Fairfax County were built the Alexandrians were exempt and we in the County part of Alexandria had to pay a very grievious tax. I think it just and right that if a jail is now to be built in Alexandria that we should likewise be exempt from paying anything towards it..."[4] It was not, however, until an Act passed May 20, 1826, that Congress appropriated the sum of $10,000 for its construction.

When Alexandria's jail was finally built, it was a small structure with a gabled roof, located on N. St. Aspah Street in the Town of Alexandria. There is reason to believe that the gabled portion of Alexandria's present city jail is the same one designed by the Architect Charles Bulfinch and built in the early 1830s. An article appearing in the <u>Port Packet,</u> a local Alexandria newspaper, September 8, 1982, entitled "Suit Seeks Closure of City's Ancient Jail" notes: "The 200 year old structure on N. St. Aspah Street was deeded to Alexandria in 1846 and was originally designed as a city poor house."[5] An additional source notes that "An Act of Congress of March 2, 1831, provided for a payment to the Architect Charles Bulfinch, 'for extra services in planning and supervising the building of a jail in Alexandria.' The central section, with gable roof, may be the original structure, enlarged from time to time."[6]

The newly formed City of Washington had been laid out by the French Engineer Major Pierre Charles L'Enfant and others, but it was only partially completed in 1800 when President John Adams and family became residents of the White House. The population of Washington County, including the City of Washington consisted of 5,151 persons.

When it became necessary for officials of the City of Washington to confine offenders or to detain those who were awaiting action of the county court, a log house at New Jersey Avenue and D Street, Southeast, was used as a jail. While it remained in operation for only a few months, this structure is usually referred to as the first city jail and the foundation upon which the District of Columbia's penal system was built. Unfortunately, very little information is available regarding the physical aspects of the building or the events that may have taken place while it was used to confine prisoners.

The second facility to be used as a jail by the City of Washington was a small brick structure located on the North side of C Street, a short distance East of Sixth Street, Northwest, and served as a temporary jail until the completion of the First Circuit Court Jail in 1802.

It was while C Street building was in use that the first execution in the District of Columbia took place. James McGurk was found guilty of the murder of his wife, and was sentenced to be executed by hanging on August 28, 1802. He was, however, granted a reprieve of several months by the President of the United States. The following account of the hanging of McGurk appears in the June 18, 1900 edition of the Washington Post newspaper:

> ...He (McGurk) was the first important prisoner in the jail, also the first person hanged in the new center of government...By trade a bricklayer and a heavy indulger in liquid stimulants, he was likewise a wife-beater.
>
> Staggering home one day, he began to abuse and maltreat his spouse. Her condition was then too delicate for her to resist his inebriated onslaught. The unfortunate woman died of her injuries. McGirk (sic) was arrested, tried and convicted of murder and sentenced to be hanged. He was confined in the jail until the day of execution, when he was marched to the gallows...The scaffold could be seen from Pennsylvania Avenue, then little more than a country road...
>
> Old chroniclers recorded the dying sentiment of McGirk (sic) as 'When a man's character's gone, his life's gone.' Having uttered these words, the condemned murderer glanced toward the sun, and surprised the

> spectators by hurling himself from the scaffold, with the rope around his neck, before the 'jack ketch,' or executioner, had adjusted the cap over his head. The Priest called to McGirk (sic) not to end his life and the hangman began to pull and tug on the dangling body of McGirk (sic). He succeeded in getting McGirk's (sic) feet on the edge of the platform when the condemned man again pushed himself from the platform. There were three or four convulsive shrugs of the body, and the culprit died.
>
> The corpse was cut down and placed in a coffin for burial. Spectators slashed off portions of the rope as souveniors, it being believed by the superstitious that the bits of rope would cure aches and pains. The body was carted to Holmead's graveyard north of the city for interment.
>
> This caused a stir among those who had relatives buried there, and they were indignant to think a murderer had been buried in the cemetery. A party of citizens exhumed the body and reburied it in a ravine on ground owned by Col. M. Nourse. Acquaintances of McGirk (sic), determined not to be outdone, took up the coffin and buried it again in the cemetery, which only served to excite the citizens more. When the McGirk (sic) faction was off its guard the body was removed from the third grave and sunk in the ground in a perfect quagmire, near a stream east of the graveyard.[7]

Although the C Street building was used temporarily as a make-shift jail until the First Circuit Court Jail could be completed, it served the District for many years in other capacities. An article appearing in the _Times,_ a local Washington newspaper, dated May 2, 1896, noted that the building was still standing, although "it had fallen into decay." The article further commented that orders issued by the City's building inspector demanded that the structure either be repaired or torn down. Reflecting on the building's history, the article noted that in addition to having been used as an early jail, it was considered one of the antebellum landmarks of the City. The article also cites the building's use as a slave pen, noting: "Slaves captured in their efforts to escape from their masters were placed there for safekeeping until reclaimed, and those offered for sale were also incarcerated in the pen for the brief time necessary prior to the auction."[8] The article further mentions the use of the building as a bath house, citing that it was "in its day the only one in the District. All Washington patronized it and naturally the business flourished, there being no opposition and the establishment having really first-class accommodations."[9]

The C Street building has long since been dismantled and replaced by a more modern structure.

SOURCES

[1.] Bryan, Wilhelmus Bogart, A History of the National Capital, Vol. I (New York: The MacMillan Company, 1914), p. 286.

[2.] Moore, Gay Montague, Seaport in Virginia, George Washington's Alexandria (Richmond, Virginia: Garrett and Massie), p. 37.

[3.] Ibid., p. 37.

[4.] Summers, Simon, Copy of Letter to The Honorable Joseph Lewis, February 4, 1814, on file Alexandria Library, 717 Queen Street, Alexandria, Virginia.

[5.] Phillips, Rene, "Suit Seeks Closure of City's Ancient Jail," Port Packet, September 8-25, 1982.

[6.] Cox, Ethelyn, Historic Alexandria Street by Street, 1976, Historic Alexandria Foundation, p. 158.

[7.] "City's First Hanging," The Washington Post, June 18, 1900, (Clipping Packet) Washingtoniana Room, Martin Luther King Library, Washington, D.C.

[8.] Times, May 2, 1896, (Clipping Packet) Washingtoniana Room, Martin Luther King Library, Washington, D.C.

[9.] Ibid.

The C Street Jail also known as the McGurk Jail. Photograph copyright Washington Post; reprinted by permission of the D.C. Public Library.

CHAPTER 2

THE FIRST CIRCUIT COURT JAIL

The First Circuit Court Jail became the third facility to be used by the City of Washington to confine offenders of the law. In 1801, the First Congress appropriated $12,000 for its construction. The site chosen for the jail was Judiciary Square near E Street, just to the rear of City Hall. It was a two-story brick structure measuring 100 feet in length and 25 feet in width. The jail was ready for occupancy in 1802, and commitments were restricted to offenders sentenced by the circuit court. "In 1826, this limitation was removed and the marshal was directed to receive all persons committed by justices of the peace as vagrants and for disorder, etc."[1]

From the beginning, the physical structure was defective in many respects. An article appearing in the Washington Star newspaper, December 16, 1902, entitled "An Old-Time Prison" described it as "...having no modern conveniences and being no more than a mere prison house possessing no facilities - not so much as a yard in which the prisoners could enjoy exercise."[2] The article further noted: "Besides those confined there for trial or under sentence, there were others, including insane persons, runaway slaves, unfortunate debtors, and, in a few instances, the most incorrigible offenders of corporation law."[3] One such "incorrigible" offender, "...a celebrated gambler, known as Major Robert Bailey, who was confined under a charge of making a false affidavit, made his escape from the E Street building and went to a point beyond the jurisdiction of the District. When he found that the marshal had offered a reward for his capture, he in turn issued a hand bill, asking for the arrest of Col. Tench Ringgold, the marshal."[4]

Within a short time, the First Circuit Court Jail became too small to meet the needs of the growing prison population. By 1825, conditions in the jail had become so deplorable that Congress requested the Committee on the District of Columbia to investigate the matter. Doctor Louis Dwight, Secretary of the Prison Discipline Society, declared before the Committee, that the jail was radically defective in its plan and so totally unfit that it ought to be torn down. The Committee's findings verified Dr. Dwight's criticism as shown by the following excerpts from the report to Congress, February 1, 1825:

> ...They (the committee) are constrained to say, they have seldom witnessed a scene more shocking to the feelings of humanity than that exhibited in the prison of this city. The plan of the building is defective. It is much too

small also, to contain, with comfort, the number of persons often required to be kept in it. It is, therefore, frequently impossible for the keeper, by any care and attention, to render the condition of those committed to his charge, tolerable.

On the lower story are sixteen cells, each of eight feet square. In each cell is a small window, but no means of free ventilation. We are informed by the Marshal, that he is frequently under the necessity of confining to these cells, at one time, sixty or seventy unhappy human beings; some are convicted of crimes, and others committed for trial. It needs no arguments to prove, that, crowding four or five people together in a room of only eight feet square, and there closely confining them for several months, with no more means of enjoying fresh air than is furnished by these squalid cells, must occasion great human suffering. But this is only one sixteenth part of the misery which this wretched abode often contains.

* * *

By confining the convict and the person committed for trial, to the same room, all distinction between innocence and guilt, within the walls of the prison, where it ought most rigid to be maintained, is entirely lost. An innocent man who is poor and suspected, is condemned to suffer the same duress - breathe the same polluted air - eat the same provisions - associate with the same company - and partake of the same moral degredation, with the convicted felon.

* * *

The roof on the present jail in this city is in such a state of ruin and decay, that the rain comes down through the rooms and cells in every part of the building. The privies, sewers, and other parts of it are in such condition, that your Committee think it will be almost impossible, for any human being to inhabit it, during the heat of the approaching summer.[5]

An epigram on the First Circuit Court Jail describes the misery the prisoners must have endured: "To the debtors of old no burial was given! Here debtors, at present, are buried whilst living."[6]

The Committee first considered recommending that the jail be enlarged by building a third story, and repairing the existing structure. On closer investigation, however, it found that the repairs would be costly and the jail would still be defective. The Committee finally concluded that it would be advisable to build a new structure, and made that recommendation to Congress. The recommendation was not carried out. Instead, funds in the amount of $5,000 were appropriated by Congress in 1826, "...to alter and repair it and make it 'a suitable, convenient, healthy and comfortable prison.'"[7] The repairs were made, and although it was still defective and greatly overcrowded, the First Circuit Court Jail served the city for another 13 years. In 1839, it was replaced by an entirely new structure, known as the Second Circuit Court Jail.

Although the First Circuit Court Jail was defective, it did not remain vacant when the prisoners were transferred to the new jail. Instead, it was occupied by the Asylum, which included several public charities, from 1842 until 1846. After it was vacated by the Asylum, it was used by "...the medical faculty of Columbian College (now part of the George Washington University)...'for purposes of an infirmary, medical instruction, and scientific purposes...'"[8] The First Circuit Court Jail was destroyed by fire in 1861.

SOURCES

[1.] Peters, F.E., A Short History of the Jails of Washington (1802-1952), Unpublished, On file in the D.C. Department of Corrections Museum, Lorton, Virginia (2)

[2.] "An Old-Time Prison," Washington Star, December 16, 1902, Martin Luther King Library (Washingtoniana Room), Washington, D.C.

[3.] Ibid.

[4.] Ibid.

[5.] Report of the Committee on the District of Columbia (on the subject of prisons in the District), 18th Congress, 2nd Session, 1825, Gales and Seaton, Washington, D.C., pp. 1, 2, 4.

[6.] The Intelligencer, January 9, 1818, Washingtoniana Room, Martin Luther King Library, Washington, D.C.

[7.] "An Old-Time Prison," Washington Star, December 16, 1902, Washington, D.C.

[8.] A Brief History of District of Columbia General Hospital, District of Columbia Department of Public Health, Undated, On file in the D.C. Department of Corrections Museum, Lorton, Virginia, p. 1.

CHAPTER 3

ORIGIN OF THE WORKHOUSE IN THE DISTRICT OF COLUMBIA (1813-1910)

The District of Columbia's first workhouse was established to meet the need for dealing with vagrants, disorderly persons, and the more serious problem that arose from the increasing number of free Negroes who were entering the newly formed Nation's Capital. The city had the right to use the Circuit Court Jail for confining these petty offenders and vagrants, provided it could pay the charges that were conferred on the magistrates to keep them confined. Money, however, was in short supply in the city treasury, and the cost could not be met. As a result, the magistrates would return these individuals immediately to the community, thus perpetuating the problem.

A City Ordinance passed November 15, 1813, provided that a workhouse be established where "...negroes, free mulattoes, and vagrants..."[1] could be sent to work producing goods that could be sold to help defray the cost of their keep to the city. A house located at Greenleaf Point was rented to serve as the workhouse until a more permanent arrangement could be made.

Because money was not available for building institutions such as schools and other public buildings, a resolution was passed by the City Council and approved by the President of the United States permitting the City of Washington to hold lotteries for the purpose of public improvement. In the year 1814, and for several years following, lotteries were held with the hope of realizing a profit of $80,000, to be used to build the much needed workhouse, a school, and a penitentiary. The enterprise was not successful, and only the school fund was finally achieved. To make matters worse, the manager of the lotteries absconded with the prize money, and the city was placed deeply in debt to pay for the prizes.

In 1815, the workhouse was administratively combined with an almshouse, or poor house as it was commonly referred to, located on M Street between 6th and 7th Streets, Northwest. The two institutions were placed under the supervision of a Board of Guardians of the Poor, who in turn reported to the City Board of Aldermen. City officials did not see this as a satisfactory arrangement, but there was no alternative, since funds were not available to build a separate facility for the workhouse. Nevertheless, on April 15, 1821, a City Ordinance was passed naming the combined institutions the Washington Asylum. The two institutions remained together for almost a century. In 1839, the M Street building was declared unfit for use as an asylum.

An appeal was made to the President of the United States for the erection of a new asylum. The request was granted on May 10, 1843, and an Ordinance was passed providing for its construction on a portion of Public Reservation 13, on the eastern branch of the Potomac (Anacostia River).

From 1842 until the new building on Public Reservation 13 was completed in 1846, the Washington Asylum occupied the old First Circuit Court Jail. It was during that time that the third public institution, the first public hospital in the District, was added to the Washington Asylum:

> In 1832, the Board of Health presented to Congress the need for a general hospital for the Nation's Capital. Finally, on August 29, 1842, 10 years after the matter first was brought to the attention of Congress, this body appropriated $10,000 to be spent fitting up the old jail on Judiciary Square for use as an insane asylum. Repairs were completed, but it was found expedient to continue to send some insane patients to hospitals in other cities, and to confine others in jails and almshouses.
>
> * * *
>
> In 1846, the almshouse and workhouse, which had been consolidated...moved to the same site as that occupied by the new asylum, which consisted of over 60 acres of ground, now bounded by 19th Street, S.E., from E to B Streets...The inmates of the original Washington Infirmary (Poor House) were transferred along with other indigents, and the combined institution became known as "The Washington Asylum Hospital." Even so, it remained a place for the poor, infirm, diseased, vagrant, and disorderly persons, prisoners, and paupers.[2]

In 1842, George Watterson's book, <u>A New Guide to Washington,</u> was published. His description of the Asylum provides a glimpse into its operation:

> The Corporation maintains an Alms House or Asylum, for the accommodation and support of poor, infirm, and diseased persons, and lunatics, at an annual expense of near $5,000. The Asylum is a large but badly constructed edifice of brick, and has attached to it a

> Workhouse or Penitentiary, where offenders against the penal laws of the Corporation are confined; but from the defective system existing, are not punished by being made to labor much. The Asylum is under the direction of six guardians, appointed annually by the Mayor, &c, and who must meet once a week at least, to superintend the affairs of the Asylum, to attend to the wants of the poor, and to provide for the interment of such as have not the means of burial. They receive $50 per annum each, and employ a clerk at $100, and a physician, who receives $200 annually. The want of a Hospital for lunatics renders it necessary, though very inconvenient, to provide for their accommodation, in the same building with the poor and infirm. These unfortunate persons are allowed two dollars a week each for their support, and the amount annually appropriated varies from five to seven hundred dollars.[3]

Watterson further mentions the reform in the practice of confining insane persons in penal institutions in the District:

> ...Congress sympathizing in their (the lunatics) miserable condition, and desirous to meliorate it, passed an Act, in 1841, directing the Marshal of the District to cause all lunatics who are paupers, now confined in the jails of Washington and Alexandria, and who may hereafter be committed as lunatics, to be conveyed to the Lunatic Asylum of Baltimore, at the expense of the Government, provided the whole expense does not exceed three thousand dollars per annum. This Act is to continue in force until the 4th of March, 1843.[4]

Shortly after the Asylum took occupancy in the new building located on Reservation 13, the Board of Aldermen appointed a Select Committee to investigate the management of the institution, alleging that the Guardians had "departed from the precepts of the law, and the wholesome regulations previously made for the Government of the Asylum...destroyed to the great degree, all proper accountability in the purchase and issue of the supplies for the house,"[5] and failed to "furnish those additional comforts to the inmates of the Institution and effect such a reduction in its expenses as might be reasonably expected from the ample house and grounds furnished by the Corporation."[6]

The Board of Guardians resented the allegations made by the Select Committee, and their response tells of the problems they encountered in operating the Asylum:

> ...If they (the Committee) were so shocked at the state of it (the Asylum) at present, what would have been their feeling had they visited the department in the old house, with all the vagrants crowded into three small rooms, one 12' by 30' and two of them only 12 feet square. These vagrants are taken up from the gutters of the city, and the lowest filthy brothels, ragged, without shoes, many without shirts, and half clothed, drunken, and filthy in the extreme, when brought to the house for 30, 60, or 90 days; they must be confined in those rooms; this is done by having a closed stool set in the chimney, with a flue attached, and so closed as to be not offensive. They are cleansed when brought in as far as practicable, and required to keep themselves so; where work can be given to them in the garden or elsewhere; they are clothed as well as our limited means will permit; the shower-bath is used as a punishment for them and others, as it is in many other establishments in the country; but is never so used improperly, and is never intended with bad effects upon health; as there are not enough rooms to be had, the males must occupy one room (large) 14 by 35; the females another; there is not space enough to put up separate beds for all, would be doing injustice to those unsupplied; the rooms are always warm, of summer temperature - they therefore do no suffer from cold; they are probably more comfortable there than they ever were when out. When they are sick, they are better cared for. The objections of the Committee to the workhouse are increased in consequence of the vagrants having to suffer all the enormities pictured for having 'committed only trivial offenses, and in many instances, doubtful whether any offense was committed.' The Board may properly hand over this charge to be answered by the Council and the police magistrates. The Council makes laws, and the magistrates execute them -- our duty consists only in keeping them safe, providing what work for them, under such rules as we may make for their government, whilst in the house. In

fact, the evils of this matter lie in the want of a proper house, with separate cells, wherein each one could be confined and made responsible for its cleanliness, and by which means alone order and regularity could be preserved and in want of a variety of employment, under the custody of a proper man, paid for that purpose, under the Gardener and Intendant.

* * *

...As for the milk of the cows, the few eggs, and chickens, and ducks which the Committee have dignified by the title of 'produce of the cows and the barnyard'...There are at present two milch cows, the usual number; what they produce (small quantity) is used for the house. The poultry and cattle are the property of the asylum. There are 12 chickens, 6 geese, 6 ducks, raised last year...they are fed from offal from the house and by Mrs. Butt; part of the food for the cows is offal, slops, &c., from the house, and part is bought; they are fed by some of the inmates under the direction of Mrs. Butt who attends to all dairy duty personally...

* * *

...the Appropriation remains the same this year, which it was 20 years ago, though the population of the city has doubled, viz: $3,500. This, together with about five or six hundred dollars received from the garden, release of penitentiaries, sale of hogs, &c., is the amount with which we have to support an average of 90 to 100 inmates daily; provide for all the outdoor poor, pay the physician, purchase medicines and hospital stores, pay the gardener and wagoner, &c., giving only about 10 cents per day for each inmate. Could anything be spared from this to invest in improvements? Yet Council has been informed of this before. So far from increasing our means, our expenses have been increased by the addition of a hospital on the grounds for the reception of smallpox patients, placed in our charge, and required to be maintained out of the annual appropriation; no furniture provided; no means of procuring nurses, or accommodating them in

> that hospital -- so that, having to be furnished from the Asylum, the disease was introduced into the house, causing the death of many, and heavily increasing our expenses, already onerous. Against this we protested, setting forth the danger -- for want of proper means to make suitable arrangements -- of introducing it into the house...but in vain.[7]

In the year 1857, the building located on Reservation 13 was destroyed by fire. It was replaced by a new structure on the same site, which was first occupied by the Asylum on January 24, 1859.

In the latter part of the 19th Century, concern was shown for the women and children who were confined in the Workhouse. The Annual Report of the Commissioners of the District of Columbia, dated December 1, 1875, to the President of the United States reads:

> Attention is again called to the very large number of young persons confined from time to time in this institution. During the period covered by this report, there were 63 persons under 13 years of age; 78 were under 16 years of age; 339 persons who were under 18 years of age. Many of them were mere children, sometimes for petty offenses, and while confined here are necessarily the companions of bad and hardened characters. Cannot some provision of law be made to meet such cases, and provide for them in reform school or some other reformatory institution?[8]

No action was taken to relieve the situation of the children until the Board of Children's Guardians was established in 1892.

The annual report of the Commissioners of the District of Columbia for 1876 contains a plea by Timothy Lubey, Commissioner, for improvement in the conditions under which the women were confined in the Workhouse:

> ...There are now confined in the workhouse of the District a number of women for the crime of 'vagrancy,' enticing prostitution, and the like. These poor creatures repeat their offenses so often that the majority of their lives are passed in the workhouse, during which

> no special effort is made toward their reformation, nor are the influences of the surroundings of a workhouse calculated to direct a change in their mode of life; in other words, they are poor outcasts, heartily shunned by their own sex and abandoned by the others.
>
> * * *
>
> The object of this communication is to call your attention to the necessity existing for a reformatory institution of some kind, under the direct control of the District government, where these women can be sent and cared for and where their time and labor can be utilized both to themselves and the state, and where a special effort can be made and certain influences thrown around them looking to a change and reformation in their lives, and molding their minds and character toward a happier and better end.[9]

Unfortunately, no steps were taken to remedy the situation of the women until early in the 20th Century.

The inmate population of the Workhouse grew steadily throughout the 19th Century. In the early years of its operation, the average daily population was around 90 inmates. By 1897, however, the population had reached 400, making it necessary to build a new wing to accommodate the prisoners. In 1904, Congress appropriated additional funds for still another wing, which was completed in 1907.

Although there is mention of a "chain gang" made up of Workhouse prisoners during the 1880s for cleaning up the Eastern Market and the streets, idleness still prevailed. Because of the constant overcrowding, there was never enough work to keep the entire population occupied. One interesting note in connection with the "chain gang" is a complaint made by the Superintendent of the Asylum that too many of the inmates were escaping from the gang. He "...recommended that all escaped prisoners from the 'chain gang' be put in irons for the remainder of their confinement."[10]

The overcrowded conditions of the Workhouse, together with the idleness that accompanied it, and the dilapidated condition of the structure itself, generated widespread concern and criticism both locally and throughout the nation. The public felt that such deplorable conditions should not exist in a penal institution in the Nation's Capital. As a result of the adverse publicity, both federal and local officials were prompted to seek measures to provide more suitable accommodations for the inmates of the Workhouse.

In the year 1900, the Board of Charities was created and the Washington Asylum was placed under its supervision. In 1903, the Alms House was moved to Blue Plains. In 1910, the Workhouse was separated from the Washington Asylum Hospital.

SOURCES

[1.] Bryan, Wilhelmus Bogart, _A History of the National Capital,_ Vol. I (New York: The MacMillan Company, 1914), pp. 8, 9.

[2.] A Brief History of the District of Columbia General Hospital, D.C. Department of Public Health, Undated, Copy on file in the D.C. Department of Corrections Museum, Lorton, Virginia, pp. 1, 2.

[3.] Watterson, George, _A New Guide to Washington,_ (Washington, D.C.: Peter Force Printer), 1842, pp. 110, 111.

[4.] _Ibid.,_ p. 111.

[5.] Report of the Select Committee on the Asylum, January 18, 1847, Washingtoniana Room, Martin Luther King Library, Washington, D.C., p. 61.

[6.] _Ibid.,_ p. 61.

[7.] _Ibid.,_ pp. 58-62.

[8.] Annual Report of the Commissioners of D.C. to the President of the U.S. (Washington, D.C.: Government Printing Office), 1875.

[9.] Annual Report of the Commissioners of D.C. to the President of the U.S. (Washington, D.C.: Government Printing Office), 1876.

[10.] Peters, F.E., A Short History of the Jails of Washington (1802-1952), Unpublished, On file in the Museum of the D.C. Department of Corrections, Lorton, Virginia.

CHAPTER 4

THE DISTRICT OF COLUMBIA PENITENTIARY (1831-1862)

Although the urgent need for a penitentiary in the District of Columbia was seen as early as 1814, when the lotteries failed to raise money for construction of public buildings, it was not until May 20, 1826, that the 19th Congress passed the Penitentiary Act. The Bill contained an appropriation of $40,000, "...to defray the expense of erecting said building,..."[1] and authorization for the President of the United States to appoint a three-man commission to select a proper site on which to build the institution.

Since offenders convicted under the laws of both the United States and the District of Columbia would be confined in the penitentiary, Congress and city officials expressed concern as to whether it should be a local or a Federal penitentiary. A decision was finally reached, and the Penitentiary became a Federal institution, with the distinction of being the first national penitentiary in the country.

Additional penitentiary legislation was enacted March 3, 1829, which approved an additional $27,000 for its completion. With regard to the upkeep of the Penitentiary, the Bill stated that once in operation "...if it be possible, the proceeds of the labour of the said convicts shall pay all expenses for the penitentiary and more."[2] In addition, the Bill gave the sanction of Congress to the Convict Labor System, authorizing the warden to let out the labor of the convicts by contract.

The three commissioners appointed by the President selected the foot of Four and One-Half Street, Southwest, on the grounds of the Arsenal (presently Fort McNair) as the site for the Penitentiary. The structure was designed by Architect Charles Bulfinch, and constructed under the supervision of the Commissioner of Buildings, as set forth in the Penitentiary Bill of 1826. The building was designed to contain 160 cells which were located in the center of the main structure, with a section for the men and one for the women. The cells were seven by three and one-half by seven feet in size. In addition, the Penitentiary grounds contained a hospital, a chapel, and workshops, all of which were enclosed by a secure wall. The warden's quarters were located in one wing and the deputy keeper's quarters in the other. The Penitentiary opened in April 1831, and served both the District and the Federal government for the following three decades. While the Penitentiary was officially known as the Penitentiary for the

District of Columbia, it was sometimes referred to as the U.S. Penitentiary.

The Penitentiary legislation of March 3, 1829, stipulated that a board of five inspectors be chosen annually by the President of the United States from residents of the District of Columbia, who would "...severally hold their offices for one year, from the date of their appointment."[3] The first board was appointed by President Andrew Jackson, and they were "...Henry Ashton, Thomas Carbery, William O'Neale, all of the City of Washington, Thompson F. Mason of Alexandria, and James Dunlop of Georgetown."[4]

The Penitentiary legislation of 1829 specified that it would be the duty of the Board of Inspectors to prepare a system of rules and regulations by minutely providing for the discipline, health, and cleanliness of the Penitentiary as well as the government and behavior of the officers and convicts.

The Board of Inspectors originally reported to the U.S. Treasury. With the creation of the Department of Interior in 1849, the Board of Inspectors was placed under the supervision of the Secretary of that agency.

The District Penitentiary, along with other early penal institutions of its kind, such as the Walnut Street Jail of Philadelphia and the Auburn Prison of New York, formed the foundation from which modern corrections evolved. The methods used for reformation of the men and women confined in those early penitentiaries influenced penological thinking for many years, and remnants of that philosophy are still found today. The rules and regulations written by the Board of Inspectors from the guidelines contained in the Penitentiary legislation of 1829, reflect that philosophy and provide us with insight into the daily routine of those early prisons. The entire operation of the District's Penitentiary, including the duties of staff and convicts alike, was set forth in a small booklet by the first Board of Inspectors, entitled "Rules and Regulations of the U.S. Penitentiary." I have seen fit to quote freely from that booklet in order to convey the philosophy of that important era in the history of corrections in the District of Columbia.

Since the government was counting on the Penitentiary to be self-supporting, one additional duty of the Board of Inspectors was to inspect the accounts regularly. In the event it failed to support itself, the inspectors would state "...in their annual report to Congress, what they suppose to be the reason of such failure."[5]

The Penitentiary legislation further provided, "That the President shall also appoint one warden of the said penitentiary, who shall hold his office during the pleasure of the President.[6] Since no geographical limits were set for selection of the warden, President Jackson appointed Benjamin Williams of Virginia to be the first to serve in that capacity. By law of February 25, 1831, however, appointment of the warden was made subject to confirmation by the Senate, and the Board of Inspectors was reduced to three members.

The warden's function was clearly stated in the Penitentiary legislation. His duties including keeping "...accurate accounts of all material bought and furnished for the use and labour of the convicts, and, also, the proceeds of their labour...making all contracts and purchases for supplies necessary for the penitentiary."[7] The warden was given the power to "...let out the labour of the convicts by contract, subject always however to the rules and discipline of the Penitentiary."[8] Under the superintendence and inspection of the inspectors, the warden managed all affairs of the Penitentiary and was responsible for enforcing the rules and regulations of the institution.

Before the warden entered upon the duties of his position, he was required to give bond to the United States with security in an amount approved by the Board of Inspectors. He was further given the power to punish any convict of the Penitentiary who willfully violated or refused to obey the rules or refused to perform the work assigned to him. The punishment consisted of solitary confinement with a diet of bread and water, by putting the convict in irons, or in the stocks.

Both the warden and the deputy keeper were required to live in the Penitentiary in the quarters provided for them. The warden could not leave the grounds for one night without permission in writing from two inspectors.

Serving directly under the warden, the deputy keeper was responsible for overseeing matters regarding the conduct and industry of the convicts and any negligence on the part of the keepers and officers. The keepers and other officers who supervised the several departments and workshops of the institution were charged with enforcing the rules and regulations:

> ...they (the keepers) shall not converse with the convicts or listen to them, further than is necessary to direct them in their work; nor shall they converse or talk among themselves in the presence or in hearing of the

> convicts or suffer any other person to do so, except in the presence of the warden or one of the inspectors. They shall not, while in their shops or on duty, employ their time or give their attention to any other subject or thing except a constant and vigilant observance and overlooking of the convicts under their charge, and making the necessary entries in their books.
>
> * * *
>
> No other officer of this prison shall be allowed to drink any spiritous liquors or wine or fermented liquers, while on duty or in the prison. No assistant keeper or other officer or agent of the penitentiary, shall be guilty of cursing or swearing or any other indecent language, or conduct, or of inhumanity to the prisoners.[9]

The wall guards or sentinals kept watch on all movement within the prison compound, ensuring that only authorized persons were permitted on the walls, and to make certain no conversation was carried on between the convicts within the prison and persons on the outside.

The staff included a prison physician who conducted a physical examination on each prisoner who was admitted to the Penitentiary before he or she was assigned to a cell or "put to labor" as a precaution against infectious or contagious disease on his clothing or person. In addition, the physician prescribed medicine for the sick convicts, a regimen for cleanliness of the prisoners in the hospital department, and kept a journal of patients in the hospital, in which he noted the time of entry of each and the time of discharge or death, the nature of the illness, and the medicine he prescribed. The journal was open to the inspection of the warden and the Board of Inspectors.

The emphasis on moral and religious instruction as major factors in the reformation of the prisoners made the role of the prison chaplain one of importance and respect. The rules and regulations required that each cell be furnished with a Bible and other books the warden and the inspectors thought suitable to improve the morals and conduct of the prisoners. In addition to his role as religious instructor, the prison chaplain performed another valuable service, that of teaching illiterate convicts to read. The warden's annual report of December 31, 1836, praised the work of the chaplains:

> Religious and moral instructions, by preaching and the Sabbath school, is continued to the prisoners once or more every week. My confidence in the usefulness of this department, I am proud to say, is not only undiminished, but is likely 'to grow with its growth, and strengthen with its strength.' Its exercises have been attended with the happiest consequences, both by the instruction of the school, and the revelation of evangelical truth. There are about twenty, whose rapid advances in the spelling book have been truly surprising; and two, that have given hopeful assurances of an interest in the divine Saviour; and these facts, important as they are, do not alone demonstrate the usefulness of this branch of our system. It sheds a benignant influence upon the very order of the prison; diverting the minds of its inmates from schemes of danger, or a repining under their misfortunes, to nobler and more profitable thoughts; and, not infrequently, bringing them to the sober resolution 'to cease to do evil, and learn to do well.' It has been a subject of remark, by different ministers officiating here, that they never addressed a more attentive audience anywhere.[10]

Typical of the Penitentiary Movement, the discipline prescribed for the prisoners by the Board of Inspectors, stressed silence and absolute submission to the administration of the institution.

> 1. Every convict shall be industrious in the performance of any duty assigned to him; he shall labor diligently and in silence, and obey implicitly the orders of the officers of the institution.
>
> 2. No convict shall secrete, or hide or carry about his person any instrument or thing, with intent to make his escape, or in any other manner endeavor to make his escape.
>
> 3. No convict shall dispute, quarrel with, or in any other manner misbehave to another convict, nor converse with any other prisoner without the leave or by the order of an officer; not absent himself from his work, nor look at or speak to visitors,

not go into the prison yard without orders, not go into the lodging rooms after being turned out in the morning till ordered, nor leave the hospital when unwell and sent there.

4. No convict shall drink any spiritous, wines, or fermented liquers, unless prescribed by the physician, when sick in the hospital, nor game in any form or by any device whatsoever, nor chew or use tobacco.

5. No convict shall write or receive a letter to or from any person whatsoever, nor have any intercourse with persons without the prison by any other means.

6. No convict shall burn or in any other manner waste, destroy, or injure any raw materials or manufactured articles, or other public property, nor default or injure the prison, or any of the buildings or fixtures connected with it.

7. No convict shall laugh, dance, whistle, sing, run, jump, or do anything which will tend to alarm or disturb the prison.

8. Convicts shall always conduct themselves toward the officers of this institution with deference and respect; and cleanliness in their persons, dress, and bedding is required.

9. When the convicts go to meals, or to or from the shops, they shall proceed in a regular order in silence, marching in such order as the warden may prescribe, accompanied by the proper officers. They shall eat their meals in the Hall.[11]

The rigid discipline of the Penitentiary authorities is further reflected in the rules that controlled the daily routine of the prisoners:

> The convicts shall be unlocked and put to work at sunrise during the year, and they shall be locked in at sunset from the 20th of September to the 20th of March, and from six to

> half past six, the rest of the year. The convicts and each of them, shall be rigidly inspected before marching to their cells at night, in the manner prescribed by the Warden, and at such other times as he shall order.
>
> The hour for breakfast, from the 20th of March to the 20th of September, shall be seven o'clock A.M.; and from the 20th of September to the 20th of March, eight o'clock. The hour for dinner shall be one o'clock P.M. The convicts shall be allowed forty-five minutes for breakfast and one hour for dinner; as the expiration of which time they shall be turned out of their cells and again put to labor.[12]

Infractions of the rules by the prisoners were punishable with confinement "...in a solitary cell, on a diet of bread and water, not exceeding twenty days for each offense."[13] The punishment could, however, be suspended by an inspector at his weekly visit to the Penitentiary or by the entire Board of Inspectors at its monthly meeting.

> Some sort of punishment was administered almost every day. The most usual offenses were making noises (including talking), destroying property, refusing to work, disobeying orders, and fighting. Here are some offenses and their corresponding punishments taken from the Penitentiary Book of Punishments:

Offense	Punishment
Improper conduct at table	Stocks - 2 hours
Refusing to go to Chapel	Stocks - 2 hours
Fighting in line	10 strokes with paddle
Striking another prisoner	Dungeon 10 days Bread and water
Betraying his trust	In cell 6 days Bread and water
Making noise in cell	In cell 3 days Bread and water
Whistling	In cell 1 day Bread and water
Caught talking to women	Thriced up for 3 1/2 hours
Running about neglecting work	Ball and chain on leg

Crazy fit, occurring at intervals	Dungeon 3 days Bread and water
Making great noise in cell and otherwise annoying officers	6 lashes
Using vulgar language towards another prisoner	Whipped with cat
Went to privey on false pretense—instead went to cell where a convict was confined	Whipped 5 lashes over shirt and placed in dungeon 1 day
Attempting to converse with woman convict	Hoisted up for 2 hours
Beating on lap to a tune causing merriment for others	Put in dungeon
Disobeying orders and swearing	In dungeon 1 day
Fighting in yard	Whipped 5 lashes
Talking in dining hall	Reproved
Attempting to escape	Whipped 11 lashes, locked in dungeon[14]

The philosophy with regard to punishment of prisoners developed by the early Penitentiary Movement was a complete departure from the harsh physical torture practiced during the Colonial Era. This reversal is seen in the following excerpt from the rules and regulations regarding the warden's duties:

> ...In exerting the duties of his office, the warden should never lose sight of the reformation of his prisoners, and should carefully guard himself against personal and passionate resentment. With the powers invested in him and the other officers, it cannot be necessary for him or them to strike or abuse the prisoners, much less can it answer any good purpose to give orders in a violent tone, or attend with oaths of indecent language. All orders should be given with mildness and dignity and they should be enforced with promptitude and firmness.[15]

It is important to note that the philosophy employed during the early years of the Penitentiary forbidding the use of corporal punishment on the prisoners changed in later years of its operation:

> In 1854, in tandem with a national trend to tighten prison discipline, the inspectors of the District Penitentiary modified the regulations of 1830 by authorizing corporal punishment. Initially, perhaps because of the personal views of the warden, this new power was used sparingly, but beginning in early 1859, following a sharp rise in the prison population and the arrival of a new warden, whipping and tricing became regular occurrences, constituting about twenty percent of all punishments.[16]

The Penitentiary legislation of 1829 stipulated that the convicts were to be clothed at public expense. The material for their clothing and bedding was to be coarse and the cheapest kind. "The convicts shall be fed on the cheapest food which will support health and strength, with as little change or variety in the said diet, as may be consistent with the health of the convicts and the economy of the penitentiary."[17] The daily rations received by the prisoners, as the standard amount of prison clothing was set forth in the Book of Rules and Regulations:

> The rations shall be such as may be prescribed from time to time by the Inspectors, and shall not exceed the following rates: 12 ounces of pork or 16 ounces of beef; 10 ounces of wheat flour, not bolted; 12 ounces of Indian meal; one-half gill of molasses; and two quarts of rye, 4 quarts of salt, 4 quarts of vinegar; 1 1/2 ounces of pepper, and 2 1/2 bus. potatoes to each hundred rations. The rations of the women and boys shall be as nearly in proportion as possible, taking into consideration age, health, etc.
>
> The clothing for each convict shall be a rounderabout or overjacket, a vest and pantaloons, made of wool for the winter and cotton or linen for the summer, with stripes running round or up and down the body and limbs, a cap of the same cloth, leather shoes and woolen socks, and shirt of coarse cotton or linen. Each convict shall have a mattress, two blankets, made of coarse woolen yarn, not less than one and a half yards wide and two and a half yards long, and one coarse sheet of the same size. They shall not be permitted to lie down or to rise up from their beds until notice

> is given by the bell for that purpose, nor shall they be permitted to sleep in their clothes.[18]

Although much simpler, the procedures for reception and discharge of prisoners of the District Penitentiary bear some resemblance to those in use today. Upon entering the Penitentiary, the convict was bathed and given a hair cut, "close" as prescribed by law. The classification procedure consists of the following:

> He shall be examined by the Warden and Clerk, in the presence of as many Keepers as can conveniently attend, that they may become acquainted with his person and countenance; and his name, height, apparant age, alleged place of nativity, complexion, color of hair and eyes, and length of feet to be accurately measured, and all visible scars or marks, the court convicted in, the crime found guilty of, and length of sentence, shall be entered in a book provided for that purpose, with such other general description as may tend to his or her future identification, and if the convict can write, his or her signature shall be written under the said description of the person.[19]

The personal effects and clothes of the prisoner were taken from him and placed in safekeeping while he was serving his term. Upon discharge of the prisoner, his belongings were returned to him. In the event the prisoner's own clothes were unfit at the time of discharge, "...a new cheap and suitable laborer's dress"[20] was issued to him at the expense of the Penitentiary.

Newly committed prisoners were instructed carefully by the officers with regard to the rules and regulations of the prison. Those prisoners who were in good health were assigned a trade that the warden felt was most suitable to them. Those who had no trade were assigned to duties that seemed "best suited" to their strength and capacity.

If the inspectors and warden were satisfied with the "industry, good order, and morality" of the prisoner's conduct, a certificate to that effect was issued to him at the time of his release from the Penitentiary.

The Penitentiary's annual reports show that men and women of all ages could be found in the prison population; with some as young as 14 years. In the early years of its operation, the

Penitentiary's population averaged around 50 to 80 prisoners. By 1862, however, the population had increased to 332 "...because of the addition of some 100 military prisoners."[21] Women accounted for only a small portion of the prison population. With the Penitentiary serving both the City of Washington and the United States Government, less than fifty percent of the prisoners were actually District residents. The remainder of the prisoners were from various states, and even some foreign countries. The racial makeup of the prisoners averaged about sixty percent White and forty percent Black. The offenses for which the men and women were convicted were quite similar to those of today, with property crime (larceny in particular) being by far the major offense of that era.

Shoemaking was the major industry in the Penitentiary, employing about seventy-five percent of the male prisoners. There were other workshops where brooms were made and carpentry and tailoring work was done. The women performed such duties as cooking, laundry, sewing, and shoe binding.

The high hopes of Congress that the Penitentiary would be self-supporting through the labor of the prisoners were not fulfilled. In fact, the annual reports of both the wardens and the inspectors go to great lengths to explain why the Penitentiary could not be self-sustaining, as shown by the warden's report of October 1, 1854:

> That this institution can be maintained under existing circumstances by the labor of the convicts is improbable, so long as we have committed to our charge convicts unfit for labor, being incapacitated by age and infirmities; and others, who are reckless and desperate, having no interest in their labor, and whose principal desires seem to be to waste and destroy material. The greater number of the convicts are sentenced for short periods, and are unacquainted with the use of tools; hence it follows, by the time they become familiar with their use the terms of sentence expires, and thus we are required to feed and clothe the most worthless class of apprentices. Nor are these the only causes to be assigned why the institution is unable to maintain itself; for, necessary to enforce discipline, guards have to be employed; and whether there be few or many convicts capable of laboring, the incidental expenses are nearly the same, as inspectors, physician, chaplain, and clerk, are necessary attaches. In fact, no one but he who

> has a practical knowledge of the several causes which tend to prevent institutions of this description from supporting themselves, can form an adequate idea of the several difficulties to be surmounted.[22]

The warden's annual report of June 30, 1855, contained the following plea:

> The suggestions made in my former reports to allow each convict a pro rata of his earnings on being discharged, my every day experience satisfies me would add incalculably to the discipline of the prison as well as to tend to bring about a general reform in the convict; at present the convict has no tie or interest to induce him to labor other than that arising from the fear of being punished, which is, in my opinion, a mode badly calculated to accomplish a moral reform amongst persons of mature age, whose habits, temperaments, and passions are habituated to vice and who are skilled in the art of deception and callous to the opinions of the Christian and moralist. Had the convict an assurance he would be remunerated for his services; had he any assurance that if he conducted himself properly whilst in prison, it would entitle him to something more than that given to the idle, mischievous and vicious prisoner on being discharged, it is more than probable it would convince him that the right path to pursue is industry and honesty in accordance with the law; were a small sum, the result of his own industry, paid him when discharged, it would tend not only to restrain his actions whilst in prison, but induce him to pursue a better course through life. It too, would enable him to travel beyond the sphere of the prison circle, and where, unknown, commence an honest pursuit, having there no prejudice to contend with because of having been a convict.[23]

There is no indication that the warden's suggestion was ever acted upon.

When the Penitentiary became unprofitable and could not be self-supporting, the inspectors were required to give the reason for its failure. They, like the wardens, agreed that the convicts were stupid, and inept and wasted material, and were determined to do as little work as possible. In addition, they argued "Washington not being a commercial city, there is a slow sale for such manufactures as are practicable in a prison, and the cost of the raw material is much greater here than at the north. The cost of living is also comparatively higher here than in most localities where penitentiaries are established."[24]

The annual report of the inspectors to the Secretary of the Interior dated October 21, 1861 reads: "The contract system has been tried and failed, the contractor frankly admitting that he found it impossible to fulfill the stipulations of his contract, from the loss of stock in teaching a trade to such ignorant and wasteful hands, and the difficulty of disposing of his manufactures at anything like a remunerative price."[25]

The contract of prison labor as a means of making the Penitentiary self-supporting had fallen far short of its goal. The Penitentiary concept itself did not achieve the success predicted by the reformers who initiated the movement. In 1862, therefore, when the Secretary of War submitted a petition to President Abraham Lincoln requesting that the District Penitentiary, which was located on the Arsenal Grounds, be turned over to the War Department, "...the comment was made that the closing was not much regretted."[26]

The Arsenal had become very active making ammunition for the Union forces during the Civil War and the Penitentiary buildings were needed by the War Department. On September 19, 1862, President Lincoln issued the order transferring the prisoners to Albany, New York, and turning over the buildings and their contents to the War Department. "The facility was transferred to the adjacent Washington Arsenal for the use as an arms warehouse."[27]

"Transfer of the prisoners to Albany was made with the greatest secrecy. Some of the prisoners were released to go to the front and a few who had but little time to serve were pardoned. A number, however, were retained as prisonors and late one night were marched to a steamer nearby and were obliged to complete their sentences."[28] The cost of transportation and maintenance of the prisoners was paid by the United States Government and the responsibility for the transfers was assumed by the Department of Justice.

Bill H.R. No. 169, recommending the construction of another Penitentiary in the District of Columbia, was introduced at the first session of the 28th Congress (1864). The Secretary of the Interior in his annual report for that year noted a total of 179 convicts under sentence from the District. Of that number, 143 had been sent to the penitentiary at Albany, New York. Since the cost of transportation from the District to Albany was about fifty dollars and the maintenance of each prisoner, $1.25 per week, the Secretary felt it would be cheaper to have them confined in a penitentiary in the District. He stated with confidence his belief that with a penitentiary possessing the appliances necessary for judicious application of labor of the convicts, they could be much more economically maintained in the District. The Bill never passed, and the practice of transferring long-term felons to Albany, New York, and later to Federal prisons, continued until 1916.

Although the Penitentiary was not used to confine prisoners after its transfer to the War Department, it gained fame as the place of confinement for eight of the nine conspirators implicated in the assassination of President Abraham Lincoln in April, 1865. "The body of John Wilkes Booth, who had been trapped and killed in a tobacco barn in southern Maryland, was secretly buried during the fog-shrouded night of April 27 under one of the cells of the penitentiary."[29] During the trial, the conspirators were placed under heavy guard in cells in the Penitentiary. When the trial ended, July 6, 1865, four of the eight suspects received prison sentences and four were sentenced to be executed in the Penitentiary courtyard the following day. Those condemned to die were Mary Surratt, Davey Herold, George Atzerodt, and Lewis Payne. The following excerpt from James Goode's book, Capital Losses, A Cultural History of Washington, details the executions:

> ...The executions took place in the penitentiary courtyard on July 7, 1865. The Potomac River was filled that day with boats crowded with spectators; within the high walls of the prison yard, the witnesses included federal troops and 100 civilians who had been issued tickets by the War Department. After reaching the top of the gallows, the four prisoners were bound, white hoods were placed over their heads, and a noose was adjusted around their necks. While photographer Mathew Brady quickly recorded the historic event, Maj. Gen. Winfield Scott Hancock, commander of the military district of Washington, gave the order for the gibbet to be dropped by clapping his hands twice. Within half an hour, the four bodies were cut down and buried in graves beneath the gallows where they had died. Several years later, the remains of Booth, and those of the four executed prisoners, were

removed by their families for reburial elsewhere.[30]

With the close of the War, activity at the Arsenal subsided and the Penitentiary was no longer of use to the military. It was decided that most of the structure be dismantled and the remaining sections be put to other uses. An article appearing in the Evening Express Newspaper of Saturday, March 7, 1868, tells of the planned renovation:

> The outside walls of the old institution are now prostrate, and the walls of the yard surrounding the grounds are also nearly demolished. The two upper tiers of cells have been torn down, leaving only the two lower stories to be removed. The bricks and other material are carefully preserved and will be used by the Government at will. The offices forming the west elevation of the building, as also the east wing, formerly the female department of the prison, left standing and will be improved for quarters for the officers. The west elevation fronting the Potomac, will be entirely renovated, surmounted with a modern French roof; a portico will surround it, and the surrounding grounds will be appropriately laid out in flower beds, walks, and carriage drives for the headquarters of General Ramsay...The east wing will be also handsomely fitted up as a residence for Major Frederick Whyte, the storekeeper and paymaster of the Arsenal.[31]

A later article, dated May 8, 1886, found in the Evening Star Newspaper comments further on the Penitentiary:

> ...The site of this building is now included within the grounds of the Washington barracks, where is quartered the larger portion of the 3rd United States artillery, Gen. H.G. Gibson, commanding. The two ends of the old prison occupied once by the officers and residences of the warden and deputy warden, now are the residences of Gen. Gibson and some of the officers. The prison portion was located between these buildings. So great has been the change that a visitor to the barracks can scarcely realize that in the space between these buildings murderers, burglars, forgers,

> and other criminals were once confined to work out their sentences.[32]

In 1903, the western portion of the penitentiary building was razed. The eastern building still stands, and is used as officer quarters. By legend, it is peopled by the famous spirits of Walter Reed and, of course, Mary Surratt.

The histories of the Penitentiary and the Arsenal are uniquely intertwined. Known today as Fort Lesley J. McNair, the Arsenal grounds, on which the Penitentiary was built, has a fascinating history of its own. Established as a military reservation in 1791, it is the oldest post in the country and it became the National War College in 1903.

SOURCES

[1.] Public Statutes at Large, 19th Congress, Sess. I, Vol. IV (Boston, Mass.: Little Brown & Co.), 1853, p. 178.

[2.] Public Statutes at Large, 20th Congress, Sess. II (Boston, Mass.: Little Brown & Co.), 1853, p. 369.

[3.] _Ibid.,_ p. 365.

[4.] Bryan, Wilhelmus Bogart, _A History of the National Capital,_ Vol. 2 (New York: The MacMillan Company, 1914), p. 87.

[5.] Public Statutes at Large, 20th Congress, p. 366.

[6.] _Ibid.,_ p. 365.

[7.] _Ibid.,_ p. 366.

[8.] _Ibid._

[9.] Rules and Regulations of the Penitentiary, National Archives Building.

[10.] Warden's Report, December 31, 1836, Copy on file in the D.C. Department of Corrections Museum, Lorton, Virginia.

[11.] Rules and Regulations of the Penitentiary, National Archives Building.

[12.] _Ibid._

[13.] Sullivan, David K., Records of the Columbia Historical Society of Washington, D.C., Behind Prison Walls: The Operation of the District Penitentiary 1831-1862, Washingtoniana Room, Martin Luther King Library, Washington, D.C., p. 248.

[14.] Records of Columbia Historical Society, Washington, D.C. 1953-1959, The Historical Society, 1959.

[15.] Rules and Regulations of the Penitentiary.

[16.] Sullivan, David K., Records of the Columbia Historical Society, 1971-1972, p. 249.

[17.] Rules and Regulations of the Penitentiary.

[18.] _Ibid._

[19.] _Ibid._

[20.] _Ibid._

[21.] Goode, James M., _Capital Losses_ (Washington, D.C.: Smithsonian Press), 1979.

[22.] Annual Report of the Warden 1854 to the Secretary of the Interior.

[23.] Annual Report of the Warden 1855 to Secretary of the Interior, p. 614.

[24.] Report of the Inspectors, U.S. Penitentiary, Washington, D.C., October 21, 1861, p. 858.

[25.] _Ibid.,_ pp. 858, 859.

[26.] Sullivan, David K., p. 266.

[27.] Goode, James M., p. 302.

[28.] O'Brien, William, J., PFC, U.S. War College, Story of U.S. Arsenal and Washington Barracks, Unpublished Paper, Washingtoniana Room, Martin Luther King Library, Washington, D.C., pp. 24-25.

[29.] Goode, James M., p. 302.

[30.] _Ibid.,_ p. 302.

[31.] _The Evening Press Newspaper,_ March 7, 1868, Clipping Packet, Washingtoniana Room, Martin Luther King Library, Washington, D.C.

[32.] _The Evening Star,_ May 8, 1886, Clipping Packet, Washingtoniana Room, Martin Luther King Library, Washington, D.C.

Cell block of old D.C. Penitentiary shows second floor and part of third where conspirators were lodged. Photograph courtesy of Special Collection of History, National Defense University Library, Washington, D.C.

CHAPTER 5

THE SECOND CIRCUIT COURT JAIL (1841-1875)

The population of the District had climbed to over forty thousand persons by 1839, making it necessary to replace the First Circuit Court Jail, which had become too dilapidated and too small to confine the number of prisoners being sentenced to serve time within its walls. An Act of Congress, passed March 3, 1839, appropriated $31,000 for construction of a larger and more modern jail.

The new jail, officially known as the Second Circuit Court Jail, was located at Fourth and G Streets, Northwest (currently the site of the old Pension Building). The structure had a frontage of 100 feet, was 80 feet in depth and 40 feet high. The exterior walls were made of brick with a covering of blue plaster in imitation stone, and because of its coloring, the jail was popularly known as the "Blue Jug." Designed to accommodate 100 prisoners, it contained 22 cells eight feet by ten feet, and ten rooms large enough to accommodate about six persons each. The prisoners began occupancy of the new jail in 1841.

The Jail was originally under the direct supervision of the U.S. Marshal for the District of Columbia, who in turn submitted reports and financial statements concerning that facility to the Treasury Department. When the Department of Interior was created in 1849, jurisdiction of the Jail was placed under that agency, and the marshal reported to the Secretary of the Interior.

Fortunately, enough of the records from the Second Circuit Court Jail have been preserved to provide interesting information regarding its management, its prisoners, and the crimes for which they were incarcerated. The jail was used for holding those who were awaiting trial, as well as, for confining sentenced misdemeanants. In addition, the registers show that prisoners designated to serve sentences in the District's Penitentiary were held in the jail while awaiting trial. Register entries for the December 1853 and March 1854 terms of criminal court for the District indicate that six men and two women were sentenced to the Penitentiary with terms ranging from one to six years. After the close of the Penitentiary in 1862, the jail still served as the holding facility for felony offenders awaiting transfer to Albany, New York, for service of sentence. The following excerpts from the register during 1865 and 1866, lists the offense and term of prisoners awaiting transfer:

11-14-1865 Larceny of a carpet bag and clothing
2 years in the Penitentiary

01-15-1866 Larceny of 20 chickens and 8 ducks
1 year in the Penitentiary

01-99-1866 Larceny of one dress valued at $7.00
1 year in the Penitentiary

03-23-1866 Larceny of one watch valued at $10.00
2 years in the Penitentiary

04-11-1866 Larceny of 6 hogs
15 months in the Penitentiary[1]

An examination of the commitment book used in the Second Circuit Court Jail indicates that runaway slaves were predominate in the offense column during the antebellum era:

> ...The name of the runaway is entered with the name of the law enforcement officer who committed the slave, the date of release and the name of the person to whom the slave was delivered upon release. The fee for keeping the slave in jail is noted (at the rate of 34 cents per day) plus what apparently is a Marshal's fee as there are countless entries showing that some or all of the total fees charged were turned over to the U.S. 'Marshal.'
>
> In another commitment book, the first entry on August 12, 1850 covers the receipt of one Noah Hanson, Negro, charged with 'Abducting Slaves.' He was convicted on March 10, 1851 and sentenced to pay a fine and costs of $1,080. On July 22, 1854, it is noted that Hanson was pardoned by the President (Millard Fillmore) and the Jailor, one D. Smith, was ordered by J.D. Hoover, U.S. Marshal, to release said Hanson from jail.
>
> ...Some of the runaway slaves were man and wife, others were women with their children - in one instance an infant. Then on March 30, 1854, an entry is found which indicated that one Sarah Williams, a Negress, who had been arrested as a runaway slave was 'Proved to be a free woman,' and there was another on October 19, 1854 covering one Harriett, a Negress,

> arrested as a runaway slave and found 'Not to be a runaway.'[2]

Among the more unusual crimes are entries in the commitment book for the period from February 4, 1858 to May 1, 1861:

> ...They concern one George Nelson and one Joseph Penny. They were received at the Circuit Court Jail on November 25, 1859 and charged with 'Attempt to scale the walls of the Penitentiary for the purpose of setting fire to it.' On the following day, November 27, 1859, one Joseph Cunningham was received at the Jail charged with 'Attempt to Rob the Penitentiary.'[3]

It was during the time the Second Circuit Court Jail was in operation, in 1863, that jail officials began keeping official records of executions taking place in the District of Columbia. The earliest official entry is dated April 1, 1864. On that date, Jermiah Hendricks was executed by hanging. Later in the same year on July 8th, the first triple execution in the District was carried out.

An unofficial account, listed in a clipping, undated and unmarked as to the newspaper from which it was taken, lists three scheduled executions between 1850 and 1863, of which two were carried out. The article relates an unusual and interesting turn of events involving the third one:

> ...The next time the scaffold was erected was for a soldier, John Foley, convicted of the murder of a corporal of his company and sentenced to be hanged in July. Foley made his preparations for death, being attended by Rev. Father Wigett, and having been pinioned he was about being led by Col. Ward H. Lamon, then marshal, to the scaffold, when a commutation of sentence to imprisonment for life was received from President Lincoln. It required the priests some time to persuade Foley that it was his duty to accept it...[4]

An article appearing in the Washington Post, August 7, 1921, reflects on the role of the Second Circuit Court Jail during the Civil War. It notes that the Jail, along with the District Penitentiary, was used to confine the overflow of Government enemies and spies who were brought to Washington from Union lines. At the time of President Abraham Lincoln's assassination, those persons suspected in the plot were temporarily housed in the Second Circuit Court Jail. It was first thought that Mary Surratt and her coconspirators would be tried by civil authorities, and if convicted, would be hanged in Judiciary Square. Later, the decision was changed and the prisoners were executed by military authorities.

The Second Circuit Court Jail was the place of confinement of Congressman Daniel Edgar Sickles after he shot and killed Philip Barton Key (son of Francis Scott Key), February 27, 1859, because of his romantic interest in Mrs. Sickles. "In a celebrated trial in which, for the first time, the defense pleaded temporary aberration of mind, Sickles was acquitted."[5]

Another dramatic incident occurred in that jail shortly after the Mexican War (1848).

> ...The Mexican War Claims Commission was meeting in the City (Washington, D.C.) at the time when two young fellows arrived in Washington with claims for extensive damages arising from the destruction of mining plants they had owned in the Southwest. Their claims were pushed through, amounting in all to something over $150,000, and shortly afterward were discovered to be clear forgeries from beginning to end.
>
> The boys were arrested and tried, and after a second trial one of them, a young Spaniard was convicted. He was carried down to the old jail and just as he stepped across the threshold, he lifted the setting of a ring that he wore and touched his tongue to the hollow beneath. It was one of the old poison rings of Oriental fame, and in less than half an hour the boy was dead.[6]

By resolution of the Senate on Februry 18, 1862, the Committee on the District of Columbia was instructed to inquire into the conditions and management of the Jail of the City of Washington, and to report such measures as in their opinion may be necessary in relation thereto. The Committee began its investigation February 20, 1862 and proceeded with the examination of witnesses at intervals up to March 6, 1862. Two causes for complaint against the conditions and management of the jail were found. One pertained to the unfitness of those having charge of it, and the other to the inadequate accommodations of the jail itself for "decent confinement of the prisoners committed to it."

The investigation brought to light a barbarous system of punishment known as "cobbing" in practice upon Black persons in the jail, for trivial offenses. This cruel treatment had been going on for quite some time prior to the investigation and it was described to the Committee by one of the jail guards who testified at the hearings:

> ...The man's breeches were unbuttoned and let to fall down below his buttox. I tied his hands by order of Mr. Wise. He was then made to lie over a barrel. The rope by which his hands were tied, was drawn under the barrel. I helped do this under the direction of Mr. Wise. He was then struck some eight or ten blows by a paddle about three feet long, an inch thick, and six inches wide. The blows were laid on with the strength of the man...they were severe, the man writhing and screaming under the infliction.[7]

Another jail guard testified that as many as 30 blows had been struck during a cobbing. This punishment was most often administered to slaves or freed men for very petty offenses or infractions, as shown by the testimony of another prison guard:

> ...One Anthony Simmes, a free Negro, was severely 'cobbed.' His offense was, he had been employed in the kitchen, and he went into the street, as those employed in the kitchen are allowed to do, and refused or neglected to come back. One Bill Adams, a free Negro, under sentence for petit larceny, or something of that kind, was severely 'cobbed.' I counted about thirty-three very severe lashes. He was employed in the kitchen and his offense was going into the street and not returning. There were three slaves whipped very severely in the early part of this month. One was Abraham Taylor, a slave, who was afterwards carried to Baltimore by Mr. Wise. He belongs to a man said to be a very strong secessionist, living in the County of Charles, Maryland. His master's name was Chapman, though his master never came after him. He was taken out of Jail the latter part of January or the first of February to avoid his release under Secretary Seward's order, and was recommitted for thirty days more to enable his master to come forward, identify him, and prove himself a loyal man, which he never did. Mr. Wise was instructed by

> Deputy Marshal Phillips to take him out of jail and recommit him. He was committed by Squire Walter. He attempted to escape, and for this put in the dungeon and afterwards sent to Baltimore, after being 'cobbed'...[8]

Testimony was also heard on the classification of prisoners according to color, offenses alleged against them, age, and sex:

> In the debtor portion of the jail there is no distinction as to color. In this portion are confined thieves, witnesses, persons charged with small offenses, fugitives from service of labor, and 'gentlemen' who have been guilty of some indiscretion, and whom the marshal does not like to put in with persons charged with grave offenses. There is no distinction as to age in any portion of the prison. Small boys are confined with persons charged with murder. In the female part of the prison there is no distinction as to crime, color, or age.[9]

As to the accommodations of the jail for sleeping, the following testimony was recorded:

> ...The prisoners are entitled to a straw mattress and blanket, but in many cases they have neither, and sleep upon the bare floor, which is made of brick and cemented. I especially called attention of the marshal at the early part of the session of Congress to the necessity of furnishing accommodations for sleeping but up to the time I left many still slept on the bare floor.[10]

The marshal was in charge of purchasing the food for the jail, for which he was allowed thirty-four cents per day for each inmate. A jail guard testifying as a witness was asked to describe the food furnished the prisoners:

> They receive two meals a day. One in the morning consists of a loaf of cornbread made of cornmeal and water; the loaf being larger than the top of a peck measure, is cut into eight parts, and one part given to each prisoner, with one Potomac herring or a small mackerel, with some ground coffee sweetened with molasses. At 2 o'clock p.m. they receive half a pound of bacon, if bacon is served, with the

> same ration of bread as in the morning, and no vegetables. About three times a week there is a quantity of fresh beef, which sometimes is made into soup, in which case they receive no bacon. I think rations could be furnished at eleven cents per day, and all over that is profit to the Marshal.[11]

The investigation resulted in dismissal of the Marshal and those who served under him, from their duties in connection with the jail. The law was amended by Act of February 29, 1864, entitled, "An Act to Authorize the Appointment of a Warden of the Jail in the District of Columbia." Authority to make rules was vested in the Supreme Court of the District of Columbia. The Act further provided that the warden submit an annual report to the Honorable Secretary of the Interior. The first Warden, Robert Beale, submitted a report for the period of April 11, 1864 to November 18, 1864, in which he described conditions in the jail as he found them when he reported for duty.

> ...I found the jail and the yards attached in a very bad condition, the yards particularly so, requiring considerable time and labor to remove the filth therefrom, and to fill up parts that were covered with stagnant water.
>
> The articles necessary for the support and subsistence of the prisoners I found very high when I took charge, and they have been on the increase ever since. Many of the articles are now over two hundred percent higher, such as bacon, molasses, and fish, which constitute the main part of the expense of subsisting and keeping the establishment...
>
> * * *
>
> There is a great and growing evil in our midst to which I beg leave to call your particular attention; it is the slowly increasing numbers of juvenile offenders from ten to fifteen years of age, who are brought into the prison. Some of these are orphans, without relatives whose aid or protection they could claim. They are often brought in without hat, shoes, or any article of apparel save a pair of tattered pantaloons. We are compelled to keep these children in the departments with the old, depraved, and desperate offenders, and their example has the most pernicious influence

> over these boys. It requires but a short association of these children with these veterans in crime to make them as bad as themselves. For the benefit and safety of society, and for the benefit of the morals of these boys, it would be both politic and humane that some provision should be made for their future safekeeping and instruction.
>
> The jail is in a dilapidated condition, and by no means safe for the keeping of prisoners; the ventilation is so bad that the air is obnoxious and unhealthy. It is next to impossible to repair or improve the present building to suit the requirements of a proper prison; a new one is indispensable; and if I may be permitted to make a suggestion, I should say, that to sell the square of ground on which the jail stands, and build another out of the proceeds, on ground more eligible, belonging to the government, would save the necessity for an appropriation of Congress. An act authorizing and directing the Secretary of the Interior to make sale of the ground and apply the proceeds to the building of a new jail would be all that is necessary.[12]

The June, 1864 report of the grand jury for the criminal court commented on conditions it found upon inspection of the Jail:

> ...In addition to the manifest insecurity of the building, two serious defects presented themselves, vis: imperfect sewerage and insufficient ventilation. In reference to the latter, it may be remarked that a stay but a few minutes in some portions of the building produced a most oppressive feeling on those unaccustomed to a confined and vitiated atmosphere.[13]

The second warden, T.W. Brown, entered upon duty August 12, 1865, and the annual report to the Secretary of the Interior for that year, confirmed the findings of his predecessor, Warden Beale, regarding the conditions existing in the Jail:

> ...I found it to be in a very dilapidated condition, and very insecure for the class of desperate characters confined therein. With all the care and watchfulness exercised in

> guarding the prisoners, still it is of frequent occurrence that they are detected in cutting holes through the walls to make their escape. I have found it necessary to ironclad three of the cells, and otherwise to improve the building, to make it more secure.
>
> * * *
>
> On account of the structure of the jail little or no ventilation is had and in warm weather particularly the air is so obnoxious that sickness is frequently the result. The rooms being all occupied and frequently crowded, we have no place to which we can remove the sick and use as a hospital. It is very important that a hospital department should be connected with the prison, that the sick may have that attention and pure air which they need.
>
> The provisions for the jail, I believe, are as good as are furnished in any other prison elsewhere. The rations consist of mackerel, with wheat bread and coffee for breakfast; beef and cornbread for dinner. Salt fish, bacon, beans, potatoes and soup are also served them on different days, while the sick have rice, tea, molasses, and good wheat bread.[14]

Warden Brown's annual report for the year 1866 read: "Since my last report of November 1, 1865, the jail has been much crowded, and crime seems not to have decreased. The crowded condition of the cells and rooms calls for a speedy completion of the new jail."[15] The report again noted the "...large number of children of both sexes committed for crime, who have to be confined with old offenders,..."[16] and further states eight White boys were sent to the House of Refuge in Baltimore, and notes: "As no house of refuge would take colored boys or girls, a great many have been dismissed by the court, after remaining in jail a limited period."[17]

It is noted that the problem of what to do with delinquent children both Black and White was not really resolved until the Board of Children's Guardians was created in 1892. Some relief for Black children came in 1887, when Professor William H.H. Hart of Howard University, "...offered the use of his 300-acre farm and buildings at Fort Washington, Maryland, for a training school for mild-delinquent colored boys."[18]

Warden Brown's annual report for 1866 further notes an increase of Black persons in the jail population resulting from the abolition of slavery. "A large majority of the persons committed to the Jail during the year have been Colored and of the class who have formerly been slaves."[19] An interesting comment on the discipline in the Jail is also found in the 1866 annual report:

> The discipline of the jail, for the past year, has been as good as could be expected. Although the building is a mere shell, and very insecure, yet not one prisoner has succeeded in breaking out for fourteen months past, although a great many attempts have been made by cutting holes in the walls, and otherwise. Much of the credit for this is due to the guards of the prison who are watchful and attentive to their duties. Instead of shower bathing, whipping, and chaining prisoners for disobedience of the rules, the only punishment inflicted on refractory persons is putting them on short allowance of food, and this alone, in most cases, has had the effect of producing obedience and good discipline.[20]

The Jail physician's report for 1866 further describes the condition of the jail and provides statistics on the physical health of the prisoners and the ailments they encountered during the year:

> ...Year after year this jail has been presented as a public nuisance on account of its insecurity and unhealthiness. The crowded state of the building, and its imperfect ventilation, have a most injurious effect on the condition of its inmates; and at present it is a reproach to the government, in the midst of its splendid edifices in the metropolis of the nation.
>
> By constant whitewashing, using chloride of lime and other disinfectants, the vitiated air has been partially purified, and disease from such causes checked.
>
> The following is the average number of cases of disease treated at the jail during the past year, including the endemic of typhus fever, which occurred there last spring:

> Diarrhea and dysentery, 75; smallpox, 3; venereal, 80; mania potu, 50; fever, 112; rheumatism, 30; miscellaneous, 150 - total 500; deaths, 3.
>
> It is remarkable and providential, under all these disadvantageous circumstances, with an endemic of typhus fever, that only three persons have died during the year. The visitation of typhus fever was fortunately of the mild, not the malignant form...[21]

Although the Second Circuit Court Jail remained overcrowded and the building itself unfit for the purpose it served, no effort to improve the lot of the prisoners was made until the Act of Congress passed June 1, 1872, which provided funds for construction of a new jail. In addition, the Act placed the jail under the jurisdiction of the Department of Justice. In spite of its many deficiencies, the old jail served the District until December, 1875, when the new jail was ready for occupancy.

In 1876, one year after its closing, the Second Circuit Court Jail was demolished to make way for construction of the Pension building. The bricks from the building were sold and the proceeds were used to make improvements in Judiciary Square.

SOURCES

[1.] F.E. Peters, A Short History of the Jails of Washington, (1802-1952), Unpublished, on file in the D.C. Department of Corrections Museum, Lorton, Virginia.

[2.] Ibid.

[3.] Ibid.

[4.] Undated Clipping from unidentified newspaper. On file in the D.C. Department of Corrections Museum, Lorton, Virginia.

[5.] Malone, Dumas, Editor, Dictionary of American Biography, Copyright 1935, 1936 American Council of Learned Societies, Charles Scribner & Sons, Renewal Copyright 1963, 1964, p.150.

[6.] Washington Post, July 2, 1893, Clipping File, Washingtoniana Room, Martin Luther King Library, Washington, D.C.

[7.] Resolution of the U.S. Senate February 18, 1862.

[8.] Ibid.

[9.] Ibid.

[10.] Ibid.

[11.] Ibid.

[12.] The First Annual Report of the Warden of the Jail, 1864, Washingtoniana Room, Martin Luther King Library, Washington, D.C., p. 1.

[13.] Ibid., p. 2.

[14.] Report of the Warden of the D.C. Jail, November 1, 1865, Washingtoniana Room, Martin Luther King Library, Washington, D.C., p. 1.

[15.] Report of the Warden of the D.C. Jail, 1866, Washingtoniana Room, Martin Luther King Library, Washington, D.C., p. 202.

[16.] Ibid., p. 202.

[17.] Ibid., p. 205.

[18.] Hart, Hastings H., _Child Welfare in the District of Columbia,_ 1924, Russell Sage Foundation, p. 60.

[19.] Report of the Warden of the D.C. Jail, 1866, p. 204.

[20.] _Ibid.,_ p. 203.

[21.] _Ibid.,_ p. 205.

CHAPTER 6

THE UNITED STATES JAIL (1875-1980)

The United States Jail holds a unique place in the history of the District of Columbia's Penal System. Unlike its predecessors, it was the first thoroughly modern jail to be built in the District, and because of its sturdy construction, it had the distinction of serving as Washington's jail for 105 years.

Authorization to construct the United States Jail was provided by Congress by Act of June 1, 1872. The public land of Reservation 13, in the 200 block of 19th Street, Southeast, was selected as the site for the new building. It was bounded on the South by the Washington Asylum and Workhouse, and on the North by the Smallpox Hospital. An appropriation of $300,000 for its construction was initially approved by Congress, and later additional funds of $140,000 were authorized to complete the construction.

Designed by Architect Adolf Cluss and Supervisory Architect of the U.S. Treasury, Honorable A.B. Mullett, the United States Jail received enthusiastic coverage by the local newspapers. The July 29, 1873 edition of the Daily Morning Chronicle described it as: "A model building of the kind. A prison within a prison, superior arrangements. The structure perfectly fireproof. No chance of an escape."[1] The article further elaborated on the unique features of the new jail:

> The building throughout will be fireproof, the materials being brick, stone, and iron and all chances of escape of prisoners have been so effectually guarded against that they who enter there under the ban of the law may rest assured that only the same strong arm will thereafter afford them release.[2]

The July 30, 1882 edition of the Star Newspaper described the new United States Jail as follows:

> ...The jail is quite an imposing looking edifice, built of Seneca stone, the outer wall being pierced with large windows, which give plenty of light to those inside. The building faces west, and is nearly 250 feet in length, the north and south wings being each 132 feet 8 1/4 inches long and 62 feet wide. In the center is the rotunda, 62 feet 5 1/2 inches by

> 77 feet 7 1/2 inches, and 60 feet from the floor to peak of roof. The building is, in fact a prison within a prison, for between the walls which enclose the cells and the outer walls there is a space of 16 feet. Each of the cells (except the double one at the end of each corridor) is 5 feet wide, 8 feet long, and 10 feet high, has a grated window opening on the space or court between the inner and outer walls, and a barred door opening upon the corridor. A thick, solid brick wall running down the center of the wings divides or separates the corridors. There are four floors or tiers of these cells and a door in a sort of cage, in which the corridors terminate at the rotunda. These cages enclose the stairway of iron which run up on either side of the rotunda. In the south wing, those prisoners who are awaiting trial are usually confined, and in the north wing, those under sentence to jail....[3]

The Seneca stone for the exterior walls, noted above, was red sandstone "...quarried in Maryland and brought up the Potomac and Anacostia Rivers on barges to a point opposite the site upon which the jail was erected."[4]

Warden John S. Crocker's annual report dated October 31, 1876, noted that the new jail was turned over to him December 2, 1875, and transfer of the prisoners to the new quarters was completed December 18, 1875. Warden Crocker's report gives details of the innovative features of the building, by stating: "...It is conveniently arranged, and is perhaps one of the best heated and ventilated buildings of the kind in the country...Its heating apparatus, laundry, and cooking arrangements are admirable, and its entire apartments are well suited to secure the health and comfort of its inmates..."[5] One of the most innovative features of the new jail mentioned by the Warden was the type of heating system.

> The jail is heated by means of a steam-heating apparatus, and the principal part of the cooking is done by steam.
>
> There is a steam-engine connected with the laundry, and one used for forcing water to the tanks in the upper part of the building. There are four large boilers and one small one used for manufacturing steam. The heating apparatus and machinery are quite extensive and somewhat

> complicated, and require an engineer and assistant engineer and four firemen to take charge of them...[6]

Warden Crocker's annual report told of the role of the inmates in completing the new jail:

> ...Most of the painting and plastering, a portion of the inside carpentrying and masonry and some mechanical and other labor on the machinery and heating and ventilating apparatus have been done by the inmates of the institution, skilled mechanics and competent workmen having been selected for the purpose from among their numbers.
>
> Besides, a large amount of prison labor has been employed in building roads, providing proper means of drainage, and grading the grounds connected with the prison...
>
> * * *
>
> When we took possession of the new building, it was entirely without furniture, and no provision had been made to furnish it. There was but little of the furniture used at the old jail that was fit for further use, and none of it was suitable for use in the new building. To supply the deficiency in this regard, some furniture has been purchased, and a large quantity, especially of cell furniture, has been manufactured within the building by prisoners, under the supervision of a mechanic employed for that purpose...[7]

The Warden was so impressed with the work of the inmates in completing the jail that he suggested workshops be installed in the jail, so "...that the labor of such prisoners as we have here in the jail can be made profitable; and besides that, as a reformatory measure, their employment in some kind of useful labor is an appliance of reformation and productive of salutary results."[8] Subsequent annual reports, however, indicate that the suggestion received no response, and idleness in the jail was widespread, developing into a serious problem in later years.

The daily average number of prisoners for the fiscal year ending October 31, 1876, representing the first year in the new jail, was 236. The 272 cells in the new jail provided ample space for the inmate population, and for the first time in many years, overcrowding did not exist in a District jail.

THE ASSASSINATION OF PRESIDENT JAMES A. GARFIELD:

The early history of the jail was uneventful according to the records and reports for those years. Then, the attempted assassination of President James A. Garfield by Charles J. Guiteau on the morning of July 2, 1881, focused widespread attention on the D.C. Jail. The attempt on the President's life occurred around 9:30 a.m., in the Ladies' waiting room of the Baltimore and Potomac Railroad Station as the President was preparing to leave the Capital on a trip. Guiteau, a disappointed office seeker and "Stalwart" fired two shots in his attempt to assassinate Garfield. The first bullet struck the right arm of the President, just below the shoulder, the second entered the right side of the back between the hip and the kidney, passing forward into the groin. The bullet that pierced the arm was removed, but the bullet that lodged in the groin was probed for but could not be removed. As noted by history, the shooting was not fatal and President Garfield remained at the White House during July and August, following the assassination attempt. Then, September 6, 1881, when it was felt that a change to the President's Summer home at Etheron, New Jersey would be beneficial, preparations were made for his trip.

The President died at his Summer home September 19, 1881, and his body was shipped to his native State of Ohio. Guiteau was indicted for murder by the Grand Jury October 8, 1881, and went to trial November 14, 1881. Because of several technicalities involved in the case, the proceedings dragged on until January 25, 1882. One was the issue of Guiteau's sanity and another was whether the trial should be held in the District of Columbia, where the President was shot, or in New Jersey where he died. In addition, Guiteau, who possessed a flamboyant personality frequently interrupted the trial to give lengthy speeches or to recite poetry which he had composed.

Guiteau's confinement in the United States Jail caused concern for his security during the trial. It was feared that an attempt might be made by a mob to storm the jail, and lynch him.

> ...In order to prevent any such eventuality, an armed military guard was thrown around the jail and especially around the North Wing (later Cell Block #2) where Guiteau was housed. This precipatated wholly unexpected results. One of the armed guards, a sergeant, while releasing the guard on duty, saw Guiteau

> in his cell through an open window. The sergeant drew a bead on the assassin and fired. The rifle ball crashed through the window, grazed Guiteau's head and imbedded itself in the cell wall beyond.[9]

Another attempt was made upon Guiteau's life while he was being returned to the jail from the courthouse the evening of November 19, 1881. "A man named William Jones, riding horseback, rode up rapidly to the rear of the open-ended Marshal's van, with Guiteau inside. Taking as good an aim as possible under the circumstances Jones fired at Guiteau with a pistol hitting him in the arm and causing a minor flesh wound."[10] Jones was captured and found to be intoxicated. He was confined to the jail himself, but "...afterward was styled 'Bill Jones the Avenger.'"[11]

When the trial finally ended, Guiteau was found guilty and sentenced to be executed by hanging on June 30, 1882. Writing in the Times newspaper, September 4, 1921, Captain J. Walter Mitchell, oldest active reporter in Washington at that time, recalls that he was assigned to cover the execution of Guiteau. The following is an excerpt from Mitchell's recollection of the execution:

> Wild revelry in the offices of the jail marked the night before the execution of Guiteau, the slayer of President Garfield. James Groggon, a venerable reporter of the old days had established the custom of spending the night before all hangings at the prison.
>
> His reason for so doing was to describe 'the prisoner's last night on earth,' the menu of the last breakfast, and other data for early copy. In those days, the Washington newspapers 'played up' the story of hangings as front-page features, giving column after column of details.
>
> So, therefore, on the night before Guiteau paid the penalty for his crime, many newspaper men, representing local and out-of-town publications, through courtesy of Gen. John S. Crocker, Warden, were permitted to stay over night at the jail. After General Crocker had departed for his home, leaving the jail in charge of Deputy Warden Russ, the newspaper men sought divertisement from the gloom that

pervades the big brown structure on the Eastern branch.

Decks of cards were produced and poker games proceeded in the offices and corridors of the jail. That being long before the Volstead era, a liberal supply of joy water and cigars were brought into the games. Soon the effect of the beverages became apparent and sounds of revelry resounded through the building.

* * *

An unwritten feature of the execution was related to me by the late Dr. Tilden of the Army Medical Museum, who represented the government at the hanging. It occurred about a half hour before Guiteau was escorted to the scaffold.

The jail was surrounded by a detail of United States regular soldiers. When the troops were marched into the building and halted in the big central corridor, the tramp of feet and the crash of their rifles as they came to 'order arms' on the stone flooring caused vibrant echoes to penetrate the cells and corridors.

Guiteau, who had been exceedingly nervous since he arose from his iron cot, crumpled into a chair at the sound and was in a state of near collapse when Dr. MacWilliams, the jail physician, and Dr. Tolden (sic) were hastily summoned.

Warden Crocker, anxious to carry out the death penalty as smoothly as possible also was present.

'Gentlemen,' he said to the doctors, 'this man must be restored at once to prevent a scene on the scaffold.'

Dr. Tilden asked the jail physician if he had any liquor in the jail apothecary shop.

'I have some brandy,' Dr. MacWilliams replied and proceeding to the medicine room,

> returned with a quart bottle of brandy. A goblet full of the liquid was administered to the assassin a few minutes before General Crocker read the death warrant.
>
> The effect on Guiteau, who had been a lifetime abstainer, can be imagined. The dose restored his nervous equilibrium but gave him a decided jag. General Crocker had several days before given Guiteau permission to make a last statement on the scaffold, but when the march of death began, the assassin was so inebriated he forgot the lines and while two Stalwart guards supported him on either side onto the scaffold, he muttered almost incoherently, a lot of jargon.
>
> 'Oh, I'm so glad I'm going to my Lordy. Where is my Lordy? I'm coming my Lordy. O-o-o-h, I'm so glad I'm going to my Lordy.'
>
> Of course, under such conditions, he was given the drop almost immediately after he had reached the trap where several guards had to support him. I was standing by the side of General Crocker when he gave the final signal. Reaching into the rear pocket of his Prince Albert coat, he drew forth a handerchief (sic) and carelessly passed it over his lips. That was the signal that ended the career of the religious fanatic who shot down the Christian President, James A. Garfield.[12]

Several additional incidents connected with the arrest and trial of Guiteau are worth noting. The first is the fact that the pistol with which Guiteau shot President Garfield was carelessly handled by the authorities. "Although brought to detective headquarters, the weapon...was with great impropriety and contrary to all precedents permitted to be taken off by the district attorney."[13] The pistol remained missing for a number of years, but was eventually rediscovered in the files of the United States Attorney, together with the handwritten confession of Guiteau. An undated clipping from the Star newspaper, contains a photograph of United States Attorney Leslie C. Garnett holding the pistol and confession. The article notes that Garnett planned to offer the pistol and confession to the National Museum. Before that could be accomplished, however, the pistol was stolen, and its whereabouts remains unknown to this day.

The bullet which was removed from the body of President Garfield on September 20, 1881, during the postmortem examination also "escaped police record and disposition,"[14] and its whereabouts was unknown for sixty-four years following the attempted assassination. It was finally found quite by accident. An article appearing in the Sunday Star Newspaper, March 16, 1947, gives the following account.

> The bullet...was found in a crevice of an old safe of obscure ownership which had been junked and not long ago was dismantled by the local firm of John G. and James H. Miller, safemasters. The safe had been stored by the safemasters for a long time and no one in the firm could remember who turned it over to the company.
>
> However, there is no reason to doubt the authenticity of the parcel it contained - a letter signed by Dr. D.W. Bliss, chief physician, who attended President Garfield up until his death at the Chief Executive's Summer home at Eberon, N.J. Wired to the letter was the bullet.
>
> The letter reads:
>
> I hereby certify that the within pistol bullet was, in the presence of Surgeon General J.K. Bayes Agnew, S.A. Boynton, D.S. Lamb, who made the autopsy, General D.G. Swain, Col. A.F. Rockwell, taken from the body of James Abram Garfield, late President of the United States, at the postmortem examination held in Franklyn Cottage, Elberton, N.J. during the afternoon of September 20, 1881. (Signed) D.W. Bliss[15]

Finally, the page in the register of the U.S. Jail on which Guiteau's name would have appeared was removed sometime during the years that followed the assassination by person or persons unknown. The gun and the page from the register were no doubt taken because of their historical value. The bullet, it would appear, was possibly placed in the safe for security reasons and in time forgotten.

Mystery still surrounds the disposition of Guiteau's remains. The Sunday Star, dated July 2, 1933, offers the following:

> As to Guiteau's skeleton. Upon apparently good authority it was once said to be in the Army Medical Museum. Some years ago the report was also current that the head had been stolen and exhibited for awhile at Atlantic City and a more recent story informs us that certain Government officials purposely scrambled the bones, or placed them untagged with other homo skeletons in order to lose their identity, which like some of the other stories we see in print about this matter from time to time, is probably without foundation.[16]

Information supplied to your author by the Special Exhibits Section of the Armed Forces Medical Museum, Washington, D.C., indicates that a portion of Guiteau's spleen is all that is preserved in that museum.

THE JAIL ONCE MORE OVERCROWDED AND IN DILAPIDATED CONDITION:

The decade following President Garfield's assassination revealed a sharp rise in the inmate population of the jail, due to the ever increasing population of the District. Once again, the need for a larger jail was apparent. The warden's annual report dated November 1, 1891, indicated an increase in the inmate population from 203 prisoners as of November 1, 1890, to 303 as of October 31, 1891, with an average daily population of 326 for the year.

During the early 1890s, there were numerous requests by various Attorneys General to transfer the power for making rules for the United States Jail from the Supreme Court of the District to the Attorney General. The judges were in favor of the transfer, citing their reasons in a letter dated April 4, 1892, that overcrowded court calendars, the difficulty of getting all of the judges together at one time to consider matters relating to jail management, their inability to make personal inspections of the jail and their lack of power under the law to take testimony. The request was not granted, and the Supreme Court still held the power to make the rules as late as 1900.

The final decade of the 19th Century showed a consistant escalation of the Jail's inmate population as well as deterioration of the jail as a consequence of the overcrowded conditions. At the close of the fiscal year, October 31, 1900, the population had climbed to 373, compared to 334 on November 1, 1899. The Attorney General's annual report to Congress for the year 1907 cited the congested conditions in the Jail:

> The attention of the department was called recently to the condition of the jail in the District of Columbia, which has become so crowded by reason of the large number of prisoners confined there as to render it inappropiate as a place of confinement and to endanger the health, discipline, and safekeeping of its inmates. Under the authority conferred upon me by law, I directed the removal of a large number of prisoners to the jail at Fort Smith, Ark., which had become nearly empty by reason of the admission of Oklahoma to statehood. This measure temporarily relieved the congestion, but the relief has been temporary only, and conditions have again become very unsatisfactory in the District by reason of the inadequate provision for the detention of criminals. I respectfully urge upon the Congress the necessity of prompt and effective action in dealing with this situation.[17]

Despite the overcrowded conditions, efforts were made to provide humane treatment for the prisoners as well as offer them spiritual guidance noted in the warden's report (1909).

> ...the moral condition of affairs at the jail have been greatly improved. Much of the harshness incident to its history has been abated. We have been trying to lift men up and to put them in a way of better living, both by example and instruction, and the means possible at our hand - such as literature and the religious opportunities that are afforded to them on all occasions. The public service on the Sabbath day is held twice - in the morning for the Catholic people, where all attend; in the afternoon for the Protestant people where all attend. The prisoners are brought into the rotunda and seated, where the services are conducted with marked effort. We have no chaplain, but are served by voluntary offerings of the people of Washington. The People's mission have been conducting the services in the afternoon two Sundays in each month. John Roberts, who for many years has been distinguished as the colored chaplain of the jail continues his faithful work with acceptance. The Catholic church occupies the

> open door offered to them by sending laymen and ministers to the various services.
>
> We have collected a small library, and are constantly distributing literature of a healthy character, which is proving to be a source of help in the government of the prisoners, as it affords them opportunities for reading rather than for lying idle in their cells.[18]

The physician's report for 1909 makes a plea for medical supplies and surgical equipment for the jail, stating: "It is no longer possible, and it has not been possible for several years past, to treat the sick prisoners in this institution on humanitarian principles without an adequate supply not only of surgical dressings and instruments, but also of medicines."[19] The physician's report goes on to add that if not for the friendship of himself and the warden with physicians in other hospitals in the city, he would have been "utterly helpless in rendering proper aid and relief to sick prisoners."

> Many serious (capital) surgical operations have been successfully performed upon United States prisoners at the above mentioned hospitals and dispensaries, solely as a matter of courtesy to the warden and the physician to the jail, and upon humanitarian grounds. All of this has been done without any expense to the jail, solely through the personal efforts of the warden and the visiting physician, through the courtesy and at the expense of public and private hospitals, upon whom we have no claim whatever. It assuredly is a haphazard, undignified, and at times very embarrassing procedure for the United States officials (in the person of the warden and the visiting physician) to be continual supplicants for help from neighboring but independent institutions in the treatment of their sick and injured wards.
>
> A surgical dispensary, properly equipped with modern sterilizing apparatus, operating table, instrument stand, instrument case, basins for containing sterilizing fluids, and washstands for cleansing and sterilizing the operator's hands, are imperatively needed in the jail. To properly equip this dispensary will cost $1,200, for which an itemized statement will be furnished.[20]

The warden's annual report for the year 1909 noted that the inmate population on November 1, 1908 was 570. His report paints a vivid picture of the conditions under which the prisoners lived:

> The general conditions at the jail continue to be bad. They have been so enlarged upon in the previous reports of the warden that it is not necessary to repeat here, except to emphasize, the sanitary conditions, which must be well known to the department and to the public. The jail is still without any sanitation in the cell rooms. The old bucket system of centuries is still in vogue. These buckets must be emptied two or three times each day, which fills the entire jail with the fowlest and most unwholesome air possible. The heating plant throughout the jail is in bad shape; it was inspected a short time ago by an officer of the Government and report thereon was made to the department. The lighting of the jail is very deficient and was also reported upon, as I understand. I therefore must earnestly request that the heating plant of the jail be changed at the earliest possible date after the meeting of Congress, as it is liable to break down at any time and leave the jail wholly without heat. We ought to have electric light in the prison, as all the other prisons in the country are supplied with it. Our system of gas is old, antiquated, and worn out; it leaves us to grope around in the cell wings with lanterns in the nighttime - something unheard of in almost any other prison in the country.
>
> The current from the electric-light plant of the city is now at hand running down B Street to the buildings east of us. We could very easily have current turned on at the jail if we had the wiring necessary. This I earnestly urge as a reasonable thing for the safety as well as the convenience of the jail.[21]

The Attorney General in his report to Congress for the year 1909 made the following plea:

> The attention of Congress has been called by the reports of my predecessors, during a

> period of at least six years past, to the shocking condition of the jail in the District of Columbia. Following a message from the President of the United States to the Congress on January 11, 1909, transmitting the report of the Commissioners appointed to investigate the condition of the jail and the workhouse, Congress enacted a law for the acquisition of property on which to erect a reformatory and workhouse. No action, however, was taken with respect to the present condition of the jail. A personal inspection made by me in the early part of June brought sharply to my attention what the President characterized in his message to Congress as 'the really outrageous conditions' in that institution.[22]

The Attorney General and the warden were joined in their pleas for a solution to the overcrowding in the jail by the press and others who felt that such deplorable conditions should not be permitted to exist, especially in the Nation's Capital. This pressure prompted President Theodore Roosevelt to appoint a commission (in 1908) to review conditions in both the jail and the workhouse, and to recommend remedial measures to alleviate the overcrowding as well as the idleness that prevailed among the prisoners. The Commission's report to the President and Congress confirmed the fact that indeed the jail and workhouse were in a deplorable state. The proposed reforms recommended by the Commission introduced a philosophy so new that it completely revolutionized the methods of treatment for prisoners in the District penal institutions.

SOURCES

[1.] _Daily Morning Chronicle,_ July 29, 1873, Clipping file, Washingtoniana Room, Martin Luther King Library, Washington, D.C.

[2.] _Ibid._

[3.] _Star Newspaper,_ June 30, 1882, Clipping file, Washingtoniana Room, Martin Luther King Library, Washington, D.C.

[4.] Peters, F.E., "A Short History of the Washington Jails," Unpublished, May 2, 1952, On file in D.C. Department of Corrections Museum, Lorton, VA.

[5.] Annual Report, John S. Crocker, Warden, U.S. Jail, Washington, D.C., Department of Justice Library, Washington, D.C., p. 36.

[6.] _Ibid.,_ p. 36.

[7.] _Ibid.,_ p. 36.

[8.] _Ibid.,_ p. 37.

[9.] Peters, R.E., pp. 18, 19.

[10.] _Ibid.,_ pp. 18, 19.

[11.] Proctor, John Clagett, "Garfield Assassinated 52 Years Ago, _Sunday Star,_ July 2, 1933, p. 7.

[12.] Mitchell, Capt. J. Walter, _Times Newspaper,_ Washington, D.C., September 4, 1921.

[13.] Proctor, John Claggett, "Garfield Bullet Unearthed, _The Sunday Star,_ Washington, D.C., March 16, 1947, Sec. C-2.

[14.] _Ibid.,_ Sec. C-2.

[15.] _Ibid.,_ Sec. C-2.

[16.] Proctor, John Clagett, July 2, 1933, p. 7.

[17.] Report of the Attorney General, 1907, Justice Department Library, Washington, D.C., p. 16.

[18.] Report of Warden Thomas H. McKee, November 1, 1909, Department of Justice Library, Washington, D.C., pp. 351-352.

[19.] *Ibid.*, p. 355.

[20.] *Ibid.*, p. 355.

[21.] *Ibid.*, pp. 348-349.

[22.] Report of the Attorney General, 1909, Department of Justice Library, Washington, D.C., p. 13.

Original U.S. Jail (later known as D.C. Jail), before any additions or changes were made to it. Photograph courtesy of Washingtoniana Division, D.C. Public Library.

PART II
(1910 - 1945)

CHAPTER 7

THE PENAL COMMISSION'S REPORT

The Commission appointed by President Theodore Roosevelt, usually referred to as the "Penal Commission," consisted of three members: Associate Supreme Court Justice of the District of Columbia, Wendell P. Stafford; Mr. Juno Joy Edson; and Mr. Robert V. LaDow. The recommendations set forth in their report to the President and Congress called for revolutionary changes that greatly benefitted the District's penal institutions as well as its courts. The innovative concepts and the foresight of those three men are evident in the "Scope of the Report" that follows:

> If it shall seem to you, Mr. President, that in some portions of our report we have gone somewhat far afield, our reason is that the problem presented has seemed to us to be of such magnitude and to involve such far-reaching consequences that it could not be wisely solved without looking to the future, as well as to the present, without considering the probable growth of the city as well as its present needs, without considering those new and better methods of dealing with prisoners, which have been successfully adopted in many states, without, in short considering the whole penal system of the District, both as it is and as it ought to be, and without taking note of the conditions which produce crime, and whose removal it is possible and practicable for us to secure. The system we are invited to propose is a system for the District of Columbia, the seat of the National Government. The capital of a nation, though it lie at the level of the sea, is a city set on a hill - it cannot be hid. Whether we wish it or not, it will be observed of all observers, and its influence will go out for good or for evil in every direction and possibly to every nook and corner of the land. We wish to see a system adopted which may become a model to all who are seeking to improve their own institutions and policies, and which shall be worthy to form a part of the law of a wise and just people.[1]

The Commission's recommendations contained six specific points for expanding the District's penal institutions as well as providing its courts with a greater degree of flexibility in sentencing than ever before:

> There should be -
>
> 1. A jail, to be used only as a house of detention, never as a place of confinement for those under sentence.
>
> 2. A probation system for those cases which may be safely dealt with without sending the offender to any place of confinement.
>
> 3. A reformatory for all who must be sentenced to confinement and who nevertheless are hopeful cases.
>
> 4. A workhouse for those who must be confined and who are not proper subjects for reformatory treatment, and yet, those offenses are not such as to require that they be sent to a penitentiary.
>
> 5. Confinement in the federal prison or penitentiary for those worst offenders who are not proper subjects for either the reformatory or the workhouse.
>
> 6. A carefully guarded parole law for prisoners in these various institutions who may be safely released upon conditions.[2]

All of the recommendations proposed by the Penal Commission were acted upon immediately, except the parole law which was not passed in the District until 1932. Appendix B contains detailed information regarding the origin of parole in the District of Columbia. A probation system was established in the District June 25, 1910, (Sec. 24-101 D.C. Code),[3] and placed under the jurisdiction of the District Court of the United States for the District of Columbia. The Commission recommended that the practice of confining long-term felony offenders in penitentiaries outside the District be continued for the time being.

The role of the District Jail was significantly broadened as a result of the Commission's recommendation that it be used only as house of detention. In addition, living conditions were much improved. The extent of these changes in the operation of the jail will be discussed in detail in Chapter 12.

The "industrial farm" concept was popular in some of the more progressive state penal systems throughout the country at the time the Commission was preparing its report. The philosophy of this type of institution was based on "hard work" for every able-bodied prisoner, together with humane treatment, fresh air, wholesome food, and sanitary living quarters. The Commission favored this idea and felt it could "...arouse confidence and self-respect in even the lowest type of humanity."[4] With that in mind, it added the following recommendation:

> For the workhouse, then, as for the reformatory, we recommend the purchase of a large tract of undeveloped farm land, which may be either within the District or in one of the adjoining States, as may be found most advisable - a farm of not less than a thousand acres, to which the institution now known as the 'workhouse' should be removed. Land adapted to this purpose may doubtless be obtined at a very low price per acre.[5]

It was thought that "...clearing and cultivation of the land itself, with the construction of necessary buildings, would furnish occupation for hundreds of those sent there."[6]

The Penal Commission viewed the men who should be confined in a reformatory and those in the workhouse as two distinctly different classes of offenders. In fact, it recommended that the institutions in which the two groups were to be confined be physically located some distance apart. The rationale of that way of thinking was to lead the reformatory inmate "...to regard himself as not sunk to the level of the criminal classes, to preserve his self-respect so as to enable him to go out at the end of his term feeling that he has not been branded as a felon."[7] The Commission's concept of the reformatory type inmate follows:

> What we need is an institution to which the courts can send such offenders as can not be safely released upon probation, who must for one reason or another be confined for a time at least, and yet who are susceptible to good influences, capable of being trained to some useful form of labor, by being improved in body and mind and made more fit to meet the temptations of life - who have not abandoned themselves to criminal courses nor come to look upon themselves as at serious odds with society, but who will almost certainly turn out

> habitual criminals if they are not immediately turned from the path they have entered. It is not so much a question what is the name of the crime they have committed (barring a few of the gravest) as it is a question of how they came to commit it and under what circumstances it was done, and what the general disposition and character of the offender has been. Most of those who would be eligible to such an institution are between the ages of 17 and 30 years. We believe that the court before whom the case is tried will be able to make a generally wise decision upon the question whether the culprit is a hopeful subject for such treatment. It is believed that if there were such an institution now established in the District there are between 500 and 600 prisoners, now confined in jail, workhouse, or penitentiary, who would be receiving the benefit of its course of discipline and education.[8]

It was further recommended that there should be shops in the reformatory where the "...men could be taught to use their hands in trades of skill and engage in the manufacture of useful articles."[9] In addition, classes should be offered where "...at some hours of each day the young men should be taught the rudimentary branches and hear lectures on practical subjects."[10]

The workhouse type of offender was described as follows:

> There is a large class of offenders whose crimes are not of that magnitude to demand a sentence in the penitentiary, and yet who are not proper subjects for reformatory treatment. They may be too old, they may have offended too often, or they may be of such a character that it would be useless to send them to a reformatory, and moreover to send them there might be to undo the work which is there being done upon hopeful ones. At the same time they may not have deserved a long term sentence, or for other reasons it may not be best that they should be sent to a penitentiary, either state or federal. Among this class will be found many who have committed assaults, many vagrants, drunkards, deserters of their families, abusers of their wives, and the like. Usually these are men to whom hard work is the

> most dreaded form of punishment. They should be put to hard labor at long hours. Even among these some cases may be found that will deserve attention under a parole system, but most of them will need to be kept to, or near to the end of their terms. For such men as these work in the open air, upon the farm or in construction of buildings or in redeeming waste places, is admirably fitted.
>
> * * *
>
> That such men are not fit subjects for a reformatory does not mean that they are not to be treated with any reference to improvement or that they are not to be released the sooner by reason of exemplary behavior. Still less does it mean that they have forfeited their right to be treated as men and to receive every encouragement of which they prove worthy. Least of all does it mean that they should be unnecessarily degraded by marks or badges of shame or compelled to look upon themselves as beyond hope. They should not be put in stripes. On the contrary, we believe in stimulating them to self-respect in all practical ways, and especially by setting apart a substantial portion of their earnings to be paid to their families, or for want thereof to be paid to them on their release; and we believe that their sentences should be somewhat elastic and responsive to their behavior and indications of a change in disposition.[11]

On the matter of how the line of jurisdiction should be drawn between the District and the Federal Government, the Penal Commission believed that the jail as well as the workhouse and the reformatory, "...should be under the exclusive direction and control of District Authorities."[12] The rationale of the Commission was that the majority of the prisoners were residents of the District. Further, the Federal government was in the process of building prisons at Leavenworth and Atlanta, and there would be ample space for United States prisoners as well as those long-term prisoners from the District.

The Bill authorizing purchase of sites for the reformatory and workhouse was enacted in 1909 by the 60th Congress, Sess. II, Chg, 250, and read:

> ...by the Senate and House of Representatives of the United States of America in Congress assembled, That the Commissioners of the District of Columbia are hereby authorized and directed to purchase two tracts of land, widely separated of not less than one thousand acres each either or both of which may be in the District, or in the States of Maryland or Virginia; one of which shall be used as a site for the erection of a reformatory and the other as a site for the erection of a workhouse.[13]

It further specified the inmate capacity of the reformatory as being 1,000 and the workhouse about 500. Other stipulations of the Bill included authorization for the Commissioners of the District to appoint a commission to consist of three persons, one of which would be one of the District Commissioners, who would act as chairman. This special commission would select the sites for the workhouse and reformatory as well as an architect with expertise in construction of prison buildings, who would prepare the plans and estimate the cost of building the two institutions. In addition, the District Commissioners were authorized by the Bill to employ prisoners who were confined in the workhouse to work as laborers in constructing the buildings. The Attorney General was also authorized to permit prisoners of the jail to work on the construction of the buildings.

Upon authorization by Congress to acquire sites for a reformatory and workhouse, the special commission publically advertised and accepted proposals for tracts of land that complied with the recommendation of the Penal Commission. A number of bids were received, and after careful consideration, a tract of land consisting of approximately 1,155 acres was found near the Town of Occoquan, along the Occoquan River, in Southern Fairfax County, Virginia. The land was undeveloped, except for a small stone crushing operation located along the river. Although the site was situated in a remote area of the county with no means of access to it by roads, its location on the Occoquan River at the point where it flows into the Potomac, made transportation of prisoners and equipment by boat or barge easy to attain as well as economical. That factor, together with its potential for development into farm land, convinced the special commission that the site would be an excellent location for the workhouse.

An article appearing in the Fairfax Herald newspaper, dated March 25, 1910, entitled "Condemnation Proceedings," gave an account of the legal matters that were involved in acquiring the land for the workhouse site:

> Condemnation proceedings over a tract of land comprising about 1,155 acres, located in Fairfax County near Occoquan, which the government desires as a site for a District of Columbia Workhouse, were heard in Alexandria last week, in the United States Court for the eastern district of Virginia, Judge Edmund Waddill, presiding.
>
> All the court officers were present, Judge L.I. Lewis, United States District Attorney, represented the government, and Judge C.E. Nicol represented all the property owners in the case, viz:
>
> L.A. Denty and wife, T.D. Violett and wife, G.W. Dawson and wife, J.L. Dawson and wife, Katherine U. Holt and R.O. Holt, her husband, W.S. Lynn and wife, Geo. Selecman, Redmond Selecman and wife, and George A. Selecman.
>
> After the legal papers in the case had been received, Judge Nicol for the property owners stated that by consent all his clients had agreed that the proceedings should be conducted as in one case, and that all had agreed as to the price at which they held their lands.
>
> Twenty-four men had been summoned from which a jury of twelve could be selected to appraise the lands.
>
> ...the price had been agreed upon and the jury returned a verdict assessing the value of the 1,154.70 acres in question at $28,648.84, which includes interest for about nine months and the price of a rock crusher, or at an average of about $18 per acre. The court thereupon entered an order approving the verdict of the appraisers and ordering a distribution of the money by Judge Nicol.[14]

The deed was recorded April 1, 1910, in Fairfax County Court House, with title vested in the United States Government, in Deed Book F-7, Pages 212-218. The Appropriation Act authorizing purchase is Public Law 303 (HR 25392). The land contained in the deed became known as the "Workhouse Tract." It is noted that over the years from 1910 until 1953, eight additional parcels of land, adjoining the Workhouse Tract, were acquired by the United States Government for use by the District of Columbia penal institutions. The "Workhouse Tract," however, is the only acquisition over which the United States Government has exclusive jurisdiction. The additional ones share joint jurisdiction with Fairfax County. (Detailed information can be obtained from document entitled "Jurisdictional status of criminal laws within the Lorton Reservation which comprises both Lorton Reformatory and the Occoquan Workhouse.((CCO: 3.CO-1))-Jurisdiction and arrest procedures on Lorton Reservation, dated October 10, 1966."). Appendix C contains a complete listing of the nine acquisitions of land by the District in Fairfax County, Virginia.

At the time the workhouse site was purchased, the Special Commission had also selected a tract of land for the reformatory. This tract was known as the "Belvoir" or "White House" tract and was located approximately three miles from Mount Vernon, on the Potomac River. The site included within its boundaries, the home of the Fairfaxes, and fronted on Gunston Cove. Just across the cove was Gunston Hall, the former home of George Mason, and just North was Woodlawn, the former home of Nellie Custis. This land was thought to be particularly well suited for the reformatory for two reasons: 1) it was located on the Potomac, which would afford economical transportation of prisoners and equipment, and 2) its location was in compliance with the recommendation of the Penal Commission, that reformatories should be isolated from other institutions.

The decision to purchase this tract of land drew much opposition from concerned citizens of Fairfax County, particularly the Mount Vernon Ladies Association. Several law suits were filed and a committee from the Ladies Association filed a petition with Congress protesting the location of a penal institution within three miles of the tomb of George Washington. On June 30, 1911, the House of Representatives voted to prohibit the location of the reformatory on this site, noting that "...the location of a criminal reformatory within 10 miles of the home and tomb of George Washington at Mount Vernon would desecrate a national shrine."[15] An amendment was adopted stating that no funds would be spent on any penal institutions within 10 miles of Mount Vernon, except the workhouse at Occoquan. This development made it necessary for the Special Commission to continue its search for a suitable tract of land on which to build the reformatory. The search did not end until 1913. Construction of the workhouse, however, got underway in late Spring, 1910.

While the prospect of having two of the District's penal institutions in their midst was disturbing to some of the citizens of Fairfax County, particularly those in the Mount Vernon area, not all of the residents were opposed to the idea. George I. Alling, who lived near the workhouse site, saw the economic aspect of having the penal institutions in southern Fairfax County. He expressed his views in the December 9, 1910 issue of the Fairfax Herald:

> As to the Workhouse: As I live as near to it as any one I should be able to see it fairly well. It is located in a territory almost isolated and of very little value to any private parties. The taxes on the whole tract were about $75 per year, I am told by a county official.
>
> Now look at it. Outside of convicts there are employed probably 100 men with families, who live near by, and they are paid much better wages than they would get elsewhere. It has made a market for all that the farmers have to sell as far away as they want to haul it from.
>
> As to the society side: There are none of those upper 400 living in this end of Fairfax and not likely to be any. From the just plain people here I have yet to hear an adverse report, or of any annoyance whatever. I say give them credit for what they do. Even among our neighbors some are not altogether as desirable as others.[16]

Both the workhouse and the reformatory continued to employ local residents of Fairfax County and neighboring Prince William County. Over the years, as the institutions expanded, they became one of the major sources of employment for the community. This not only aided the economy of the two counties, but in time the institutions were accepted as part of the community, since most of the employees were local citizens.

SOURCES

[1.] Report of the Penal Commission, Jail, Workhouse, etc., in the District of Columbia, on file in the D.C. Department of Corrections Museum, Lorton, Virginia, p. 28.

[2.] Ibid., p.12.

[3.] D.C. Code (1951 ed.), Title 24, Sec. 101, Chap. 1 - Probation (Washington, D.C.: U.S. Government Printing Office, 1952), p. 769.

[4.] Report of Penal Commission, p. 18.

[5.] Ibid., p. 18.

[6.] Ibid., p. 16.

[7.] Ibid., p. 16.

[8.] Ibid., p. 16.

[9.] Ibid., p. 17.

[10.] Ibid., p. 17.

[11.] Ibid., pp. 17-18.

[12.] Ibid., p. 20.

[13.] Ibid., pp. 47-48.

[14.] "Condemnation Proceedings," Fairfax Herald, March 25, 1910, Fairfax County Library, Fairfax, Virginia.

[15.] "House Votes to Prohibit Location of Reformatory Near Mount Vernon," Fairfax Herald, January 27, 1911.

[16.] "As to the Workhouse," Fairfax Herald, December 9, 1910.

CHAPTER 8

THE WASHINGTON ASYLUM AND JAIL (1911 - 1921)

Upon recommendation of the D.C. Commissioners, the 61st Congress (34th Sess.) approved the transfer of the United States Jail from the jurisdiction of the Justice Department to the District of Columbia, effective July 1, 1911. The same Act provided for combining the jail with the Washington Asylum Hospital. The jail was placed under the Board of Charities, and the two institutions became officially known as the Washington Asylum and Jail. L.F. Zinkhan, warden of the jail, was named superintendent of the joint operation of both institutions. It is noted that the title "warden" was never again used in the District's penal institutions.

Although joining of the two institutions was viewed as an important step in unifying local institutions, the asylum hospital authorities voiced the disadvantage of being associated with a penal institution.

> The legislation authorizing the combining into one the two institutions formerly known as the Washington Asylum and Jail has resulted in making the Washington Asylum Hospital an integral part of the same institution as the jail, just as it formerly was an integral part of the same institution as the workhouse. The hospital renders an indispensible service to the community, and the demands upon it are constantly increasing, but its work is seriously hampered in many ways because of its intimate association with the penal institutions. It is difficult to induce patients who greatly need its care to enter the hospital, and it is difficult to secure proper nurses and other attendants to care for them.[1]

Ever since 1846, when the asylum hospital became a part of the almshouse and workhouse, it had served as the only public institution of its kind in the District. As a result of its long struggle in caring for the poor without sufficient resources to do so, its buildings were dilapidated and considered unfit "for purposes of the sick."[2] In addition, the hospital was greatly overcrowded. As early as 1903, the Board of Charities urged that greater effort be made to provide a municipal hospital for the City of Washington, citing that there were a number of persons who should be in a hospital but "they were denied admission because there was no room"[3] in the asylum hospital. Also, in 1903, when the almshouse was moved to Blue Plains, the brick building which had been occupied by the inmates of that institution was converted into a psychopathic unit for the hospital. Nevertheless, it continued to treat vagrants and disorderly persons.

A potters field, which had been located on the same grounds as the asylum and jail, was moved to Blue Plains at the same time as the almshouse, making room for expansion of the asylum. It is interesting to note that the District built a crematorium in 1907 near the site of the asylum and jail for the poor who had no relatives or friends to take care of funeral expenses. The building was closed in 1929 because it was badly deteriorated. The city resumed the use of potters field at Blue Plains. The crematorium was razed in 1948.

The desperate need for an adequate municipal hospital in the District is shown by the numerous recommendations that were made to secure better physical and mental health care facilities for those residents who could not afford private hospital care. In 1908, "...the Board of Charities recommended facilities be provided for treatment of the acutely insane."[4] Also in 1908, a quarantine station for smallpox suspects was erected on the hospital reservation at a cost of $15,000. New Hampshire physician and Senator, Jacob H. Gallinger, introduced Bill (S-6594) at the first session of the 60th Congress (1909) making special provisions for the treatment of "alcoholics and drug habitues." In 1910, the Board of Charities again recommended that buildings be constructed to replace the one-story wooden structures that comprised much of the asylum hospital. "The medical profession and social workers called attention to the need for psychopathic wards to care for acute mental disease."[5]

The opening of the new workhouse at Occoquan in 1910 made available two buildings which had been previously occupied by inmates of that institution. In 1912, the District Commissioners submitted a report to Congress noting the availability of the buildings. The Commissioners, however, "...were indisposed to recommend those buildings be used for hospital accommodations."[6] The Board of Charities, too, was of the opinion that it would be a mistake to spend money in an attempt to convert the workhouse into a hospital. It also stated that the hospital should not be associated with the jail.

It was not until 1914 that $15,000 was appropriated for construction of "...a hospital for municipal purposes."[7] The original site chosen for the new facility was located at 14th and Upshur Streets. "There was so much opposition on the part of citizens in that community against the location of a municipal hospital in that neighborhood, that action was deferred."[8] Finally, in 1917, Congress decided to "...abandon the idea of erecting a new municipal hospital on the Upshur Street site, and to construct it on Reservation 13,"[9] i.e., the location of the asylum hospital. An appropriation of $600,000 was provided by Congress, but construction of the hospital was delayed "...due to World War I."[10] Later, an additional appropriation, increasing the amount to $1,500,000, was necessary because of post-war inflation. During the decade of the 1920s, an entirely new group of buildings were constructed.

"In 1921, the administration of the jail and hospital were...separated,"[11] and each institution reported directly to the Board of Charities. By Act of Congress, June 30, 1922, the name of the asylum and hospital was officially changed to "Gallinger Municipal Hospital," in honor of Senator Gallinger who served on the District Committee for more than 20 years, and who was instrumental in securing appropriations for construction of the hospital as well as other large appropriations for improvement of the District's Health Department.

Under the name of Gallinger Municipal, the asylum hospital continued to expand and to serve as the only general institution of its kind that was owned and operated by the District of Columbia for the purpose of caring for indigent, sick, and injured persons.

Although the asylum hospital severed its official ties with the District's penal institutions in 1921, after having been combined first with the Workhouse for over fifty years, and then with the Jail for another ten years, it continued to share the site of Reservation 13 with the Jail under the name of Gallinger Municipal Hospital. In earlier years, gangs of male prisoners were detailed to the Gallinger Hospital to perform various maintenance duties. While the arrangement benefited the hospital by providing free labor, it was not always satisfactory with the jail. A letter of complaint by W.L. Peak, Superintendent of the Jail, dated March 24, 1931, to M.M. Barnard, General Superintendent of the D.C. Penal Institutions, included a long list of escapees from the hospital detail. Excerpts from that letter follows:

> I am submitting herewith list of prisoners who have escaped from the hospital grounds since July 1st, 1930; also a list of those who have been turned in in an intoxicated condition during that period. The Hospital Authorities do not seem to know when a man escapes as

> reports to that effect are seldom made. Escapes are usually discovered by the jail officers when the prisoners are turned at the jail at night by the hospital watchman, and when the watchman's attention has been called to the fact that a prisoner is missing he seems to be surprised and claims no knowledge of how or when the escape occurred. This indicates poor supervision.
>
> A few days ago a white prisoner working on the hospital detail became intoxicated and the hospital authorities, I understand, called the police from No. Five Precinct, and had him arrested and taken to court and given another sentence. We carried this man as an escapee, but learned later that he had been turned over to the police.
>
> Two white prisoners became intoxicated last Sunday at the Hospital, presumably, from drinking wood alcohol. One of them died Sunday afternoon and the other died last night. These two cases are in the hands of the Coroner at the present time.
>
> * * *
>
> About eighteen men attempted to strike last week because of the poor food that is served them at the Hospital. They claim that the food served to them at the Hospital is not near as good as the jail fare. They were going to march in a body to my residence during the noon hour to make a protest, but I understand were persuaded from doing it.[12]

Around 1950, the name "Gallinger Municipal" was discontinued and it became known as the D.C. General Hospital. While the practice of detailing gangs of prisoners from the Jail to the hospital has long since been discontinued, through the years a close association has been maintained between the two institutions. Today, most of the prisoners from the D.C. Department of Corrections who require hospital care are transported to D.C. General Hospital for treatment, and a special secure "locked-ward" is maintained by the hospital for the prisoner patients.

SOURCES

[1.] Annual Report to the Commissioners of the District of Columbia, November 1, 1910 - October 31, 1911 (Washington, D.C.: U.S. Government Printing Office), p. 387.

[2.] A Brief History of District of Columbia General Hospital, undated, D.C. Department of Public Health, on file in D.C. Department of Corrections Museum, Lorton, Virginia, p. 6.

[3.] _Ibid.,_ p. 7.

[4.] _Ibid.,_ p. 8.

[5.] _Ibid.,_ p. 8.

[6.] _Ibid.,_ p. 9.

[7.] _Ibid.,_ p. 10.

[8.] _Ibid.,_ p. 10.

[9.] _Ibid.,_ p. 10.

[10.] _Ibid.,_ p. 10.

[11.] _Ibid.,_ p. 10.

[12.] W.L. Peak, Letter to M.M. Barnard, General Superintendent of D.C. Penal Institutions, March 24, 1931, on file D.C. Department of Corrections Museum, Lorton, Virginia.

CHAPTER 9

BUILDING THE WORKHOUSE AT OCCOQUAN (1910 - 1945)

William H. Whittaker, in his first annual report to the Board of Charities, recalled what he found upon his arrival at the Workhouse Tract July 1, 1910, to assume the duties of first superintendent:

> On taking charge of the institution,...I found 29 prisoners had been transferred from the old workhouse, Washington, D.C., and were located in tents on the Occoquan River, where a stockade was under process of construction, within which were to be erected dormitories, dining rooms, and hospital facilities for the care of about 300 prisoners.[1]

The 29 prisoners noted in Mr. Whittaker's report had been transported to the workhouse site by barge, to the point where the Occoquan flows into the Potomac River, and then about one half mile up the Occoquan to the workhouse site. It is noted that in September, 1910, the District "...accepted a United States tugboat, the 'General Warren,' from the Federal government in payment of a debt of $3,000 for dredging machinery purchased for use by the War Department."[2] The "General Warren" was placed in operation between Occoquan and Washington for transportation of prisoners and supplies. "In 1912, a system of water transportation between Washington and Occoquan was inaugurated. The Ninth Street Wharf in Washington was officially transferred to the jurisdiction of the superintendent of the workhouse in August, 1915."[3]

Mr. Whittaker's first report further read: "The work of the first 30 days at the institution was in completing the stockade and the necessary tents to care for the prisoners as they were transferred from the workhouse in the District."[4] By the end of August, 1910, the stockade and tents were completed and equipped to handle about 300 inmates. "The next work was the building of a road from our location on the bank of the Occoquan River to the permanent site, a mile and a half North, near the center of the 1,150 acre tract."[5]

Very little of the land had been cleared, and most of it was covered with second growth timber and underbrush. Mr. Whittaker noted: "This made our task of handling prisoners more difficult, so that we could not give to each officer a great number of prisoners."[6] This was a problem that required some experimentation, as described in Mr. Whittaker's report:

> It being a new proposition to work with this class of prisoners, we necessarily had to be cautious and to proceed with a great deal of care, in order that there might be no criticism from the standpoint of discipline, or from the proper care of the prisoner, as to his health and safekeeping.
>
> * * *
>
> We started with six inmates to a squad. This we continued for a short period and increased the number from time to time until at the end of this fiscal year we find the average number of prisoners successfully handled and worked by each officer is 20.[7]

Upon completion of the road to the permanent site, which required about 60 days, construction of the temporary wooden buildings began. "The plans and number of buildings constructed were laid out by the engineer commissioner of the District and built under the direction of a superintendent of construction furnished by the Engineer Department." The goal was to make every effort to "...get these quarters in shape for winter."[8]

The health of the prisoners during the first year was described as exceptionally good by Mr. Whittaker:

> There has been very little sickness, in fact, most every case in the hospital was where the individual had some disease or trouble before coming to the institution. We find this locality practically free of malaria. The open-air-treatment given the inmates in the one-story, well-ventilated dormitories, dining rooms, and lounging quarters, in my judgment, are reasons for the good health of the inmates of the institution.
>
> Our policy has been to keep the prisoner clean and give him good wholesome, and substantial food, well cooked, and to see that he is given fair treatment by the officer in charge. Our policy, also, is to have each and every prisoner do a good, honest day's work, all of which is beneficial to him and conducive to his good health.[8]

Although there were nine deaths among the inmates that first year, only two resulted from accidents sustained while the inmates were working on construction of the buildings. Of the other seven deaths, five were caused by pneumonia, one from a stroke, and one from traumatic epilepsy.

In his first annual report, and repeatedly in the years that followed, Mr. Whittaker urged the D.C. Commissioners, through the Board of Charities, to press Congress to strengthen the penal code under which the workhouse operated. He felt the new philosophy provided a healthy and practical employment for the prisoners, but he believed that two important amendments to the law were necessary before beneficial and lasting results could be achieved:

> First: A fixed sentence, such as the courts are now compelled to give those who violate the law and especially those who have short terms such as 15 to 30 days, is the cause of much of the crime and vagrancy committed in the District. I recommend that the criminal code be so amended that prisoners committed to the workhouse should be sentenced for a period of not less than 30 days and no more than 2 years, the time of release to be vested in the Commissioners of the District depending upon the ability of the prisoner to maintain himself as a self-supporting and law-abiding citizen.
>
> Second: Let the law provide that before the prisoner is released on parole a position be provided for him for at least six months, during which time he would be under the supervision of an officer of the institution to see that he honestly and faithfully performs the labor that he agreed to do at the time he is released on parole, and also see that the employer gives the man a square deal. Let the law further provide that should the prisoner violate any of the terms and conditions of his parole he can be returned to the institution without cost to the taxpayers to serve part or all of his unexpired sentence.[10]

It is noted that many of the prisoners were arrested on vagrancy and intoxication charges. Intoxication was punishable by a fine and/or short term sentence in the jail or workhouse of five to 90 days, depending on the severity of the case. Most of the men and women arrested for intoxication were alcoholics, and the same individuals kept returning to the workhouse time and time again. For this reason, Mr. Whittaker believed that the indeterminate sentence would provide enough time to assure that these offenders could receive help before they were released to the community. He pointed out:

> No greater injustice can be meted out to an individual who is 'down and out' than to give him a short sentence of 15 to 30 days, at the end of which he is discharged, with no money, with a suit of clothes that 50 percent of the time is a disgrace to him and a detriment to his efforts in procuring a job, with no opportunity in view and no friends to assist him. Such treatment only means for the individual another sentence of the same old charge of vagrancy.[11]

In spite of Mr. Whittaker's pleas, and the pleas of others who shared his views, legislation providing for indeterminate sentence and parole was not passed in the District of Columbia until 1932.

The cost of transforming the undeveloped Workhouse Tract of land into a thriving industrial farm was kept to a minimum by careful planning, together with the use of the natural resources available on the land itself and the inexhaustable supply of cheap labor provided by the prisoners. The wood for construction of the temporary buildings was provided from trees felled on the workhouse site and sawed into lumber.

One of the most innovative plans for the development of the workhouse site was the opening of a brick yard as an adjunct to the small stone crushing operation that was on the site when it was purchased. The annual report for 1911 noted:

> Much progress has been made during the year in building necessary roads through the site and in clearing and improving land for agricultural purposes. Two brick kilns have been constructed and are now in use. It is planned to build 10 additional kilns. It is expected that these kilns will furnish approximately 40,000 bricks per day. The entire product can be used on public work by the District of Columbia. During the past year stone has been furnished for road making in the District from the quarries on the workhouse site, the stone having been quarried and crushed by the prisoners. Practically all the labor of making the improvements indicated has

been performed by the prisoners under the direction of a few hired foremen...

> The development of this interesting work thus far has been accomplished under the immediate supervision of a special commission on buildings and the Commissioners of the District of Columbia. The work of establishing the institution has now been completed to such a degree that the commissioners have requested the Board of Charities to take supervision, and arrangements to this effect will soon be made.[12]

By 1914, the building project on the workhouse site had progressed as follows:

> On this land there has been constructed some 30 buildings, including dormitories, dining room, lounging hall, hospital, horse and dairy barns. These are all one-story buildings, made of wood, with a view of giving ample light and ventilation. The plan for the prisoners is that of the congregate or dormitory system. There are no cells, locks, or bars about the institution. Two hundred prisoners are taken care of during the night in each dormitory, and as we have 600 male prisoners these require three buildings. Cots are arranged side by side in these dormitories on raised platforms, and sufficient bedding, consisting of mattresses, sheets and pillow, blankets and comforts, are given to each prisoner. All the buildings are equipped with steam heat and electric lights, and have ample water, both hot and cold, in each of the buildings with modern up-to-date sewerage system.
>
> * * *
>
> In one of the buildings referred to there is a shower bath and arrangements for the inmates to make their toilets. In this building 125 men can be taken care of at one time. We have no washbasins, but have a faucet for each man, which makes it more sanitary, and the men are also furnished with individual towels and soap.[13]

Agricultural pursuits were developed on the workhouse site simultaneously with the brickyard, sawmill, and stone crushing operations. During the first several years of operation, land was cleared, but before crops could be grown, it was necessary to cultivate the soil and prepare it for planting. The 1911 annual report notes: During the winter..."we constructed on the bank of the Occoquan River a wharf, 160 feet long and about 25 feet wide.[14] One of the functions of the wharf was to aid in unloading manure collected on the streets of Washington and brought to the workhouse site by barge, to be used as fertilizer for the farm land. In 1911, over seven tons of manure were collected, and Mr. Whittaker noted that the workhouse would be able to handle at least 10,000 tons of fertilizer for an indefinite number of years.

A copy of the menu at the workhouse for the week ending February 25, 1911, indicates that the men were given three meals a day.[15] The menu contained a variety of foods including roast beef, roast pork shoulder, liver, fish, and frankfurters. The vegetables consisted mostly of potatoes, beans, onions, pickles, vegetable soup, and rice. The only fruit on the menu was stewed prunes. Bread and coffee were served with each meal. The meals, although somewhat starchy, were a vast improvement over the food that was served to prisoners of the workhouse and jail during the 19th century. It is noted that the inmates were segregated by race.

An interesting table included in the 1911 report, shows the weight gains from a random sampling of 50 men from the workhouse population. The men in the sample were all serving 30 day sentences, and the results indicated weight gains among the men of "...one to 18 pounds."[16]

As the institution developed a dairy herd was added, along with an orchard, hennery, and a hog raising industry. An article appearing in the <u>Fairfax Herald,</u> September 15, 1916, read:

> Hog-raising is becoming one of the big industries at the District of Columbia Workhouse Farm, near Occoquan in this county. Approximately 700 pigs compose this year's output, and facilities are about completed for raising double this number next year. It is Superintendent Whittaker's plan to slaughter 700 hogs annually for consumption at the institution, and sell an equal number, which should bring in about $10,000 cash to the District every year.

> The Occoquan hog plant is one of the largest in the country. There are six large cement feeding pens, each connected by a runway with a five-acre field.[17]

As buidings were erected on the permanent site of the Workhouse, more roads were also laid out. An article appearing in the _Fairfax Herald,_ dated May 17, 1912, stated: "The D.C. Workhouse has made great improvement in its property, and has certainly been helpful to this part of Fairfax County. They have a good road from Lorton to Occoquan; have cleared lots of land and have it under cultivation."[18] The road from Occoquan to Lorton was extremely important because it provided the residents of that area as well as the workhouse, with the first means of access to the Richmond, Fredericksburg, and Potomac Railroad, which had an accommodation train stop at Lorton on its run from Washington, D.C. to Richmond, Virginia. Access to the railroad permitted transportation of prisoners by train to the workhouse. Return of the prisoners to Washington from Occoquan was made by way of the Potomac River in the early years.

> ...In the early days of its use the 9th Street Wharf boasted quarters for a work detail of prisoners who acted as longshoremen in loading and unloading the barges.
>
> According to tales told by the old timers of the District Jail and Workhouse, one of the sights along the waterfront in the days when the barges were used to transport prisoners from Occoquan to Washington was the prisoners themselves. Many of them had gone to Occoquan in the summer, dressed in lightweight clothing and wearing straw hats. They would often return to Washington in the middle of winter after completing their sentences dressed in the same lightweight clothes and wearing their straw hats and sitting on top of the barges completely indifferent to what was often extremely cold weather. Just to get back to Washington was all they wanted.[19]

The method of transporting materials, supplies, and products by barge between Washington and the institutions in Occoquan and Lorton was officially discontinued in July 1941.

The early rules and regulations that governed the prisoners of the workhouse were few and to the point, as noted by the following which were issued in 1915 by Mr. Whittaker:

> With a perfect record for 30 days, a prisoner will be permitted to write to father, mother, brother, or sister, wife, son or daughter upon arrival, and one letter each month thereafter, so long as the prisoner maintains a perfect record. Prisoners will be given permission by the Superintendent to write special letters pertaining to business.
>
> Money coming in letters will be held in office until the prisoner is discharged.
>
> Smoking and chewing of tobacco not permitted.
>
> Prisoners will be permitted to receive from their relatives by mail 1 tooth brush, 1 pair of suspenders, 1 weekly paper, 1 weekly or monthly magazine.
>
> Packages sent to prisoners by express will not be receipted for.
>
> Letters must be sent to Superintendent's office without folding.[20]

In keeping with the recommendations of the Penal Commission, the workhouse was designed to be a model institution, based on the philosophy described by Mr. Whittaker: "We believe beneficial results cannot be obtained successfully in the old-time prisons, with high walls, locks and bars. We believe that for every bar of restriction removed more rays of sunlight and hope will reach the heart of the convicted man."[21]

While the new philosophy of the "open air" prison was designed to give the prisoner a sense of freedom, it also provided an opportunity for escape. Not all of the inmates responded positively to the new approach, and escapes from the workhouse were frequent occurrences. An article in the _Fairfax Herald,_ dated February 10, 1911, noted:

> A general riot broke out at the reformatory (should read workhouse) of the District of Columbia, at Occoquan, Wednesday night of last week. One guard was struck down, and when order and quiet were finally restored six prisoners were missing. They were later captured at Cherry Hill and returned to the

> reformatory. All six will probably be indicted and tried for jail breaking...[22]

In an article appearing in the Washington Star newspaper, entitled "Wants Rigid Guard Kept at Occoquan," dated February 24, 1912, Judge Pugh of the Police Court expressed his alarm at the frequent escapes from the workhouse:

> Declaring that if a more rigid guard is not kept over prisoners sent to Occoquan, Washington and the District will soon be overrun by a horde of thieves, swindlers, and vicious criminals. Judge Pugh of the Police Court today made a demand that the authorities at the workhouse be required to take whatever steps are necessary to prevent the escapes which it is declared have been of frequent occurrence.
>
> * * *
>
> Judge Pugh has taken up the matter of the frequent escapes with Assistant United States Attorney Ralph Given, by whom it was referred to United States Attorney Wilson. The latter has written officially to the District Commissioners and asked that a stronger guard be placed over the prisoners, and that the 'golden rule' administration at Occoquan be abandoned, at least so far as concerns the vicious and habitual criminals sent there.[23]

The May 21, 1915 edition of the Fairfax Herald carried an article entitled "Escape from Work House in Automobile:"

> Saturday afternoon, two prisoners at the Occoquan Work House managed to slip out unobserved, and, jumping into an automobile belonging to Mr. Withers Hall (son of School Superintendent M.D. Hall) made a dash towards Alexandria. The police of that city were notified, and soon the runaways whisked by them at a rapid rate of speed. A nearby machine was pressed into service to give chase, but was unable to overtake the runaways. When the latter approached the Highway bridge they abandoned the automobile and took to the bushes, the police being unable to find them. The automobile was taken back and delivered to

> Mr. Hall, having sustained no perceptible injury from the wild chase.[24]

While the grounds of the workhouse were not enclosed by fences, a system of sentinal boxes was used as a means of alerting the guards in the event of an attempted escape. There were about 30 such outposts placed at strategic points throughout the workhouse reservation. They were manned by prisoners who were chosen by the authorities to guard the other prisoners who were working in the fields or at other assigned tasks. When a prisoner attempted to escape, the alarm was sounded.

An old record book dating back to 1910, provides interesting information regarding the methods that were used in the early days of the workhouse to punish escapes as well as other disciplinary infractions. The book notes that a special building, known as the "punishment house," was used to administer punishment for attempted escapes, and for those who made good their escape and were later apprehended. The escapee was taken to the punishment house and placed in chains. The chain gang method of controling the prisoners was still in vogue in those days. Other infractions such as refusal to work or disrespect to an officer was punishable by a diet of bread and water for a specified number of days. This practice was later replaced by loss of privilege, and the chain gangs were discontinued around 1934.

The record book noted above also contains records of assaults by inmates on staff. One particularly interesting assault reads: "Dennis Baker, colored, while working with Mr. Hall, officer of the twenty-three squad, above prisoner assaulted Mr. Hall with an axe, therefore Mr. Hall shot him in the leg."[25]

In addition to punishment and assaults, the old record book lists the deaths of inmates and staff alike, during the early days of the workhouse and reformatory. The entry includes the date and cause of death. When there was no relative or friend of the deceased inmate to provide for a funeral, the institution authorities took care of the preparation for burial through an arrangement with Hall's Funeral Home in the nearby Town of Occoquan, Virginia. A special plot of ground, known only as Stoney Lonesome, was set aside on the workhouse site for interment of those men and women who died while incarcerated with no relatives or friends to take care of the burial. According to the recollection of William Leatherland, now retired from the D.C. Department of Corrections, Stoney Lonesome is an old prison name and it seems fitting for the prison equivalent of a potters field. In more recent years, other arrangements have been made for those inmates who require the services of the District's penal institutions for burial. Today, Stoney Lonesome is all but forgotten, and only a few of the institutions' present employees are aware that it ever existed.

In March of 1918, Mr. Whittaker resigned his position as Superintendent of the workhouse and reformatory because of poor health. He was succeeded by Charles C. Foster, who in 1919 became the first General Superintendent of penal institutions. "Mr. Foster served until July 1921, at which time William H. Moyer was appointed General Superintendent and served until his death in October of 1923."[26] Morris M. Barnard was then appointed to the position of General Superintendent.

A decrease in the inmate population was noted during the years 1918 and 1919. This was attributed in part to the general prosperity brought about by World War I, which created a demand for labor in the free community, and in part to the prohibition law. The daily average population for 1918 was 373, and in 1919, it was 433. These figures were much lower than the average population of around 600 in 1917 and for several prior years.

By the year 1920, the concept of the industrial farm on the workhouse site had achieved the success that the Penal Commission had hoped it would. Despite the constant turnover in the workhouse population and the fact that horses were still being used to move most of the farm equipment, the administration had managed to turn 1,150 acres of wilderness into a productive operation that was hailed by many penal authorities throughout the country as a model of its kind.

Religious and recreational activities for the prisoners of the workhouse expanded over the years from very limited leisure time in the beginning to a well developed program by the end of the 1930s. The annual report for 1914 described the recreation activities as follows:

> During the evening and after the day's work is done and on Sundays, the men are taken to a large building known as the rest hall and library, where they are permitted to talk, play checkers, or read the daily newspapers, which are bought for them by the management. They have access to the library of over 4,000 volumes. On summer evenings and on Sundays the inmates are permitted to take the benches out into the yard, where it is possible to enjoy more freedom and have an abundance of fresh air.[27]

By 1922, William H. Moyer, General Superintendent of the workhouse reported:

> Fresh air and sunshine are very beneficial to the diseased mind as well as to the diseased body. That is why I advocate the greatest amount of outdoor work and play at penal institutions consistent with security and good training. The institution of baseball and other clean sports at the workhouse and the continued use of those already instituted at the reformatory have had much to do with the creation of a better spirit and a better sense of honor among the inmates.[28]

The annual report for 1922 tells of a unique organization at the workhouse known as the "Inmates' League:"

> The inmates of the workhouse organized and maintained a league of inmates designed to be a means of self-help. This league has had nothing whatever to do with the administration of the workhouse, but it has in fact, indirectly been of much assistance. Every fair-minded officer of that institution will admit that this league has been of real value in obtaining and maintaining a more friendly spirit among the inmate population as well as an earnest desire to cooperate with the officers as far as permitted. That it has been successful in this is reflected in the low percentage of escapes. The value of any system of administration of penal institutions which will give the inmates an opportunity to show in what way and to what extent they can be trusted can no longer be reasonably questioned.[29]

In 1930, Mr. Arthur Pettit, Superintendent, reported that a new athletic field "for the development of both the inmates and the institution"[30] had been completed, and recommended that a stadium be added. Mr. Pettit was responsible for getting a stadium built at the workhouse. He further noted: "The religious denominations of Washington, D.C. have continued to send representatives to the workhouse to conduct services, and have lent a helping hand to the inmates.[31] By the close of the decade of the 1930s, the annual report commented: "Recreation facilities have been improved. Baseball, softball, vollyball and football and other field day activities were permitted to as many as were able to participate. Moving pictures were shown bi-weekly, films being furnished without charge by the Washington exchanges. Two visits per month from relatives of inmates were permitted."[32] Religious services were conducted throughout the year by various churches of Washington, D.C. for those inmates of the workhouse who wished to attend.

As early as 1919 the annual report of the Board of Charities to the District Commissioners noted that the workhouse buildings were only temporary structures, and offered a plan for replacing them with permanent construction. "The buildings will be of brick manufactured by the institution, and the work of construction will be done by prisoners under skilled supervision. It will require a number of years to rebuild the plant by this method but the cost will be much less than would be the case if the buildings were erected by contract."[33] The brick yard was producing around 5,000,000 bricks a year during that time and lumber was available on the workhouse site. These resources, together with inmate labor, made the cost of constructing the buildings a mere fraction of what a contractor would have required. Construction of the permanent buildings began in 1924, and the first brick dormitory was completed in 1925. Much of the construction took place during Mr. Barnard's tenure as General Superintendent. By 1928, 21 permanent brick buildings had been completed; enough new buildings to house 75 percent of the inmate population. It is noteworthy that construction of the permanent buildings marked the second time the prisoners had built their own prison.

The Board of Public Welfare for the District of Columbia was created March 16, 1926, and the District's penal institutions were placed under its supervision. Mr. Barnard continued to serve as General Superintendent of the penal institutions. Mr. Charles C. MacCloughy was named Assistant Superintendent of the workhouse in 1926, and served until his death in 1927. He was replaced by Mr. Julian A. Schoen who served as Assistant Superintendent until 1930. Mr. Schoen was replaced by Mr. Arthur Pettit.

The decade of the 1930s brought with it the great economic depression in America which was responsible for the upward trend in the inmate population of the workhouse. At the onset of the depression in 1929, the daily average population of the workhouse was 684. By the year 1935, the population had reached 833, and by June, 1937, it was 1,117. An article appearing in the <u>Washington Star</u> newspaper, December 2, 1937, noted: "The population of the District of Columbia Workhouse at Occoquan has grown so fast that tents are needed to house the inmates...the workhouse is close approaching its all time record."[34] The annual report for 1938 describes conditions as follows:

> No new construction has been put on at the Workhouse. Coupled with the meager - practically negligible - means of segregation and showers, the congestion there can not prevent whatever dangers emerge from contagion.
>
> The tremendous turnover is the baffling problem, yet it is obvious that this group presents more potential danger at release to the District than the felon group.
>
> We will try to put in showers in each dormitory - imagine 150 men bathing once a week and sleeping in a dormitory, eating in one room, and congregating in a room where space makes personal continued contact inevitable.
>
> For 1940, if funds permit, we should complete this unit and make further provisions for segregaton by revamping existing buildings located elsewhere, and to arrange for small units of low cost housing for such groups as the inebriate, the aged and physically incompetent, and such other groups as prove susceptible to segregation.[35]

One of the major problems brought about by the overcrowded conditions was the spread of communicable diseases among the prisoners, especially tuberculosis. The workhouse hospital reported 27 cases of tuberculosis in isolation during 1938. In addition, the hospital cared for 866 bed patients, and treated 47,607 outpatients. There were, however, only six deaths at the workhouse during that year. Efforts were made to control the spread of disease among the prisoners by having all mattresses and bedding material aired at least once a week, the inmates were issued individual drinking cups, and portable outhouses were constructed for the men who were detailed in outlying sections of the reservation. In addition, a water filtration and sedimentation plant was put in operation, and the water mains were cleaned.

A step forward for the workhouse occurred in 1938, when the security guards were uniformed for the first time, and plans were underway to uniform the non-custodial officers. Captains of the guard were rotated from one shift to another for the first time that same year.

The depression of the 1930s, followed by World War II during the first half of the 1940s greatly hampered the normal progress in the operation of the workhouse. Not only was it difficult to recruit employees during the war years, but all major construction was virtually halted because of shortages in materials. The most that could be accomplished was repair and maintenance of the buildings and equipment already at hand.

Despite the personnel shortages during the war years, the conduct of the inmate population was considered satisfactory. With about 1,000 acres of land under cultivation, the farm continued to produce fruits, vegetables, and meat. In 1945, for example, the farm yielded produce in the amount of $35,595.69, and after expenses showed a net profit of $18,045.27. In addition 2,397 cases of number 10 cans of fruits and vegetables were preserved. The hog ranch contributed 170,000 pounds of pork, of which 42,305 pounds were cured for later use.

When the war ended in 1945, once again the time had come to update the physical plant and equipment at the workhouse, but more important, it was time to turn to more modern methods of penology.

SOURCES

[1.] Annual Report to the Commissioners of the District of Columbia 1911, p. 200.

[2.] "The Occoquan Prison," Fairfax Herald, September 8, 1910.

[3.] Perspectives for Correctional Practices, Department of Corrections, Industries Division, 1960, p. 38.

[4.] Annual Report to the Commissioners of the District of Columbia 1911, p. 200.

[5.] Ibid.

[6.] Ibid.

[7.] Ibid.

[8.] Ibid.

[9.] Ibid.

[10.] Report to the D.C. Commissioners, 1911-1912.

[11.] Ibid.

[12.] Report to the D.C. Commissioners, 1910-1911, p. 386.

[13.] Report to the D.C. Commissioners, 1914, p. 479.

[14.] Report to the D.C. Commissioners, 1911, p. 200.

[15.] Ibid., p.203.

[16.] Ibid.

[17.] "Hog Raising at Occoquan," Fairfax Herald, September 15, 1916.

[18.] Fairfax Herald, May 17, 1912.

[19.] P.F. Peters, A Short History of the Jails of Washington, unpublished, May 2, 1952, Appendix I, p. 3.

[20.] Rules and Regulations, on file in the D.C. Department of Corrections Museum, Lorton, Virginia.

[21.] Report to the D.C. Commissioners, 1914, p. 479.

[22.] Fairfax Herald, February 10, 1911, Fairfax County Library, Fairfax, Virginia.

[23.] Ibid., February 24, 1912 edition.

[24.] Ibid., May 21, 1915 edition.

[25.] Record Book, on file in D.C. Department of Corrections Museum, Lorton, Virginia.

[26.] Perspectives for Correctional Procedures, 1960, p. 39.

[27.] Report to the D.C. Commissioners, 1914, p. 479.

[28.] Report to the D.C. Commissioners, 1922.

[29.] Ibid., p. 30.

[30.] Report to the D.C. Commissioners, 1930.

[31.] Ibid.

[32.] Report to the D.C. Commissioners.

[33.] Annual Report of the Board of Charities, 1919.

[34.] Washington Star Newspaper, December 2, 1937.

[35.] Annual Report of the Board of Charities, 1938, on file in the D.C. Department of Corrections Museum, Lorton, Virginia.

CHAPTER 10

THE WOMEN'S WORKHOUSE AT OCCOQUAN (1912 - 1945)

The Penal Commission made no special recommendations for the women who were confined in the District's penal institutions. The women were simply included with the recommendations for treatment of male prisoners. For this reason, the early history of the women's workhouse at Occoquan is meshed with that of the workhouse for men. Since there were few women prisoners compared to the number of males, the early annual reports elaborate on the activities and programs for the men, and devote much less attention to the women.

Although the workhouse for women was originally intended to be used to confine short-term misdemeanant offenders, the Act of September 6, 1916 (D.C. Code, Sec 24-402)[1] made it possible for prisoners who were serving one year or more to be confined in an institution within the District of Columbia. For that reason, eventually women with felony sentences were also confined there. In time, the title "workhouse" was discontinued and the institution became commonly known as the "women's division."

The women's workhouse at Occoquan opened during the fiscal year ending June 30, 1912. Mr. Whittaker's duties as Superintendent of the workhouse included the women as well as the men. Mrs. Minnie Herndon, however, was named Assistant Superintendent of the women's workhouse, and matrons, as they were known in those days, supervised the day-to-day activities of the prisoners.

A section of the workhouse site located about 1,000 feet from where the men were housed was set aside for the women. By 1912, sufficient housing had been completed on the women's section to accommodate about 100 prisoners. Mr. Whittaker noted: "The women's buildings are therefore completely segregrated from the men's department and no communication between the inmates of the separate groups is permitted."[2]

Like those of the men, the women's sentences were of short duration. Their offenses, however, were mostly for violation of the excise law, soliciting prostitution, disorderly conduct, vagrancy, and intoxication. The ages of both Black and White women prisoners covered a wide range, with the youngest being 15 and the oldest 65. There was one exception, a Black woman who served a sentence in 1917 was 85 years old. The age range for most of the women, both Black and White, fell between 20 and 45 years.

The women were expected to perform a full day's work, and Mr. Whittaker's report for 1914 notes:

> We handle the women prisoners from the City of Washington with the same system of buildings provided for the men. The female department is managed by women, and the two institutions are some distance apart. The average number of prisoners in the female department is about 100. The women do laundry work and make the clothes for the prisoners of the two institutions. In addition, a number of them work on the lawn and in the garden, do the painting and other sanitary work about the buildings. The female department, like the male department, has neither cell, lock, nor bar. The buildings are one story with neither wall nor fence around them. We have handled 3,000 women in the past 3 1/2 years and have only lost 3 through escaping.[3]

Mrs. Herndon's annual report of June 30, 1917 notes that it was necessary to issue 59 disciplinary reports during the year, most of which were to "women whose parents died when they were infants."[4] She described the prisoners as women who "drifted into homes of poverty and vice and grew up with no desire to work or live clean lives."[5] She further noted:

> We find this class of women are being continually sent to us with only 15 and 30 day sentences. We are interested so much in this class and we want to help them. Is there not some way by which they may be sent to us with longer sentences?
>
> We request further that if the courts of the District of Columbia see fit to continue committing to this institution expectant mothers and mothers with infants, that we be provided with a suitable room or ward in our hospital where the mother and child may have the quiet and privacy they need during the convalescent period.[6]

The Board of Charities' report for the year 1918 noted that "one colored male child was born in July 1917,"[7] in the women's workhouse, and further commented: "Mrs. Herndon, aided by the attendants, rendered kind, thoughtful, courteous, commendable service such as wins the respect of the inmates and unquestionably elevates their view of right and better living."[8] The report further noted: "A feature of the treatment of women is to make their surroundings absolutely clean. This, in itself, acts as an impressive lesson to women in discipline and the proper way to live."[9]

Aside from the daily chores of cooking and cleaning, two industries were introduced at the women's workhouse. The first was a laundry operation and the second a sewing room. Mrs. Herndon's 1918 report states: "The women become skillful as seamstresses and they are instructed in laundry work...and they are permitted to work in the gardens among the flowers."[10] It is noteworthy that over the years, the flower gardens and landscaping in general became outstanding features of the women's division of the workhouse. The institution was never enclosed by a fence or wall, giving an added air of attractiveness to the grounds.

The year 1917 is notable in the history of the women's workhouse as the period when the National Women's Party, organized by Alice Paul in 1916, began to picket the White House in an effort to gain the support of President Woodrow Wilson and the Democratic Party on the Susan B. Anthony Amendment to the Constitution. The issue of voting rights for women was extremely controversial at that time, and many of the Suffragists were arrested and charged with unlawful assembly or obstructing traffic. Those who were found guilty were fined $25.00 or given misdemeanant sentences. Many of the women who were arrested chose to be incarcerated rather than to pay fines, as a means of giving added attention to their cause. Once confined, the Suffragists insisted upon being treated as political prisoners rather than as common criminals. The officials, including Mr. Whittaker, however, refused to grant their request. Several groups of Suffragists were incarcerated at various times during 1917. They were first placed in the D.C. Jail where some remained during the term of their sentences. A number of the Suffragists were transferred to the workhouse for women at Occoquan. According to Inez Haynes Irwin's book entitled, A Story of Alice Paul and the National Women's Party, the women Suffragists related stories of harsh treatment at the hands of the jail and workhouse officials. The following excerpts from that book indicate that the treatment grew progressively worse with each group of Suffragists who served their sentences in that institution:

> In the Suffragist of July 28, 1917, occurs the first account of Occoquan, by Mrs. Gibson Gardner. Mrs. Gardner, it will be remembered, was one of the early group of sixteen pickets whom the President pardoned after three days.

She says:

The short journey on the train was pleasant and uneventful. From the station at Occoquan the women sent to the Workhouse were put into three conveyances: two were filled with white women and the third by colored women. In the office of the Workhouse we stood in a line and one at a time were registered and given a number. The matron called us by number and first name to the desk. Money and jewelry were accounted for and put in the safe. We were then sent to the dining room. The meal of soup, rye bread, and water was not palatable...

From the dining room we were taken to the dormitory. At the end of the long room, a white woman and two colored women were waiting for us. Before these women we were obliged, one by one, to remove all our clothing, and after taking a shower bath, put on the Workhouse clothes. These clothes consisted of heavy unbleached muslin chemises and drawers, a petticoat made of ticking, and a heavy dark gray cotton mother hubbard dress. The last touch was a full, heavy, dark blue apron which tied around the waist. The stockings were thick and clumsy. There were not enough stockings, and those of us who did not have stockings during our sojourning there were probably rather fortunate. We were told to wear our own shoes for the time being, as they did not have enough in stock. The prisoners were permitted to have only what they could carry.

The dormitory was clean and cool and we longed to go to bed, but we were told we must dress and go into the adjoining room where Superintendent Whittaker would see us. Mr. Whittaker brought with him a man whom we afterward learned was a newspaper man. The Superintendent informed us that for about an hour we could do as we chose, and pointed to the piano and said that we might play and sing...but that night no one had a desire to sing. Although Mr. Whittaker's words were few and not unpleasant, we realized that our presence did not cause him either embarrassment or regret.

* * *

The days were spent in the sewing room. We were permitted to talk in low tones, two or three being allowed to sit together. While we were there, the sewing was very light. We turned hems on sheets and pillow slips and sewed on the machine...The work was monotonous and our clothing extremely heavy.

The great nervous strain came at meal time. All the women ate in one big room. The white women sat at one side. The meal lasted thirty and sometimes forty minutes. The food to us was not palatable, but we all tried to be sensible and eat enough to keep our strength. The real problem, however, was not the food; it was the enforced silence. We were not allowed to speak in the dining room, and after a conscientious effort to eat, the silent waiting was curiously unpleasant.

The use of the pencil is forbidden at all times. Each inmate is permitted to write but two letters a month, one to her family and one business letter. All mail received and sent is opened and read by one of the officials. Next to our longing for our own toilet articles was our desire for a pencil and a scrap of paper...

* * *

It will be remembered that this was that early group of pickets whom the President pardoned after the appeals of J.A.H. Hopkins, Dudley Field Malone, and Gibson Gardner. Before leaving they were taken to Superintendent Whittaker.

Asking for the attention of Miss Burns and the rest of them, he said:

'Now that you are going, I have something to say to you.' And turning to Miss Burns, he continued, 'And I want to say it to you. The next lot of women who come here won't be treated with the same consideration that these women were.'[11]

An article appearing in the Fairfax Herald, August 24, 1917, entitled "Suffragists at Occoquan" reads:

> The six militant suffragists, sentenced by Judge Pugh in the Washington Police Court to thirty day terms in the Occoquan workhouse, for violation of Washington police regulations, were received there Saturday night and were immediately inducted into the routine of prison life. Supt. Whitaker states that the suffragists will receive the same treatment as does any other person sent to the prison for violating the law. The leniency shown the first batch of suffragists sent to Occoquan with respect to receiving visits from relatives and attorneys will be considerably curtailed with respect to the latest commitment. Prison rules regarding such practices will be strictly adhered to and no favoritism will be shown. Relatives of the prisoners may visit them twice a month, provided arrangements are made in advance with Supt. Whitaker...[12]

The following account of the treatment of a later group is expressed by Suffragist Katherine Rolston Fisher whose group entered the Occoquan Workhouse for Women in late August, 1917:

> Upon entering Occoquan Workhouse, we were separated from the preceding group of Suffragists. Efforts were made by the officers to impress us by their good will towards us. Entirely new clothing, comfortable rooms in the hospital, and the substitution of milk and buttered toast for cold bread, cereal, and soup, ameliorated the trials of the table. The head matron was chatty and confidential. She told us of the wonderful work of the superintendent in creating these institutions out of the wilderness and of the kindness shown by the officers to the inmates. She lamented that some of the other Suffragists did not appreciate what was done for them...
>
> 'Why are we segregated from all the white prisoners?' I asked the superintendent of the Workhouse. Part of the time we were not segregated from the colored prisoners, a group of whom were moved into the hospital and shared with us the one bathroom and toilet. 'That is

for your good and for ours,' was the bland reply...

That was quite in the tone of his answer to another inquiry made when the superintendent told me that no prisoner under punishment - that is, in solitary confinement - was allowed to see counsel. 'Is that the law of the District of Columbia?' I inquired. 'It is the law here because it is the rule I make,' he replied.

We learned what it is to live under a one-man law. The doctor's orders for our milk and toast and even our medicine were countermanded by the superintendent, so we were told. Our counsel after one visit was forbidden, upon a pretext, to come again.

On Tuesday, September 18, we were made to exchange our new gingham uniforms for old spotted gray gowns covered with patches upon patches; were taken to a shed to get pails of paint and brushes, and were set to painting the dormitory lavatories and toilets. By this time we were all hungry and more or less weak from lack of food. A large brush wet with white paint weighs at least two pounds. Much of the work required our standing on a table or stepladder and reaching above our heads. I think the wiser of us rested at every opportunity, but we did not refuse to work.

All this time we had been without counsel for eight days...

The food, which had been a little better, about the middle of the month reached its zenith of rancidity and putridity. We tried to make a sport of the worm hunt, each table announcing its score of weevils and worms. When one prisoner reached the score of fifteen worms during one meal, it spoiled our zest for the game.

We had protested from the beginning against doing any manual labor upon such bad and scanty food as we received...

Mrs. Kendall, who was the most emphatic in her refusal, was promptly locked up on bread and water. The punishment makes a story to be told by itself. It clouded our days constantly while it lasted and while we knew that half of what she suffered.

All this time - five days - Mrs. Kendall was locked up, her pallid face visible through the windows to those few Suffragists who had opportunity and ventured to go to her window for a moment at the risk of sharing her fate.

* * *

The most atrocious experience of the pickets at Occoquan was, however, on the night known to them generally as 'The Night Of Terror.' This happened to that group of Suffragists who were arrested on November 14, sentenced to Occoquan, and who immediately went on hunger-strike as a protest against not being treated as political prisoners and as the last protest they could make against their imprisonment. Whittaker was away when they arrived, and they were kept in the office which was in the front room of one of the small cottages. Out of these groups there always evolved a leader. If the group included the suave and determined Lucy Burns, she inevitably took command. If it included Mrs. Lawrence Lewis, equally velvet-voiced and immovable, she inevitably became spokesman. This group included both. The Suffragists were then still making their demand to be treated as political prisoners, and so, when the woman at the desk - a Mrs. Herndon - attempted to ask the usual questions, Mrs. Lewis, speaking for the rest, refused to answer them, saying that she would wait and talk to Mr. Whittaker.

'You will sit here all night then,' said Mrs. Herndon. The women waited for hours.

* * *

Suddenly the door burst open, and Whittaker came rushing in from a conference, it was later discovered, of the District of Columbia Commissioners at the White House —

followed by men -- more and more of them. Mrs. Lewis stood up.

'We demand to be treated as political pris...' she began. But that was as far as she got.

'You shut up! I have men here glad to handle you!' Whittaker said. 'Seize her!'

Two men seized Mrs. Lewis, dragged her out of the sight of the remaining Suffragists.

In the meantime, another man sprang at Mrs. Nolan, who, it will be remembered was over seventy years old, very frail and lame. She says: I am used to being careful of my bad foot, and I remember saying: 'I will come with you; do not drag me. I have a lame foot.' But I was dragged down the steps and away into the dark. I did not have my feet on the ground. I guess that saved me.

* * *

As Mrs. Nolan entered the hall, a man in the Occoquan uniform, brandishing a stick, called, 'Damn you! Get in there!' Before she was shot through this hall, two men brough in Dorothy Day, - a very slight, delicate girl; her captors were twisting her arms above her head. Suddenly they lifted her, brought her body down twice over the back of an iron bench. One of them called: 'The damned Suffrager! My mother ain't no Suffrager! I will put you through hell!' Then Mrs. Nolan's captors pulled her down the corridor which opened out of this room, and pushed her through the door.

Back of Mrs. Nolan, dragged along in the same way, came Mrs. Cosu, who, with that extraordinary thoughtfulness and tenderness which the pickets all developed for each other, called to Mrs. Nolan: 'Be careful of your foot!'

The bed broke Mrs. Nolan's fall, but Mrs. Cosu hit the wall. They had been there but a few minutes when Mrs. Lewis, all doubled over like a sack of flour, was thrown in. Her head

> struck the iron bed, and she fell to the floor senseless.
>
> The other women thought she was dead. They wept over her.
>
> Ultimately, they revived Mrs. Lewis, but Mrs. Cosu was desperately ill all night, with a heart attack and vomiting. They were afraid she was dying, and they called at intervals for a doctor, but although there was a woman and a man guard in the corridor, they paid no attention. There were two mattresses and two blankets for the three, but that was not enough, and they shivered all night long.[13]

The Suffragists who were incarcerated on November 14, 1917, at the Occoquan workhouse persisted in their efforts to be treated as political prisoners by continuing their hunger strike. "In the meantime, Superintendent Whittaker began to fear that Mrs. Lawrence Lewis and Lucy Burns would die...had them taken to the hospital of the District Jail. They had been forcibly fed at Occoquan, and the feeding was continued at the jail."[14] The following account is given by Lucy Burns:

> Wednesday, 12 M. Yesterday afternoon at about four or five, Mrs. Lewis and I were asked to go to the operating room. Went there and found our clothes. Told we were to go to Washington. No reason, as usual. When we were dressed Dr. Gannon appeared, said he wished to examine us. Both refused. Were dragged through halls by force, our clothing partly removed by force, and we were examined, heart tested, blood pressure and pulse taken. Of course such data was of no value after such a struggle. Dr. Gannon told me that I must be fed. Was stretched on bed, two doctors, matron, four colored prisoners present, Whittaker in hall. I was held down by five people at legs, arms, and head. I refused to open mouth, Gannon pushed the tube up left nostril. I turned and twisted my head all I could, but he managed to push it up. It hurts nose and throat very much and makes nose bleed freely. Tube drawn out covered with blood. Operation leaves one very sick. Food dumped directly into stomach feels like a ball of lead. Left nostril, throat and muscles of neck very sore all night. After this I was brought

> into the hospital in an ambulance. Mrs. Lewis and I placed in same room. Slept hardly at all.
>
> This morning Dr. Ladd appeared with his tube. Mrs. Lewis and I said we would not be forcibly fed. Said he would call in men guards and force us to submit. Went away and we not fed at all this morning....(sic)
>
> * * *
>
> The final barbarity, however, in the treatment of the pickets came out of the experience of Alice Paul. Of course, the Administration felt that in jailing Alice Paul, they had the "ringleader." That was true. What they did not realize, however, was that they had also jailed the inspired reformer, the martyr-type, who dies for a principle, but never bends or breaks. Miss Paul was arrested, it will be remembered on October 20. The banner that she carried had, in the light of later events, a grim significance. It bore President Wilson's own words:
>
> THE TIME HAS COME TO CONQUER OR SUBMIT. FOR US THERE CAN BE BUT ONE CHOICE. WE HAVE MADE IT.[15]

Miss Paul was sentenced to a term of seven months in the D.C. Jail, and during the time she spent there, she was also force fed when she attempted to go on a hunger strike. Eventually, she was placed in the psychiatric ward of the Asylum Hospital, in an attempt by the administration to have her declared insane. Eventually, the court decided that the pickets had been illegally transferred from the jail to the Occoquan workhouse, and they were released from Occoquan in the custody of their counsel one night with instructions to report to the jail the next morning. "They went immediately to Cameron House and broke their hunger strike - spent the evening before the fire - talking and sipping hot milk. The next day, they were committed to the jail again and immediately started a new hunger strike."[16] As the news of the harsh treatment received by the Suffragists at the hands of penal officials reached the public, the cause of voting rights for women gained support. In addition, the sentences were reversed upon appeal, and the women who were incarcerated in the Occoquan workhouse and the D.C. jail for the cause of woman suffrage had made a major contribution in the fight that eventually led to ratification of the Susan B. Anthony amendment in August, 1920.

The official records of the jail and the Occoquan workhouse for women contain very little information concerning the imprisonment of the women Suffragists. In fact, the annual reports of the D.C. Commissioners for the years 1917 and 1918 carry only one brief reference to the Suffragists, by Superintendent Zlinkhan of the jail, which states: "There were two unusual incidents in the District jail during the fiscal year; the first was the commitment of about 100 suffragettes, whose persistent insubordination made it very difficult to maintain wholesome discipline,..."[17] No mention at all could be found in the reports by Mrs. Herndon for that period. The register, however, contains the names of Alice Paul, Lucy Burns, and the others who were incarcerated for picketing.[18] An old record book contains the following entries for the year 1917:

> November 14. Twenty-seven white, female prisoners, suffragettes transferred from the female department to cellrooms in the punishment house.
>
> November 15. Twenty-seven white female prisoners suffragettes transferred from the cell room in the punishment house to hospital.[19]

The reason for which the women were transferred to the cell house and the hospital is not given. It is noted, however, that those dates coincide with the dates Lucy Burns and Mrs. Jacobs were incarcerated in the Occoquan Workhouse.

The story of the Suffragists at the Occoquan Workhouse was recently brought to light through the untiring efforts of Joseph Flakne, who, in March 1982 along with the League of Women Voters of Fairfax County and the D.C. Department of Corrections, succeeded in having a historical marker placed at the site of the Workhouse as a tribute to the Suffragists who were incarcerated there.

Throughout the decade of the 1920s, the sewing and laundry operations at the women's workhouse increased. The 1927 annual report notes 3,238 garments made and 20,000 pieces repaired by the women, and 199,202 pieces were laundred. By 1931, the women had expanded the sewing activities to making shirts, bedticks and sheets for the men's department of the workhouse in addition to weaving rugs and making layettes for the Gallinger Municipal Hospital.

The annual report for 1929-1930 noted that Carolyn La Mar had succeeded Mrs. Herndon as Head Matron of the women's workhouse. Her report included the following: "There is a great need for a course of training for house maids, which could be done with our present staff."[20] In addition, Miss La Mar suggested that the women be trained in weaving basketry, shopping bags, etc.). She further commented: "We are now carrying an average population of 60 women. The health of the inmates has been excellent, no deaths occurring during the past fiscal year. One of the great needs is absolute separation of inmates, white and colored. This will tend for a better morale. At present we are carrying this into effect as far as practicable under our present housing arrangements."[21]

The depression of the 1930s decade brought about an increase in the population of the workhouse for women as well as for the women's department at the jail. In fact, conditions became so overcrowded that it was necessary to board some of the women in Federal prisons at a cost of from $1.86 to $2.52 per day. The buildings in which the women were housed were in a severe state of dilapidation, as noted in an article appearing in the Star newspaper, May 18, 1927, reporting on a visit by the grand jury to Occoquan:

> At Occoquan they found some 51 women prisoners housed in immaculate but weather-beaten dormitories, with cracks in the walls through which daylight found no difficulty in passing. The buildings for the women there were constructed for a life of five years. Capt. M.M. Barnard, in charge of local penal institutions, told the grand jury, but they have now stood for more than 16.[22]

It was not until 1938 that additional permanent dormitory space was completed for the women. The annual report for that year notes:

> Two brick dormitories have been completed and occupied; 6 control cells have been opened and used; matron's quarters have been changed; the old box like control cells of wood have been opened and used as contagious rooms; mess hall floors have been reinforced; an additional mess hall has been made by shifting the Matron's dining room, and certain storage space for the inmate's clothes has been expanded and relocated. Before October we should open the two brick dormitories to give more housing space. If population keeps up we will have to

> retain the present wooden dormitory. If not we will use it for an assembly hall. Such a place is necessary especially while new building goes on and the presence of the workmen restricts the use of outdoor space.[23]

During the decade of the 1930s, the population of the women's workhouse grew to a daily average of about 200 inmates. In addition, about 50 percent of the women were serving felony sentences that were long enough for them to benefit from institutional programs. Those women presented a problem different from the short-term police court women. "Weekly church service under the leadership of several denominations, a weekly Bible class, semi-weekly moving pictures, an occasional dance, and Sunday night 'sing'..."[24] were helpful but the women with sentences of more than a year needed academic and vocational training if they were to make positive adjustments in their lives. Those types of programs, of course, were not available at that time. Although the position of Superintendent of the Women's division, created in June 1940 and filled by Blanche La Du, one of the nation's outstanding penologists, did much to focus more attention on the needs of women inmates, it was not until after World War II that academic and vocational programs were introduced and made available in that institution.

SOURCES

[1.] D.C. Code, 1951 edition, Parts I-IV, Sec. 24-402, p. 778.

[2.] Annual Report to the Commissioners of the District of Columbia, 1912, p. 386.

[3.] Annual Report to the Commissioners of the District of Columbia, 1914, p. 480.

[4.] Annual Report to the Commissioners of the District of Columbia, 1917.

[5.] _Ibid._

[6.] _Ibid._

[7.] Annual Report to the Commissioners of the District of Columbia, 1918, p. 386.

[8.] _Ibid._

[9.] _Ibid._

[10.] _Ibid._

[11.] Irwin, Inez Haynes, _The Story of Alice Paul and the National Women's Party_ (Fairfax, Virginia: Denlinger's Publishers, Ltd, 1977), pp. 273-275.

[12.] "Suffragists at Occoquan," _Fairfax Herald,_ August 24, 1917, Fairfax County Library, Fairfax, Virginia.

[13.] Irwin, Inez Haynes, _The Story of Alice Paul and the National Women's Party_ (Fairfax, Virginia: Denlinger's Publishers, Ltd, 1977), pp. 277-281.

[14.] _Ibid.,_ p. 288.

[15.] _Ibid.,_ p. 289-292.

[16.] _Ibid.,_ p. 298.

[17.] Annual Report to the Commissioners of the District of Columbia, 1918, p. 367.

[18.] Register for Year 1917, on file at the D.C. Department of Corrections Museum, Lorton, Virginia.

[19.] Record Book, on file at the D.C. Department of Corrections Museum, Lorton, Virginia.

[20.] Annual Report to the Commissioners of the District of Columbia, 1929-1930.

[21.] *Ibid.*

[22.] *Evening Star Newspaper,* May 18, 1927.

[23.] Annual Report of D.C. Penal Institutions to the Board of Welfare Fiscal Year 1938, on file in the D.C. Department of Corrections Museum, Lorton, Virginia, p. 11.

[24.] *Ibid.,* p. 87.

Hospital, Women's Division. Original frame structure. Photograph courtesy of Bess Garrott.

Administration Building, Women's Division. Original frame structure. Photograph courtesy of Bess Garrott.

CHAPTER 11

THE LORTON REFORMATORY (1916 - 1945)

With the workhouse established and operating successfully, attention was turned to the construction of a reformatory for the District of Columbia. On March 5, 1913, Congress passed an Act providing for the expenditure of funds by the government of the District of Columbia to purchase land adjoining the workhouse site. This tract consisted of approximately 1,388 acres. The order vesting title in the United States Government was filed April 14, 1914, and all documents were admitted to record in the Clerk of the Circuit Court of Fairfax County, Virginia, April 17,1914 (Deed Book S-7, pages 497-505).

It is notable that included in the reformatory tract was "Laurel Hill," originally the plantation home of Major William Lindsay who served with the Virginia Militia during the Revolutionary War. According to Historic American Buildings Survey Inventory number 157, "Laurel Hill" was built around 1766. The graves of both Major Lindsay and his wife, the former Ann Calvert, a great granddaughter of Cecil Calvert, Lord Baltimore, are located on the site. The graves were marked for preservation by the National Society of the Daughters of the American Revolution. Over the years, several additions have been made to the house; nevertheless, the original structure as well as the grave site have remained intact. Although the house is presently vacant, it served as residence for reformatory superintendents in the past. Plans have been underway in recent years to restore "Laurel Hill" by the Department of Corrections.

The philosophy by which the reformatory was established was considered a daring experiment in penology for that era. The concept of no bars or fences to confine the prisoners was so new that a "wait and see" attitude was taken to determine if it worked before making plans to build a permanent institution. The December 23, 1914, edition of the Washington Herald quoted D.C. Commissioner Oliver P. Newman as saying: "We hope to establish a reformatory on principles more advanced than ever attempted...The institution will take the place of the old-style penitentiary but it will not be a prison. Reformation of criminals is the chief objective in view. In this reformatory will be kept criminals sentenced to a term of one year or more."[1]

During the year 1915 work was begun on preparing quarters for housing inmates at the reformatory site. The immediate goal was to construct sufficient housing to accommodate approximately 100 prisoners who would be utilized in building a railroad from the wharf at Occoquan, through the reformatory site, and eventually to the Richmond, Fredericksburg, and Potomac Railroad at Lorton. This railroad was necessary for transporting prisoners, building materials and supplies to the reformatory and workhouse sites.

Temporary housing was completed in October 1916 and the reformatory was officially opened November 11, 1916, under the supervision of Mr. W. H. Whittaker. The first prisoners to occupy the new institution were 60 District of Columbia felony offenders with one or more years to serve, who were incarcerated in the Federal Prison at Leavenworth, Kansas. By the end of June, 1917, 15 additional prisoners had been transferred from Atlanta, Georgia, and 43 from the District Jail, making a population of 118.

It is noted that the Act of September 6, 1916 (D.C. Code, Sec. 24-402) made it possible for prisoners who were serving one year or more to be confined in an institution within the District of Columbia. Thus, it was no longer necessary for the Attorney General to transfer long-term District prisoners to other jurisdictions for service of sentence.

The new institution contained several cells for use in handling disciplinary cases. For the most part, however, housing was dormitory style and there were no locks or bars, and no fences or walls surrounding the compound. The institution was operated on the honor system. Although there were 15 attempted escapes during the first year of operation, it did not cause great concern on the part of the reformatory's administration. In fact, a notation in the annual report for the year 1917 reads: "Considering the crude conditions under which we opened the institution, with a force of officers absolutely inexperienced in the handling of prisoners, this is evidence of our success in the new order of handling long-term criminals in the open."[2]

While the philosophy for the treatment of prisoners was the same for both the reformatory and workhouse, development of the reformatory focused on prison industry, a reformation technique that was popular around the turn of the century. The concept of the industrial shop was designed to provide all able-bodied prisoners with a full day's work while teaching him skills in certain trades. Mr. Whittaker, who served as the first Superintendent of the reformatory, in addition to the workhouse, noted in his first annual report for the institution:

> Most of these men being brought from old-established institutions such as the Government prisons at Atlanta and Leavenworth,

where employment and hard labor is not provided, and where many privileges are allowed inmates that we deem inadvisable to allow at this new institution, and the fact that we immediately started out by giving these men all kinds of rough labor for which they had not been trained, working them in all kinds of weather under primitive conditions, with but a few of them being dissatisfied and attempting to get away, makes it appear to the management that we are safe and that the experimental stage of handling these convicted people successfully in the open is past, and we are more confident now that the improved conditions that are coming in our management and organization from day to day, our percent of loss in escapes will become less each year; that the great benefit to society, which should be the first thought in handling of criminals, and, second, the benefit to the inmates in physical development, education, and moral instruction will be improved as the years go on if the same support from the commissioners and Congress is given the management as has been given in the past.

* * *

It will be our purpose from time to time to recommend to the commissioners that certain industries be established at the reformatory for the purpose of giving proper employment to the inmates, with a view that when they are paroled or discharged they will be able to go back into the community from which they were committed and make their living by working at the trade they were taught in the institution.

In addition to this it should be the purpose of the management as soon as practicable to establish in the institution a school of letters where the illiterate can be taught the common branches up to the eighth grade.

With this thought in mind we have already established a department for the manufacture of brooms, and have secured the services of a man who is a thorough broom maker; and the commissioners have given us a contract to

> furnish brooms of all weights and sizes to the various departments of the District for the fiscal year beginning July 1, 1917.
>
> In addition to the making of all the brooms required by the institutions of the District it is our purpose to have this department turn out the necessary mattresses for ourselves and the other institutions of the District...
>
> We have also organized a carpenter shop, where a number of prisoners will be taught the carpenter's trade; also a plumbing shop, where the inmates will do all of our own plumbing work and will be taught the trade. A blacksmith shop has been organized, and all the work in this line is being done by the inmates.[3]

After three years of operation, the reformatory was progressing so well that the annual report for 1919, read: "...the experiment of handling these longer term prisoners in the open dormitory system, as contrasted with the old system of cell blocks and locked enclosures, has been so satisfactory as in the minds of the penal commission, to warrant the planning of a permanent institution on the lines required by this more humane and constructive method."[4]

By the early 1920s, the workhouse and reformatory had achieved outstanding success as open style institutions. This revolutionary concept combined with the use of a humanistic approach to the treatment of inmates placed the District of Columbia amoung the most progressive penal systems in the United States. Oliver Hoyem's article, "The Prison System of the District," in <u>The Survey</u> magazine for August 16, 1920, noted:

> All of us are justified in taking a keen interest in prison development because within these restricted and thoroughly controlled industrial or farm communities there is being carried out a series of very practical experiments in the study of the individual and his relation to society which necessarily will greatly influence all social experiments outside the prisons. Problems of hygiene, vocational education, industrial management, wage fixing, psychiatry, housing, and institutional management find their solution here. Eventually the government will

> appreciate the necessity of paying adequate salaries to attract men of sufficient calibre and training to cope with these problems. Men of this type who realize their responsibilities and are trying to meet them adequately do not find in their jobs a piker's paradise or a politician's plum.
>
> The District of Columbia has been particularly fortunate in having the direction of its penal institutions in the hands of capable men and the time is not distant when the prison system can be exhibited as a model not only for the states but for inquiring foreign countries.[5]

Under the guidelines set forth by the Penal Commission both the workhouse and reformatory continued to progress, prompting the General Superintendent to comment as follows:

> Early in the history of these institutions the original intention of those creating the establishments planned only the detention of first offenders, but due to overcrowding in the Federal penitentiaries we have received those convicted for the third and fourth times. Adherence to the request of the Attorney General's office has resulted in a very material saving of expense formerly incurred in transferring prisoners to Leavenworth or Atlanta. This fiscal year (1930) only 28 prisoners were transferred to the Federal penitentiaries from the District.
>
> No serious trouble has been experienced with any of the long-term prisoners. Nearly all of this type respond to the present plan. We are working out a problem that is being watched from all sections of the country. Since the recent prison riots, fires, and disturbances of the 'shut in institutions' we have been visited by commissions from different States who are making surveys with views toward bettering conditions. All of them write praising our work. Our success is due in a large measure to the splendid cooperation and good feeling which exists between inmates and officials. While there have been spasmodic outbreaks in several institutions throughout

> the country, there has not been the slightest indication of anything of this nature here.
>
> Every man who enters our institutions is treated humanely and no attempts ever made to destroy a man's self-respect, though every encouragement is offered to a man to better himself during his stay with us. It is insisted that every man, excepting the sick, be required to perform a day's work, and idleness is in no sense a problem with us...[6]

Since the focus was on industry, the first academic education program was extremely limited, consisting of basic reading and arithmetic. In the beginning, Mr. Charles D. Reeder served as the only instructor, with the aid of an inmate assistant. Excerpts from the following early annual report give examples of the educational level of many of the inmates.

> Most of the pupils, probably actuated by a disinclination to acknowledge their actual state of ignorance, profess that they have attended school prior to conviction, but the most rudimentary examination has proved that they merely 'attended.' In arithmetic the multiplication tables are the greatest difficulty. They nearly all arrive at the next higher result by addition and not by multiplication, and the habit of finger counting is so strong that the tables are long, consequently the pupil with a sluggish mind is slow to be impressed...
>
> * * *
>
> Many have been taught to read papers who previously only looked at the pictures. A few are able to write letters. An interesting pupil is Eddie Epps, colored. He learned very slowly, but he studies hard and failure never discourages him. He is determined to learn. If he could, he would devote his entire eight hours to working out his difficulties. His advancement is encouraging. For a long time letters and figures were marks to him. He could see no difference in them worth mentioning. Now they mean something, and he is anxious to know what they mean when grouped in the myriad ways of characters.

> Generations of ignorance are evidenced in a majority of pupils in the reformatory school. They learn with the greatest difficulty and forget if not constantly drilled.
>
> * * *
>
> Most of the reformatory school pupils choose to do the right thing because teaching proves that right for right's sake pays best and is the only way.
>
> Meanwhile the educated crook is, as ever, a menace. In cases of this character there arises the question concerning surgery as a means of relief to society and the restoration of the offender to a normal condition.[7]

In addition to the large number of alcoholics in the workhouse, as early as 1920, offenses connected with the automobile were causing serious problems for the police as well as the District's penal institutions. In his annual report for that year, Mr. Foster expressed the following views:

> Motormania is spreading throughout the land. Speeders, joy-riders, and auto-car thieves, not to mention bandits who use motors in flight and those who drive recklessly and sometimes kill people are growing in numbers daily. The laws are inadequate everywhere. The trial of auto drivers occasions little comment, and the offenders make up an endless list almost everywhere.
>
> The number of men in the Lorton Reformatory and other District of Columbia penal institutions in no way indicate the extent of motormania in Washington. At this time 8 white and 15 colored men are serving sentences for violating regulations relating to automobiles. The total number of years represented by the length of imprisonment is 53 1/2. The shortest time is 18 months; longest, 5 years.
>
> The imposition of a fine against an offending driver is disturbing only to the public. The suggestion is made to pass a law providing for forfeiture of license, so wording the law that the violator may not secure a

> license in any other state. The thing to avoid is delay and confusion in the infliction of the penalty, and the system will bring the result in preventing theft and automobile manslaughter.[8]

Work on the permanent structures of the reformatory was begun in 1924. Snowden Ashford, municipal architect, designed the plans in accordance with the suggestions of the Penal Commission. An article taken from the Washington Star newspaper, no date, noted:

> ...the new plant like the existing one will consist of dormitories instead of cells. There will be no stockades or prison walls. Sunshine and good air will be counted as valuable as ever.
>
> But while the honor system is to continue in force, danger of escapes under the tenative plan worked out will be minimized. The buildings are to be grouped so as to render supervision less difficult.
>
> A more important factor in reducing escapes is promised in the proposed arrangement for two punishment rooms and two disciplinary dormitories. Inmates who become unmanagable will be sent to the punishment rooms. Those whose offenses are not so serious will have some of their liberties withdrawn by being sent to the disciplinary dormitories.
>
> * * *
>
> The site selected is in front of the existing group of buildings which are of frame construction. Brick and stone will be used in the new buildings. Much of the labor will be furnished by the inmates. All of the brick will be made at the workhouse plant and the stone will come from the reservation.
>
> Mr. Ashford has obtained a colonial effect in the lay out that dispels suggestion of a penal institution. The main set of buildings has a quadrangle arrangement. The administration building at the front end of the quadrangle will be two stories high. On its right will be an assembly hall, with a gallery

> and seating capacity for 1,000 on its left, a school building with four classrooms. The quadrangle will be flanked on the north and south by twelve dormitories, or six on each side. These will be 25 by 160 feet, having a capacity for fifty men each.
>
> The east end of the quadrangle will be closed in with a mess hall, 35 by 140 feet, having a capacity for 600. Immediately back of the dining quarters will be a kitchen, bakery and storeroom.
>
> A second group of buildings, according to the present intentions, will be located 200 feet back of the first. This will consist of the two punishment rooms and two disciplinary halls, 30 by 150 feet each. In the extreme rear will be four buildings for housing the shops and industrial trade schools, and a general storeroom. Provision is made for a hospital to occupy a separate site.[9]

Construction of the permanent buildings continued throughout the decades of the 1920s and 1930s.

The hospital unit was completed and occupied in May, 1932. The annual report for that year stated: "A full-time physician and a full-time assistant physician are in attendance. A modern operating room makes possible under the best conditions such minor operations as may properly be done at the institution. The open-air sun porches afford excellent provision for tuberculosis patients." School and library facilities, also included in the hospital building, were nearing completion that year.[10]

A railroad leading from the wharf at Occoquan to the reformatory was completed in 1925, with the right-of-way to the Richmond, Fredericksburg, and Potomac Railroad at Lorton under way. An article taken from the _Washington Star_ newspaper, February 26, 1927 edition, states:

> Using prison labor and oaken cross-ties cut from the reformatory woodlands, Supt. Barnard has built a standard gauge railroad, which links into the Richmond, Fredericksburg & Potomac system. The first freight cars ran over this new track the third week in January. An industrial locomotive belonging to the District is employed to haul the freight from the main line to the reformatory and workhouse.

> Several hundred tons of miscellaneous freight are handled annually, as well as 1,000 tons soft coal, which formerly was delivered by water.[11]

During 1927, several new industries were installed at the reformatory, the most important of which was the tag plant for manufacture of automobile license plates for the District. The inmates became proficient in producing these plates which resulted in a saving of time and money to the District. A foundry plant was under construction and a canning factory was installed to conserve the excess food produced by the farms operated by both the workhouse and the reformatory for use by the penal institutions during the winter months. Completion of a laundry in 1930 made it possible for the reformatory to assume all of the laundry work for the institutions as well as contract work from other District government agencies. By 1929, an automobile repair shop was in operation to provide maintenance and upkeep of all automobiles, including those used for industrial delivery service. A transportation unit was also established to maintain all automobile vehicles as well as the waterway and railroad systems that were in operation at the reformatory and workhouse.

The broom factory at the reformatory supplied the District government offices as well as the institutions, with handmade brooms. By 1928, the activities of the broom factory were extended to include the production of handmade baskets. The baskets were made of ash and oak strips from timber felled on the reservation at Lorton. The industrial activities at the reformatory and workhouse drew considerable attention from the local press. An article taken from the Washington Star, February 26, 1928 edition, reads: "The supply of raw material is unlimited for, after all the ash trees are exhausted, there are more than 3,000,000 oaks available."[12] The same article comments on the reformatory's bakery:

> Some of the District's best bakers are men who learned their trade at Lorton. The bakeshop is fully equipped and boasts one large oven, where 600 pounds of bread can be baked at a charge. Electrical mixing machines are employed to prepare the dough. The arrangement is such that the bakery goods are protected from all dust, dirt and smoke during preparation. Men who knew nothing about commercial baking when they arrived at the 'pen' go forth at the termination of their

> terms as qualified bakers, able to earn more money than ever before in their lives.[13]

The article further comments on the activities of the foundry:

> The new foundry at Lorton which is isolated from the other buildings to protect them from its smoke and soot, is now producing all the grate bars, alley gratings and other castings used by the District Water Department, not to mention the iron and steel work turned out for service at the reformatory and workhouse.[14]

"In May, 1928, a working capital fund was authorized, which provided funds for industrial-type shops at the institution. This in turn offered products and services at fair market value to other District and Federal agencies."[15] The working capital enabled Mr. J.E.C. Bischoff, Superintendent of Industries, to expand operations, as noted in the annual report for 1930:

> This activity (foundry) has already reached the maximum production with the present building limitations. The funds now available for the extension to this building will permit further expansion during the coming year. The value of castings disposed of to District departments during the fiscal year, 1930 amounted to $22,997.56, as compared with $22,676.20 for the previous year. The value of castings used at these institutions during the fiscal year, 1930, amounted to $3,566.90, as compared to $2,584.02 for the previous year. The total tonnage for 1930 amounted to 546 tons, as compared to 456 1/2 tons for the previous year...[16]

Legal authorization, made possible by the 1931 District of Columbia Appropriations Act provided the payment of a small wage to the inmates for the first time. The wage scale was based upon the inmate's conduct and the amount of work he accomplished. It was found that this provided incentive for the inmate to to a better job.

An article appearing in the Star newspaper, June 21, 1931, shows the diversified types of industries as well as the price list for the products at the Reformatory and Workhouse.

> Anybody who wants a coffin, a manhole cover, a corn broom, a cocoa mat, a rubber heel or any of a long and varied list of useful articles will be interested in a price list promulgated today by the District Commissioners as the "fair" prices at which products of services of the District Work House and Reformatory are to be sold to the various District institutions and the Federal Government.
>
> A good coffin, size 7 1/2 by 6 by 18 inches, sells for $1. There are several other sizes. The largest, 20 by 12 by 61 inches, sells for $6.50. The manhole covers bring $4.25 each, whiskbrooms, $1.75 a dozen, and the rubber heels, 60 cents a dozen.
>
> A schedule also is arranged for the cost of laundry service done at the institutions, which ranges from handkerchiefs and slings at 1 cent each, up to the more complicated garments, such as teddies and nurses' uniforms, which will be washed for 20 cents each. A special rate is made on washing flags of 1 cent per square foot.[17]

In keeping with the philosophy of the era, Superintendent M.M. Barnard utilized "white collar" criminals to the advantage of the reformatory, as illustrated in the following excerpts from an interesting article by Walker Stone, appearing in the Star newspaper, June 21, 1931:

> D.C. Reformatory, Lorton, Va. - Men who were cutting wide swaths along Washington's 'Little Wall Street' only a few months ago - until they got caught playing too loosely with other people's money - are now doing a good portion of the clerical work of this model penitentiary.
>
> And Capt. M.M. Barnard, superintendent of the District's penal institutions, will tell you that they are among his most trusted and valued 'helpers.' They are doing good work, he says, and are keeping his records straight...
>
> In any place other than a penal institution, the jobs held down here by Harry V. Haynes, Edmund D. Rheem, C. Elbert Anadale,

John H. Edwards Jr., William M. Moffatt and George Bennete might be referred to as 'white collar positions.' But no white collars are worn in this prison settlement which boasts a 2700-acre farm and a variety of small machine shops and factories. The man who pushes a pencil or punches a typewriter in the general office wears the same grey and blue striped seersucker uniform as the man who lays bricks or mixes mortar in the institution's million dollar building project.

The very logical explanation why Washington's ex-financiers are handling pencils and typewriters instead of picks and shovels is that they can perform more important service in keeping the prison's records, whereas there are some seven or eight hundred inmates who are more at home in the shops and the foundry or on the farm.

Herewith are some of the names, recently emblazoned across the front pages of Washington newspapers, with accounts of who they are, why they were sent 'down the river,' and what they are doing now:

HAYNES, former president of the Farmers & Mechanics Bank of Georgetown, former president of the District Bankers' Association. He was sentenced to 4 1/2 years for juggling the records of his bank, when stock market losses upset him. He is now the clerk and custodian of the records in the prison hospital...

RHEEM, the dapper, snappy former head of the Swartzell Rheem & Hensey Co., who got seven years after pleading guilty to removing $162,000 worth of notes from the vaults of his firm. He works in the main office, along wih 11 other inmate bookkeepers, all experienced men, checking over production records. He arrived at Lorton last Friday, just in time to take over the desk where Anadale had worked. Anadale is now at the District Jail where he is assisting Justice Department agents in checking the accounts of the F.H. Smith Co.

EDWARDS, former vice president of the F.H. Smith Co., who was sentenced to three years when convicted with Anadale and G. Bryan Pitts of conspiring to embezzle $5,000,000 and conceal and destroy records of the Smith Co. He is bookkeeper in the commissary, and third baseman on the prison's first string white baseball team.

MOFFATT, the broker, who was sent up for eight years for embezzlement. He is bookkeeper for the daytime Captain of the Guard...

ROBERT J. WHELAN, lawyer, who was given six years for embezzlement. He keeps the records of the supplies, tools and materials in the garage.

And then there are others who ran afoul of the law in different ways but whose names will be instantly remembered:

DR. LOUIS W. HOFFMAN, sent here for 30 years after pleading guilty to second-degree murder resulting from an alleged illegal operation. He cares for the sick at the hospital.

GEORGE L. CASSIDY, better known as 'The Man in the Green Hat,' who was notorious as the bootlegger for members of Congress. He has charge of the records in the prison tailor shop.

DEXTER DAYTON, who murdered his sweetheart while on a drunken spree at the Roosevelt Hotel. Here for life...He now has a job in the laundry front office.

* * *

There are others too numerous to mention. Down here in this prison without walls, they go about their daily tasks with apparently no thoughts of the outside world. There is almost nothing to remind an inmate that he is a prisoner - no barred cells, no guards with rifles, no balls and chains.

There is manifest 'community pride,' in the new buildings which are going up, particularly in the almost complete auditorium,

> equipped with chandeliers, the seats and the furnishings, that were taken from Poli's and the old President's Theaters of Pennsylvania Ave. torn down to make room for the new Government buildings.[18]

It is noted that while no fences or walls enclosed the reformatory and workhouse compounds, blood hounds were used to aid the prison officials in searching for escaping prisoners. An article in the February 28, 1928 issue of the Washington Star read:

> A crew of 45 officers, working in three eight-hour shifts, keeps careful tab on the Lorton inmates both day and night. None of the prisoners are allowed out of the sight of these guards. A half-dozen trained bloodhounds are also kept in prime condition for cross-country chases. An expert who had handled 'canine sleuths' of this breed most of his life, has charge of the bloodhounds. He has assisted in the capture of more than 1,000 Virginia and Maryland criminals during his lifetime.
>
> As you would imagine, these trailing dogs are kept under leash. They occupy comfortable kennels, sleep on soft cushions, are bathed daily and exercised and have the run of strong-fenced yards. Their ration includes corn meal pone, wheat bread, meat and bones.
>
> Olympic game athletes train no more faithfully than do these dog policemen. Three to four times a week the dogs engage in actual chase after human runaways. 'Trusties' serve as decoys in these exciting runs over hill and dale. The 'trusties' are given plenty of start, so that the dogs do not over take them. The chase, in every case, continues for one to two hours.
>
> This training keeps the bloodhounds in splendid condition for field service. Furthermore, the presence and practice of the dogs exert advantageous psychological effect on the prisoners. The baying of the bloodhounds is a most satisfactory source of seemly behavior among those sentenced to the District institutions at Lorton. In fact the attempts at escape are very rare and all the runaways

> have been caught. Most of them are overtaken even before they cross the boundaries of the prison farm.[19]

It is noted that the use of bloodhounds to aid in the capture of escapees was discontinued around 1960.

By 1929, however, it became obvious that certain prisoners could not be managed by the honor system alone, and it was necessary for Superintendent Barnard to propose the building of a walled area and cell blocks for unmanageable inmates. He made the proposal in a letter to the Board of Public Welfare, and cited his reasons as follows: "The congested conditions in Federal institutions throughout the country and the insistence of the Attorney General that the District take care of all prisoners convicted in this city..."[20] Mr. Barnard added that in the two previous years 570 prisoners had been received in the District, and of that number, 300 were sentenced to terms of five years and over, and some had previously served terms in other institutions. He added that: "The original intention of the reformatory was that it should be a place of confinement for all hopeful cases, but should we be obligated to accept all classes we feel that such a course would destroy the purpose for which it was intended."[21]

The annual report of the Board of Welfare for the year ending June 30, 1930, recommended the addition of a walled area at the reformatory to house those inmates who required confinement within a maximum security structure. It was hoped this new addition would not change the character of the reformatory and that as many persons as possible could continue to be housed in a dormitory style setting. Construction of the walled area consisted of two cell blocks, a dining hall, and three shop buildings. Completed in 1936, these buildings were located within a twenty-five foot brick wall, enclosing approximately ten acres of land. Approval for additional construction was granted in 1938 which added a visiting building and salle porte just inside the wall. In earlier times, this part of the reformatory was known as the "penitentiary section." It is presently known as the Maximum Security Facility.

During the decade of the 1930s, academic education was limited to the elementary level (grades one through eight). All of the instruction was on an individual basis to allow the men to proceed as rapidly as their ability would permit. Academic, vocational, and intelligence testing was conducted during the time the new prisoners were in quarantine, and the results were given to the Classification Committee for use in developing the inmate's program.

Vocational training was offered to those inmates who possessed the essential mental and physical abilities that the trade required. The classroom portion of the training in such trades as plumbing, electrical work, foundry work, and automobile mechanics was taught through the use of correspondence courses in the various subjects. It took place in a supervised study period conducted by a capable inmate instructor. The practical experience was learned by working in the shops. Training in barbering, baking, and cooking was offered to apprentices assigned to those details. The inmates who were selected to teach the vocational training courses were "workers of recognized skill and masters of the technical knowledge" of the trade they taught, and worked under the supervision of the shop foreman at all times.

In addition to academic and vocational courses, visual education was provided once a week. This consisted of a moving picture on health, agriculture, manufacturing, travel, etc., supplemented by a lecture. These presentations were attended by approximately one-half of the reformatory inmate population. The reformatory library consisted of almost 5000 books, both fiction and non-fiction, and the inmates were permitted to visit it once a week and select the books they wished to read. The education department also supervised a 25-piece band which was under the direction of an accomplished inmate musician. The band provided music for the inmate population and for special occasions. In addition, art instruction was provided by an inmate artist. It is interesting to note that all educational instruction, including the academic courses and classroom instruction in the vocational subjects, was taught at night. For the majority of the inmates at the reformatory, the days were spent at physical labor.

The economic depression of the 1930s presented a number of problems for the administration of the reformatory. The ever increasing inmate population necessitated a continued need to provide more living space for the prisoners. In 1929, the daily average population at the reformatory was 580, by the end of fiscal year 1938 it had reached 1,596. It became difficult to maintain a sufficient staff of correctional officers to handle the large number of prisoners and to fulfill one of the basic concepts in the philosophy of the era which was to assure a full day's work for each inmate.

Despite the overcrowded conditions and insufficient personnel, progress in developing the reformatory's programs continued. In 1937, a classification plan for prisoners at the reformatory was initiated. Under this system, all inmates received individual study and treatment. The plan was divided into three parts or activities: "(1) a comprehensive study of the individual at the time of admission, (2) the coordination of the findings of this study and the planning of a program by the Classification Board, and (3) a follow-up study and changes in the program during the period of incarceration."[22] Upon admission to the institution, each prisoner was placed in quarantine for thirty days, during which time he was examined to assure that he was not suffering from any communicable disease which might be transferred to other inmates, and for observation by various special methods of examination and investigation by professional members of the staff. At the expiration of the quarantine period, the Classification Board reviewed the reports of examinations and investigations by the staff members and planned the prisoner's institutional program, based on their findings. Changes could be made in the prisoner's institutional program through a follow-up study by the Classification Board. Under the classification system, pre-parole studies were prepared by the reformatory for the first time. These studies were especially helpful to the Parole Board because they provided social, educational, religious, and other information regarding the parolee. Prior to creation of the Classification Board, pre-parole studies were prepared by the Bureau of Rehabilitation. An additional innovative procedure, introduced in 1938, was the preparation of medical summaries on each new admission to the reformatory for use by the Classification Board. Although the introduction of classification to the reformatory eventually led to the wide use of academic and vocational programs in the treatment of prisoners, the reformatory was clearly an industrial institution until the mid 1940s.

An Officers In-service Training program was established in 1937. "Training officers were assigned at the Jail and the Reservation Institutions, and all new employees given a two weeks basic training course under the direct supervision of the training officers."[23] All other officers were given several days of refresher training each year. In this connection, custodial employees of the reformatory were placed in uniform in 1936. "The first uniforms were purchased by the employees, but in 1937 funding was made available for uniforms for custodial employees of the Workhouse and the Reformatory. It was not until 1940 that funds were appropriated for custodial uniforms for the Jail."[24]

The overcrowded conditions created by the economic depression of the 1930s placed a burden on the health care staff at the reformatory as well as the District's other penal institutions. The medical staff consisted of one senior medical officer, a resident physician, a resident dentist, a pharmacist, and a graduate nurse. The staff was supplemented by inmate attendants and orderlies. An indication of the volume of cases treated by the medical staff is found in the annual report for 1938. The staff performed 24 major surgical and 35 major orthopedic operations as well as 1,128 minor surgical and 507 minor orthopedic operations. The outpatient or "sick call" statistics for that year was 62,652. The incidence of tuberculosis among the inmate population at the reformatory was .05%, and the number of isolated cases under treatment at the institution was 26 for the year, in addition to venereal clinics dispensing 3,433 treatments for gonorrhea and 16,092 treatments for syphilis. The dentist performed 2,642 extractions as well as 681 admission examinations, in addition to fillings, plate work, etc. The pharmacist dispensed 40,429 medications, and manufactured fly spray, suppositories, and some triturate and compressed tablets "...at a considerable saving over the purchase price of the finished product."[25]

In addition to the routine professional services rendered to patients, as noted above, vocational training in nursing, and dental and clinical laboratory work was introduced by the medical staff of the reformatory, and instruction in first aid, preventive medicine, and hygiene were in the planning stage. The annual report for 1938 notes: "...thought has been given to rendering contributions and theses concerning medical statistics and research problems..."[26]

In expressing the personnel needs to increase the medical and dental staffs of the reformatory and workhouse to a level that would effectively meet the medical needs of the inmate populations, the following is noted in the 1938 annual report:

> ...Personnel needs include the appointment of six additional registered nurses to give twenty-four hour nursing service on each area; four dental internes; three medical internes; including one female interne; one medical laboratory technician to render necessary laboratory work on new admissions, and also on cases admitted to the hospital; a psychiatrist or psychologist who will be a member of the classification committee and whose work will be helpful in reducing the number of men at 'sick call' through therapy, and also in an advisory capacity to the custodial staff in the care of men suffering from nervous and mental disorders; and a dental laboratory technician to manufacture all dental prosthetics and aid in vocational training in this particular field.[27]

Other needs expressed by the medical staff included: "...installation of showers in dormitories to permit daily bathing; construction of a Tuberculosis Unit to permit segregation, isolation, and treatment of all tuberculosis cases on the Reservation area; installation of drinking fountains in each dormitory and shop..."[28]

America's involvement in World War II in 1941, added to the difficulty of operating the reformatory as well as the other institutions. The staffs of the institutions were made up of male employees, with the exception of the Women's Division. Although the inmate population decreased during the war years, induction of the male personnel into the Armed Services placed a hardship in recruiting male employees to replace them. A notation in the annual report of the Commissioners for the year ending June 30, 1942, illustrates the turnover in personnel as a result of the loss of male employees.

> The War services have made heavy inroads among personnel. The turnover has been 171 out of 351 and the difficulty of filling positions has increased and has led to the employment of women in some of the office positions. This has not been an easy solution of the personnel problem for the reason that, formerly, employees have been able to supervise a number of inmates in office work.[29]

The shortage of manpower was partly offset by instituting a longer workday. As for the employment of women in male institutions, this practice was not discontinued when the war ended. In fact, gradually over the following three decades, women assumed more and more responsibility in the operation of the District's male institutions, including that of correctional officer.

The inmate population contributed significantly to the war effort. Their cooperation and outstanding service received a number of commendations. A Selective Service Board was established to screen parolees and mandatory releasees for duty in the Armed Services. During the war years, 389 inmates were accepted and inducted into the Armed Services.

The inmates participated in medical war research, volunteering for experiments in the control of typhus, the penicillin drug, and the use of vesicant gas, conducted by the Army, Navy, Department of Agriculture, and Western Reserve University. The inmates donated several thousand pints of blood to the Red Cross during the war years.

The industries division at the reformatory made 350,000 bomb noses for the War Chemical Service and manufactured shirts for the Navy Department and the United Nations Relief and Rehabilitation Administration. They also renovated mattresses and furniture and manufactured deck brushes for the Navy.

The inmates organized an aircraft spotter station at the reformatory and participated in first aid training. One of the most outstanding accomplishments was the organization of a fire-fighting unit. This proved to be particularly helpful since the surrounding area was completely wooded, and brush and forest fires were frequent occurrences. The lack of civilian manpower for this duty gave the inmates an opportunity to perform a valuable service to the community.

Scarcity of raw materials for industries such as the foundry and clothing factory caused by the war had severely hampered production at the reformatory. In addition, lack of sufficient personnel to properly supervise operations at the brickyard and other industries further contributed to poor production during the war years. When the war ended in 1945, attention of the reformatory's administration was focused on returning the institution to normal operation. With the creation of the Department of Corrections in 1946, however, the experiment of the industrial farm, as such, came to an end. A more modern approach in the treatment of prisoners had been found, and it ushered in a whole new era in the history of the D.C. penal institutions. Although the experiment had ended, industrial operations remained a valuable part of the reformatory's program.

The industrial farm experiment contributed substantially to the store of knowledge in the field of corrections. Prison officials of the reformatory and the workhouse who participated in the experiment not only learned how to utilize every resource at hand, but the insight they gained from handling prisoners in open institutions proved that many of the prisoners could function under the honor system. Most of all, it proved to the officials and inmates alike that hard work and ingenuity could build successful penal institutions where once there was nothing but wilderness.

While many contributed to the success of building the penal institutions at Lorton and Occoquan, the credit for leadership belongs to one man, Captain M.M. Barnard, as noted in the January 23, 1937 edition of the Washington Daily News:

> Capt. M.M. Barnard has asked for retirement at the age of 75 from his post of General Superintendent of District penal

institutions. To his 20 years of excellent service he has added a challenge to the Municipal Government to return to the ideals it launched with his appointment in 1916.

Convinced that society's duty is to rehabilitate offenders rather than punish them, he developed the honor system at Lorton and built an institution unsurrounded by walls and watch towers.

This idea was based, in part, upon segregation of hardened from first offenders. Habitual felons were to be sent to Federal penitentiaries.

Not so many years ago, when the Federal prison system began to fall behind penological progress, Federal authorities began to reject the District's felons, forcing Barnard to house them in his reformatory. Only his extraordinary talents prevented this change from breaking down his honor system.

He finally was compelled to accept the Federal change of policy and met the new situtation by building the walled group of new cell houses at Lorton for hardened criminals.

In his request for retirement he calls attention to the crowded condition of the reformatory and the inadequacy of appropriations, stresses again the need for a farm sanatorium for inebriates and the overhauling of the probation and parole systems.

It is to be hoped that the Commissioners will exercise the greatest of care in selecting Capt. Barnard's successor. The day of the hard-boiled jailer has passed. The best available student of modern penology, tried out in administrative experience, should be appointed.[30]

SOURCES

[1.] Washington Herald, December 23, 1914, on file in the Washingtoniana Room, Martin Luther King Library, Washington, D.C.

[2.] Annual Report to the Commissioner of the District of Columbia Fiscal Year July 1, 1916 - June 30, 1917 (Washington, D.C.: Government Printing Office), p. 506.

[3.] Ibid., pp. 506-507.

[4.] Annual Report to the Commissioner of the District of Columbia July 1, 1918 - June 30, 1919 (Washington, D.C.: Government Printing Office), p. 329.

[5.] Hoyem, Oliver, "The Prison System of the District," The Survey Magazine, August 19, 1920, Washingtoniana Room, Martin Luther King Library, Washington, D.C. or D.C. Department of Corrections Museum, Lorton, Virginia, p. 261.

[6.] Annual Report to the Commissioner of the District of Columbia 1929-1930 (Washington, D.C.: Government Printing Office), p. 27.

[7.] Annual Report to the Commissioner of the District of Columbia 1922 (Washington, D.C.: Government Printing Office).

[8.] Annual Report to the Commissioner of the District of Columbia July 1, 1919 - June 30, 1920 (Washington, D.C.: Government Printing Office), p. 426.

[9.] Washington Star Newspaper, clipping, no date, in packet labeled "Reformatory 1910-1931," Washingtoniana Room, Martin Luther King Library, Washington, D.C.

[10.] Annual Report to the Commissioner of the District of Columbia July 1, 1931 - June 30, 1932 (Washington, D.C.: Government Printing Office), p. 8.

[11.] Washington Star Newspaper, February 26, 1927 edition, contained in packet labeled "Reformatory 1910-1931," Washingtoniana Room, Martin Luther King Library, Washington, D.C.

[12.] Ibid.

[13.] Ibid.

[14.] _Ibid._

[15.] Annual Report to the Commissioner of the District of Columbia July 1, 1929 June 30, 1930 (Washington, D.C.: Government Printing Office), p.37.

[16.] _Ibid._

[17.] _Washington Star Newspaper,_ June 21, 1931, in packet labeled "Reformatory 1910-1931," Washingtoniana Room, Martin Luther King Library, Washington, D.C.

[18.] Stone, Walker, unknown newspaper, unknown edition, (clipping packet labeled "Reformatory 1910-1931"), Washingtoniana Room, Martin Luther King Library, Washington, D.C.

[19.] _Washington Star Newspaper,_ February 28, 1928 edition, (clipping packet labeled "Reformatory 1910-1931"), Washingtoniana Room, Martin Luther King Library, Washington, D.C.

[20.] _Washington Star Newspaper,_ November 29, 1929, (clipping packet labeled "Reformatory 1910-1931"), Washingtoniana Room, Martin Luther King Library, Washington, D.C.

[21.] _Ibid._

[22.] Board of Welfare Annual Report to the D.C. Commissioner, 1938, on file D.C. Department of Corrections Museum, Lorton, Virginia.

[23.] _Ibid._

[24.] _Ibid._

[25.] _Ibid.,_ p. 51.

[26.] _Ibid._

[27.] _Ibid.,_ p. 50.

[28.] _Ibid.,_ p. 50.

[29.] Annual Report to the Commissioner, Ending June 30, 1942, filed in packet marked "Excerpts from Annual Reports," D.C. Department of Corrections Museum, Lorton, Virginia.

[30.] *Washington Daily News,* January 23, 1937 edition, clipping packet labeled "Reformatory 1910-1931," Washingtoniana Room, Martin Luther King Library, Washington, D.C.

CHAPTER 12

THE JAIL AS A HOUSE OF DETENTION (1911 - 1945)

Transfer of the jail from the jurisdiction of the Justice Department to the District in 1911, with supervision by the Board of Charities, marked the first step in unifying the penal institutions. For the first time in its history, the District's penal institutions were together under one local agency. The task of carrying out the Penal Commission's recommendation that the jail be used "only as a house of detention, never as a place of confinement" brought about major changes in its operation. Transition from an institution that traditionally confined sentenced misdemeanant offenders to a place for housing the accused, cast the jail in an entirely new role, a role that has not significantly changed with time.

Under the newly acquired title, house of detention, the jail became the center or "hub" for processing and holding for short periods of time, all admissions, transfers, releases, and other movement of all prisoners for the workhouse and reformatory as well as transfer of the District's felony offenders to Federal and State penitentiaries for service of sentence. In connection with the transfer of felony offenders, the jail acquired the additional responsibility of arranging for their transportation, which was by rail in the early days. Other responsibilities assumed by the jail consisted of maintaining a repository of permanent records on all prisoners who entered the District penal institutions as well as identification files on known criminals. In the beginning, the Bertillon system of identification was used. (Identification was made through recording measurements, color, markings, and deformities, etc., of the prisoner.) A little later on, around 1915, fingerprinting became popular and was incorporated into the identification process. In addition, all sentence computations were made at the jail as well as assignment of all prison numbers. In the beginning, the workhouse and reformatory had different numbering systems. Beginning July 1, 1933, however, the practice of using the same set of numbers for all new offenders entering the District's penal system was initiated, and it is still in use. It is noted that an offender is assigned a number upon entering the District's penal system for the first time, and he retains that number regardless of the times he re-enters the system.

With the opening of the workhouse at Occoquan in 1910, the inmate population of the jail was substantially reduced. By 1911, it had decreased from a daily average of 500 in 1910, to slightly over 200. Superintendent L.F. Zinkhan reported:

> Prisoners sentenced to the jail are no longer kept in idleness, but are transferred to Occoquan and required to work, unless their condition is such that they are unfitted for work. The only persons sentenced to serve jail sentences who are now kept at the jail and are fully employed are a few whose sentences are for such a short period - seven days or less - that the trouble and expense of transporting them to and from Occoquan seems hardly warranted.[1]

The Penal Commission's assessment of the jail was that if some changes were made to its interior, it would be an "adequate building for a long period of time," since the "outer jail - that is to say, the main walls of the building,[2] were in excellent condition. Further, since it would be "used only for the confinement of accused persons, it would not be regarded as a prison and its presence would be far less objectionable."[3] The Penal Commission would have preferred to have the jail in closer proximity to the courts, and noted that if a new jail was ever built in the District, it should be situtated nearer to the courthouse.

In keeping with the Commission's recommendation, the interior of the jail was greatly improved at a cost of $37,230. Between 1910 and 1911, a plumbing system was installed. This included water closets, which replaced the old bucket system, and the addition of wash basins and bath tubs. The old cells were converted by using two cells to make one larger one. This reduced the capacity of the jail to 136, making it necessary to keep two prisoners in one cell. The superintendent commented: "This is a condition that ought not to obtain when it can possibly be avoided."[4] In 1913, a modern heating plant was installed at a cost of $15,000, and new kitchen was completed in 1916.

By 1918, the jail population had begun to escalate, creating a need for further renovation and expansion. One of the major reasons for the overcrowded conditions was the long delays in the trial of prisoners. The annual report for 1919 noted: "The criminal docket is far behind, and very great hardship is placed upon poor persons accused of crime unable to obtain bail, because they must wait for many months, and occasionally as much as a year, in jail before their cases are disposed of."[5] In addition, World War I had curtailed building due to the high cost of supplies and materials as well as labor.

Charles C. Foster assumed the duties of Superintendent of the Asylum Hospital and jail on April 23, 1919, in addition to his duties as Superintendent of the workhouse and Reformatory, and served in the capacity of General Superintendent until July 1921. W.A. Peak became Assistant Superintendent of the jail in 1919, and served in that capacity until 1927, and as Superintendent until 1932.

Peak noted in his annual report of 1923: "A greater variety of food was served and a greater satisfaction recorded among the men who received it. This result is due very largely to the first year's administration of the commissary by a paid steward and to the productive capacity of the Jail's own garden."[6] The garden produced over 13,625 pounds of fresh vegetables at a cost of $185.55, "exclusive of the Guards' salaries."[7] Other interesting statistics for the same year included a daily average population of 320, and average daily per capita cost for maintainence of prisoners (all expenses) $.719, of which $.266 was spent for food.

The 1923 report mentioned that screens for the windows had been provided during the year and that the grounds had been resodded in an effort to improve the jail's surroundings.

By 1926 it was necessary for Congress to appropriate $275,000 to provide quarters for 200 additional prisoners. The inmate population had increased to 425, which was 25 percent above the crowding point, and 125 persons beyond the intended functioning of the equipment.

The following quotation indicates that Congress had some help in deciding to appropriate funds for the renovation:

> ...In this connection, it is interesting to note that Phillip C. Kauffman, then assistant editor of the _Evening Star,_ seems to have been instrumental in persuading Congress to appropriate the above mentioned $275,000 for the new East Wing - or at least Mr. Kauffman and the _Evening Star_ claimed credit for the good deed...Mr. Kauffman decided to investigate for himself. He had himself arrested as a vagrant, donning a seedy outfit of clothes for the occasion. After sentence, he was confined in 'the overcrowded District Jail' for several days when his release was conveniently arranged. After release Mr. Kauffman wrote a story which the _Evening Star_ claimed so shocked the members of Congress that funds were

> promptly appropriated for a new wing for the Jail.[8]

The new addition was completed in 1927, and it became known as the East Wing. In a letter to the Director of the Board of Welfare, January 7, 1927, Peak described how he planned to use the additional space:

> When construction work is completed, it is planned to transfer the prisoners in the North Wing (composed of those convicted of misdemeanors) to the new wing. The North Wing will then be used as a Criminal Wing to relieve the present congestion in the South (Criminal) wing.
>
> Female prisoners will be distributed over three floors of the new wing. This will require, in my judgement, a change in the present arrangement of supervision. Two matrons now alternate in covering the twenty-four hour period, making it necessary for the one on duty to sleep in her department, a practice which is most unsatisfactory and not in accordance with disciplinary requirements. As the new female department will be arranged as a dormitory, replacing the old cell block, it seems imperative that regular inspection be made at all hours of the night to insure proper conduct of prisoners.
>
> It occurs to me that in order to properly police the three floors of the new department, it would be most advisable to have two matrons on day duty; one a Senior Matron, to be in charge and should rank in authority to the Captains and should be compensated commensurate with the office.
>
> A Senior Matron would not only supervise the entire female Department, but would be able, with her assistant, to more efficiently commit new prisoners; transfer those detailed in the laundry; transfer of female prisoners to Occoquan; see that those wanted in the various courts are ready at the proper time; examine incoming packages sent to prisoners in their Department; regulate visits and visitors; and refer the sick to the attention of staff physician.[9]

Regarding the women's department, Peak noted in his report for 1927: "The women's department is now a complete and individual unit with ingress and egress independent of the main-building activities." The functioning of this department within itself is admirable.[10]

In the letter noted above, Peak listed the equipment he would need to furnish a proposed hospital unit in the jail. The equipment would be used in a Combined Physician's Office, Examining, Minor Operating and Dressing Room. It is noted that although the Gallinger Municipal Hospital was used for treatment of the penal institutions' major medical needs, the jail hospital was necessary to attend to routine procedures such as medications and dressing, minor operations, blood tests, physical examinations, etc. The 1927 annual report contains the following comment by Peak in regard to the hospital unit:

> An important step toward the complete independence of the jail has been achieved by the converting of the west wing directly over the executive offices into an infirmary, equipped with an operating room, drug dispensary, and dental office. The staff consists of a resident physician, a resident dental interne who comes under the supervision of Dr. G.A. Hewey, chief of the dental staff at Gallinger Hospital, and a graduate nurse. This very important and long-needed arrangement was made possible by the generosity of a citizen who agreed to assume the sum involved in the physician's salary pending a regular appropriation later on. The jail community is measurably helped by this addition to its functioning departments within itself and disposes of the drawback heretofore existing by its enforced dependence upon Gallinger Municipal Hospital.[11]

Correspondence between the jail and the Gallinger Municipal Hospital during the early months of 1929 concerned the possibility of voluntary blood transfusions by prisoners of the jail for the benefit of patients of the hospital. In order to permit such a practice, however, a decision by the Board of Welfare was necessary. The following statement was issued by the Board March 1, 1929: "that on proper statement of the need for transfusion by responsible hospital authorities, prisoners might be allowed to volunteer their blood for transfusion but that no compulsion or pressure of any kind should be exercised to secure such volunteers."[12]

Although some of the traditional operations of the jail were changed when it became a detention facility, it continued to serve as the legal site of execution for those offenders of the law who were condemned to death by the District's criminal justice system as cited in Title 23-706 of the D.C. Code (March 31, 1901). Until 1925, hanging was the official method of execution in the District. In that year, however, Congress issued a Decree of Condemnation of the jail's gallows. Under Title 23-701, D.C. Code (January 30, 1925), the method of execution was changed as follows: "The mode of capital punishment shall be by the process commonly known as electrocution. The punishment of death shall be inflicted by causing to pass through the body of the convict a current of electricity of sufficient intensity to cause death, and the application of such current shall be continued until such convict is dead."[13]

In keeping with the Decree of Congress, on October 7, 1925, the gallows was dismantled and burned. An article appearing in the Washington Star newspaper on that day gives a dramatic account of the event:

> The District Jail gallows, stark reminder of the inexorable penalty society exacts of some prisoners, no longer throw its sinister shadow down the long narrow confines of the dining hall in the north wing to mingle over tables, benches and prisoners with shadows from the bars in the windows.
>
> There is no more gallows at the jail. It became mere scraps of lumber early this afternoon. By tonight much of it will be charred fragments of wood or ashes blown about the courtyard of the jail.[14]

The first execution to be carried out on the jail's gallows was that of James Stone. The hanging took place on April 2, 1880, with Warden John S. Crocker as the official in charge. The last execution by hanging was that of Herbert L. Copeland, which took place January 22, 1925, for the murder of a police officer. Peak, Assistant Superintendent of the jail, was the official in charge.

In his annual report for 1923, Peak made an interesting comment regarding "The Toll of the Gallows:"

> During the year five men have paid the death penalty and 31 prisoners were received during the same period for Murder. The flaw in

> the District Code was remedied by the last Congress and the series of respites based thereon have been eliminated. In spite of the horror and the undoubted ignominy of the method, competent judges are of the opinion that this distasteful service is performed as humanely as possible.[15]

During its 45 years of use, the gallows was the scene of 51 executions.

When the gallows was replaced by electrical execution, Peak noted: "...the inauguration of electrical executions in lieu of the gallows is an achievement in the best modern trend..."[16] Philip Jackson was the first prisoner to be executed under the new method. The execution took place May 9, 1928, with Peak as the official in charge. Between the years 1928 and 1945, 28 prisoners were put to death in the electric chair. Included in that number are two triple executions; the first occurring on June 22, 1928, (Nicholas L. Eagles, Samuel Morano, and John Proctor), and all three men were involved in the same crime. The second triple execution occurred January 12, 1934, (Irvin Murray, Joseph J. Jackson, and Ralph Holms), with all three men involved in the same crime. In addition to the 28 prisoners who were put to death under jurisdiction of the District of Columbia, six saboteurs were executed in the jail under the direction of the United States Army in 1942.

Initially, there were eight saboteurs held in the D.C. Jail during the Summer of 1942 while they were facing a month long trial by a Military Commission after being charged as enemy agents. The evidence and the Commission's decision was given to President Franklin Roosevelt for his review who approved the judgement of the Commission. All the prisoners were found guilty. However, only six of the prisoners were executed because two had testified against the others. Of the two who were not executed, one was given a life term and the other was given 30 years. Beginning at noon on August 9, 1942, the executions were carried out, using the jail's electric chair. The bodies of the saboteurs were transported to Walter Reed Army hospital's morgue until they could be claimed by relatives or friends. When bodies were not claimed, they were buried in the District's Potter's Field at Blue Plains. The graves are identified only by numbers ranging from 276 to 282 painted on wooden tombstones.

Before other arrangements were made at the Jail, a makeshift space near the mess hall was used to house the gallows and later the electric chair. When there was an execution, the tables and chairs were moved out of the mess hall to set up for the execution, and then, after the execution, they were quickly put back in place for lunch. The place of execution was in full view of the prisoners as they ate their meals. This was all changed with addition of the death house which was completed around 1942. The plans for a more private place of execution were contained in the January 21, 1938 edition of the Washington Daily News:

> The death house would be the fourth story of a new administration building. The death chamber would be a small, quiet room resembling a chapel. There would be sound-proof rubber floor covering, so those awful last footsteps couldn't reverberate.
>
> No curious eyes would watch the prisoner. The room would be empty except for him, his guard and his spiritual advisor.
>
> Facing the electric chair would be a blank wall of one-way glass such as is used to shield the Dionne quintuplets from the thousands of visitors who watch them at play. Witnesses in an observation room beyond this wall could see the doomed man but he couldn't see them.
>
> There would be four cells in the fourth story of the new building. The jail often has more condemned prisoners than that, but it is planned to delay the trip to the death house until all appeals have been rejected. As long as a prisoner had hope he would stay in the main building.
>
> The switch that operates the chair would be out of sight. As far as possible, 'public spectacle' features of an execution would be eliminated.
>
> The present electric chair is a gruesome sight between executions, covered with white muslin in an alcove off the jail mess hall.[17]

An interesting letter addressed to Superintendent Peak, dated June 25, 1928, from Dr. Orthello Langworthy, Department of Pathology, Johns Hopkins Medical School, Baltimore, Maryland, reads in part as follows:

> I wish to thank you for your offer to cooperate in obtaining specimens of the nervous

> system from those killed by electricity. I have been asked by representatives of electric companies to study the pathological changes produced in the brain by electricity with a view to treating the victims of electric accidents. Such a study may be pursued in several ways. It is proposed to study animals where the voltage and amperage may be controlled. It is also important to follow the work and learn the results produced in man. It is seldom possible to obtain material from victims of accidents and I must therefore resort to a study of legal electrocution.
>
> ...It would be valuable to obtain permission for a complete autopsy so that specimens of other tissues besides the brain could be studied...I need not add that we will do all we can to avoid publicity in this matter. I really feel that you can render an important service by helping with this work.[18]

Peak's reply, dated June 28, 1928, follows:

> I have your letter of the 25th instant relative to obtaining specimens of the nervous system of those killed by electrocution and beg to advise you that I will be very glad to co-operate with you in any way that I can and will be pleased to see you in my office after September 10th.
>
> In order to obtain a complete autopsy on a person electrocuted in the District of Columbia it will be necessary to have Congress enact a law covering the subject.[19]

No record could be found that Congress ever enacted such a law.

A fire in the top floor of the West Wing of the jail in October, 1925 destroyed records and did $8,000 worth of damage to items that were stored there. Peak commended the police and fire departments on their splendid cooperation in aiding the staff of the jail in bringing it under control: "There was no serious panic among the desperate and imprisoned men and no disorders outside. The presence of the reserves of both departments prompted response of all guards off duty together with emergency efficiency of the shift within the wings saved a situation overfull of difficulties. It is a pleasure to report that the needs of the hour disclosed no weak link in the lines of defense:[20]

Mr. Peak's interest in the welfare of the jail guards is evident in his comment in the annual report ending June 30, 1926:

> A lack of playtime has been conceded to be the breeder of dull wits, and monotony to be the bugbear of efficiency. In the modern acceptance of these truths the one group of men who have been passed over is the jail guard force. The guards are surrounded by lawbreakers and have not the diversion of rounding them up nor the exhilaration of the chase. For eight hours every day they share the confinement of the men in their keeping. Much is required of the guards and much is delivered. The present training and efficient force on duty here should be permitted to share with the district police and fire department the boon to efficiency of a day off in every seven.
>
> Discipline is very often but another name for normal guardianship; irritation, slow thinking, frowns and disgruntlement are usually dispelled by a day in the open. To deal successfully with the abnormal, the guard should be normal. One day a week to adjust his perspective should be accorded him not only as a matter of justice but for the very selfish reason that he will be made more dependable in his responsible duties. Four additional guards are necessary to permit this breathing spell and to properly augment the demands of a larger area of watchfulness. The appointment of an additional assistant engineer is also recommended in order that a day off a week may be given employees of that department. A salaried record clerk to take over the work now performed by prisoners, should be made an early addition to the office force. Vital records and the confidential handling of them are not certain of either loyal or capable treatment by involuntary clerks.[21]

The same report quotes statistics that provide information regarding the misdemeanant offenses for the year. The figures on arrests for intoxication are particularly interesting, since our country was in the midst of the "Prohibition Era."

> The total turnover for the year was 10,986 prisoners, or 1,305 more than last year. As usual, the outstanding item in this harvest of chaff is the all-time record of 5,054 committed for intoxication or about 46 percent. In percentage this offense falls from its status of 54 percent last year, in spite of the fact that it makes a new record for volume. The reason is that other forms of crime also show increases, or superior detection and conviction. There were 60 more cases of disorderly conduct; 78 more cases of assault and 110 more cases of larceny. The dangerous age for moral skidding is again shown to be between 21 and 30 years. In this group are found 4,243 of this years offenders and in the group over 60 years of age there were 250. Of the total population of the District, approximately 2 percent have been fingerprinted during the year.[22]

While early records of the jail are far from complete, some that date back to the 1920s and 1930s have been preserved, and one file in particular indicates that religious and recreation activities were a regular part of inmate life. The clergy and other religious organizations of the city's churches held services on a regular volunteer basis. Other civic organizations provided entertainment in the form of boxing matches, musical programs, and educational lectures. Motion pictures were also shown. In fact, one old file from the 1920s contains a questionnaire from a motion picture distributor, asking the inmates to name their favorite movies.

Another unique activity of the inmates was a radio program reported in the January 18, 1933 edition of the Washington Herald which notes the following:

> Under direction of Mrs. Alice Washington, inmates offered a program including 'Where Is My Boy Tonight' and 'Old Time Religion.' The songs were divided among quartets, soloists and the ensemble.
>
> Mrs. Washington has for 39 years been known as 'Mother Washington' at the jail. A social worker from the Calvert A.M.E. Church, she spends much time at the institution

> arranging such events as went over the air last night.[23]

Another interesting bit of information relating to the activities of the jail in the early days was found in an article appearing in the February 27, 1921 edition of the <u>Washington Post</u>, entitled "The School in the Washington City Jail:"

> One of the most unique educational institutions in the National Capital is the school maintained in the District of Columbia under the direction of Superintendent Charles C. Foster. There are an average of 25 to 35 students in attendance and school is held in a high white-washed, blue ceilinged corridor, lighted by tall windows that, save for their bars, have a cathedral effect. Two rows of desks face a teacher's platform and a blackboard. Each desk is equipped with elementary text books, pencils, pens and paper.
>
> Individual vocational training is given and although most of the pupils are illiterate an attempt is made to give instruction of a character that will help into wage-earning positions after they have served out their terms.
>
> The teacher is himself a prisoner...[24]

The jail's inmate population reached an all time high during the decade of the 1930s. This increase was due, for the most part, to the economic depression throughout the country. The number of commitments to the jail in 1929 was 12,722, and the daily average population was 503. In 1938 the number of new commitments rose to 17,965, and the daily average population was 646. By 1935 the jail was so overcrowded that as many as six inmates were confined to one cell. It was not until 1941 that further renovation of the jail was completed and the situation was eased.

> Two additional new wings (Cell Block #3 and #4) were erected and occupied in 1941. At the same time extensive alterations were begun in the main building. The old brick cells in the north and south wings (later becoming Cell Blocks #2 and #1) were replaced with steel cells and roofs. A complete modern kitchen also was installed. Brick walls were erected around the recreation areas for prisoners

> confined in the maximum security wings (Cell Blocks #1 and #2) and a separate recreation area for the prisoners in the women's department. This work, under a P.W.A. grant, was completed in 1942 at a cost of $1,056,275. At about the same time, construction work on a new administration building and hospital began and was finally completed in 1942 at a cost of $283,861.[25]

Upon the resignation of Mr. Peak in 1932, Mr. Thomas M. Rives became Superintendent of the jail and served in that capacity until April 16, 1942. He was succeeded by Mr. E.A. Green who served until July 1, 1944. Claude O. Botkin became Superintendent of the Jail in July 1944 and served until May 20, 1946. With the resignation of M.M. Barnard in 1937, Ray L. Huff was appointed to the post of General Superintendent of the District's penal institutions. He held that position until 1944, when he was selected to become director of the Department of Welfare. Huff was succeeded as General Superintendent of the penal institutions by Howard B. Gill.

The escape of five prisoners from the jail November 24, 1945, followed by a further rash of escapes between that date and April of 1946, prompted a congressional investigation of the jail's administration. The seriousness of the escapes was compounded by the fact that two of the escapees were condemned prisoners scheduled for execution.

The escapes led to the suspension and later the dismissal of Howard B. Gill as General Superintendent of the D.C. penal institutions in April of 1946. The charges described were in the April 19, 1946 edition of the Washington Post newspaper, some were very vague and didn't stand up.

> ...The dismissal of Mr. Gill was apparently the board's riposte to the criticism directed against it after the recent and scandalous series of escapes by prisoners from the District Jail. Whether calculated or not, the implication contained in the charges against Mr. Gill is that it was his 'incompetency, inefficiency and insubordination' that made the escapes possible. These are rather large and sweeping words, and it seems to us that Mr. Gill has done well to insist that the charges be made specific.

> One of the charges is that he demoralized the prison administration by 'arbitrarily and unjustly reprimanding members of the custodial force of the jail.' This charge is not implausible; tact is evidently not Mr. Gill's most conspicuous virtue, and his habit of speaking his mind too freely has probably been at the bottom of most of his difficulties with the board. But the suggestion that Mr. Gill's manner of dealing with the jail officers was an encouragement to riots and escapes seems preposterous. Conditions at the jail were notorious and escapes frequent long before Mr. Gill's appointment. Another and more serious charge is that he refused to make use of the 'control cells' in the basement of the jail for dealing with refractory prisoners. Mr. Gill's retort to this charge is that the cells are farcically inadequate.[26]

An article appearing in the Washington Star newspaper, May 20, 1946, noted:

> Washingtonians who were alarmed by the weakness of their local government exposed by the recent jail breaks may find considerable comfort in the fact that reorganization efforts are proceeding...there is a new administrative set-up at the District Jail. With the expert assistance of J. Ellis Overlade, who was borrowed from the Federal Bureau of Prisons, the local authorities have selected Lieut. Col. Curtis Reid to replace Jail Superintendent Claude O. Botkin. This should mean the prompt initiation of reforms and reorganization at the jail itself.[27]

Investigation at the jail led to the introduction of a Bill in the House by Representative F. Edward Hebert to form the penal institutions into a department that would function directly under the control of the District Commissioners, thus freeing it from any control by the Board of Public Welfare. Creation of a Department of Corrections would form the final step in fusing the District's penal institutions into a unified system as well as ending the shifting from one government agency to another that had prevailed for 146 years.

Despite his dismissal, Gill lauded the reorganization of the penal institutions into a Department of Corrections, saying:

> ...today charactrized as 'a step forward' the recommendations of the Hebert subcommittee on reorganization of penal administration here despite the fact that the report calls for his own dismissal.
>
> 'It promises achievement of the first objective for which we have been fighting,' he said. 'It may well mark the end of paregoric penology in District prisons and is recognition of professional administration of D.C. penal institutions.'[28]

The article further quotes Mr. Charles V. Morris saying:

> Charles V. Morris, secretary of the corrections division of the Council of Social Agencies, supported the congressional recommendation for a separate department of corrections but said the District 'would be losing one of the best penologists in the country' if it fires Mr. Gill.[29]

SOURCES

[1.] Annual Report of the Board of Charities to the Commissioners of the District of Columbia, (Fiscal Year Ending October 31, 1911), p. 387.

[2.] Report of the Penal Commission Jail Workhouse, etc. in the District of Columbia, p. 12.

[3.] _Ibid.,_ p. 12.

[4.] Annual Report 1910–1911, p. 387.

[5.] Annual Report Board of Charities 1918–1919, p. 329.

[6.] Annual Report, Superintendent of the D.C. Jail to the Board of Charities, July 9, 1923, p. 1.

[7.] _Ibid._

[8.] F.E. Peters, "A Short History of the Jails of Washington," unpublished, May, 1952, on file in the D.C. Department of Corrections Museum, Lorton, Virginia, p. 25.

[9.] Letter on file in D.C. Department of Corrections Museum, Lorton, Virginia.

[10.] Annual Report to the Board of Welfare, 1927, on file in the D.C. Department of Corrections Museum, Lorton, Virginia.

[11.] _Ibid._

[12.] Correspondence on file in the D.C. Department of Corrections Museum, Lorton, Virginia.

[13.] D.C. Code, 1951 Edition, Vol. 1, (Washington, D.C: U.S. Government Printing Office).

[14.] _Washington Star Newspaper,_ October 7, 1925, Washingtoniana Room, Martin Luther King Library, Washington, D.C.

[15.] Annual Report of the Superintendent of Jail to Board of Charities, 1923, p. 4.

[16.] Annual Report to the Commissioners of the District of Columbia, 1928, p. 32.

[17.] Washington Daily News, January 21, 1938, Newspaper Clipping Packet, Washingtoniana Room, Martin Luther King Library, Washington, D.C.

[18.] Letter on file in D.C. Department of Corrections Museum, Lorton, Virginia.

[19.] Letter on file in D.C. Department of Corrections Museum, Lorton, Virginia.

[20.] Annual Report to the Commissioners ending June 30, 1926, p. 26.

[21.] Ibid.

[22.] Ibid.

[23.] Washington Herald Newspaper, January 18, 1933, Newspaper Packet, Washingtoniana Room, Martin Luther King Library, Washington, D.C.

[24.] Washington Post, February 27, 1921, Newspaper Packet, Washingtoniana Room, Martin Luther King Library, Washington, D.C.

[25.] E.F. Peters, "A Short History of the Washington Jails," p. 27.

[26.] Washington Post, January 16, 1946, Newspaper Packet, Washingtoniana Room, Martin Luther King Library, Washington, D.C.

[27.] Star Newspaper, May 20, 1946, Newspaper Packet, Washingtoniana Room, Martin Luther King Library, Washington, D.C.

[28.] Star Newspaper, April 19, 1946, Clipping Packet, Washingtoniana Room, Martin Luther King Library, Washington, D.C.

[29.] Ibid.

Holes in floor of inmate dining room of old D.C. Jail show where electric chair was bolted down for executions prior to completion of death house. Photograph courtesy Washingtoniana Division, D.C. Public Library.

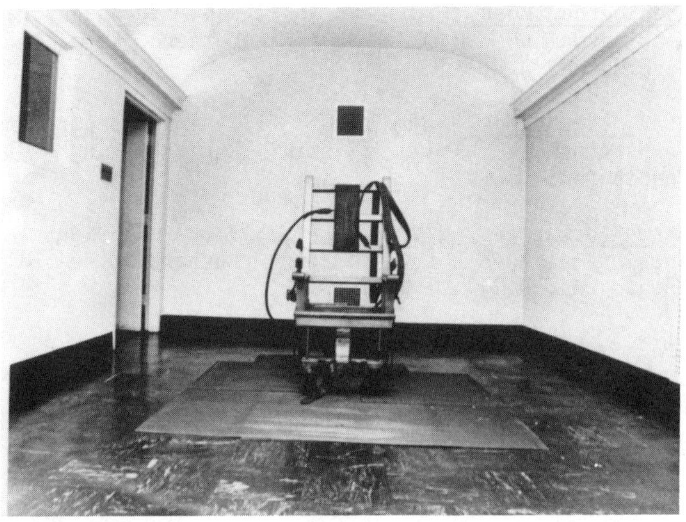

Electric chair in death house of old D.C. Jail. Photograph courtesy Washingtoniana Division, D. C. Public Library.

Numbers on graves of Nazi sabotuers in Potter's Field
Photograph courtesy of Washingtoniana Division, D. C.
Public Library.

PART III

1946 - 1959

CHAPTER 13

CREATION OF THE D.C. DEPARTMENT OF CORRECTIONS

The events leading to the creation of the District of Columbia Department of Corrections began as a result of the numerous escapes from the D.C. Jail between November, 1945 and April, 1946. Representative F. Edward Hebert headed the special subcommittee investigating those escapes. Originally, the committee's task was to investigate and reorganize only conditions at the jail. Hebert, however, believed that long-range reorganization was needed for all the District's penal institutions. He, in turn, initiated legislation designed to create a department of corrections that would function directly under the D.C. Commissioners. Signed by President Harry S. Truman, June 27, 1946, the legislation became Public Law 460 (79th) Congress, effective July 1, 1946.

Groundwork for the new department was developed through the joint cooperation of the D.C. Commissioners, the D.C. Board of Welfare, and the Justice Department's Federal Bureau of Prisons. Warden J. Ellis Overlade, on loan from the Federal Prison at Terre Haute, Indiana, was placed in charge of reorganizing the penal institutions. Much of the revamping followed the guidelines of the Federal Bureau of Prisons, and two of Warden Overlade's major tasks were reclassifying position descriptions of the penal institutions' employees to conform with Civil Service Federal Personnel Manual, and revising the in-service training program.

Upon the recommendation of Representative Hebert, the House District Committee approved the following special committee to develop legislation for operation of the new department: Chief Justice Bolitha J. Laws of the District Court; James V. Bennett, Director of the Federal Bureau of Prisons; Vernon West of the Corporation Counsel; Edgar Morris, Welfare Board Chairman. Representative Hebert served as Chairman of the committee.

Originally, it was proposed that the District's institutions for juvenile delinquents be made a part of the newly created Department of Corrections. Those institutions included the Industrial Home School, The District Training School, The National Training School for Girls, and the Industrial Home School for Colored Children. The proposal was not accepted, however, and the Hebert Committee drafted legislation (Bill 498) which placed the juvenile institutions under the Board of Public Welfare.

In addition to transferring the management and regulation of the District's penal institutions from the Board of Public Welfare to the D.C. Commissioners, the Hebert legislation provided the new department with the ability to submit its budget requests directly to the Commissioners, and not as part of the Welfare Board's budget, as in the past.

With the creation of the new Department of Corrections, the position of "General Superintendent" was changed to that of "Director." Donald L. Clemmer, who had succeeded General Superintendent Howard B. Gill several months prior to the creation of the new department, became the first Director.

The Hebert Committee drafted several additional pieces of legislation which were closely related to the operation of the Department of Corrections. The first, Bill 494, approved July 17, 1947, reorganized the system of parole of prisoners convicted in the District of Columbia. The second, Bill 2659, (P.L. 380, 80th Congress, August 4, 1947), established a program for the rehabilitation of alcoholics. It provided for "...medical, psychiatric, and other scientific treatment for chronic alcoholics; to minimize the deleterious effects of excessive drinking on those who pass through the courts of the District of Columbia..."[1] The Bill defined a "chronic alcoholic" as "any person who chronically and habitually uses alcoholic beverages to the extent that he has lost the power of self-control with respect to the use of such beverages, or while under the influence of alcohol endangers the public morals, health, safety, or welfare."[2] The Bill established a clinic for classification and diagnostic purposes, and each person committed to the clinic was required to pass through the diagnostic center for observation, examination, and classification. Although the law stated that "...the courts of the District of Columbia are hereby authorized to take judicial notice of the fact that a chronic alcoholic is a sick person and in need of proper medical, institutional, advisory, and rehabilitation treatment...,"[3] it tended to include only the most severe cases. It fell short of slowing the steady stream of offenders sentenced to the workhouse and women's division on alcohol-related charges. Alcoholism continued to be a problem among the inmate populations of those institutions for the next two decades.

Another important piece of legislation was Public Law 67, 80th Congress, passed May 16, 1947, which provided "meritorious good time" credits to inmates performing "...outstanding services in institutional operations."[4] It is noted that "industrial good time" credits for inmates performing outstanding work in the industries division were approved by Act of May 27, 1930, and "statutory good time" was approved March 3, 1901 (3) Stat. 134, D.C. Code.

SOURCES

[1.] D.C. Code, Title 24, Sec. 501, 1951 ed. (Washington, D.C.: U.S. Government Printing Office), p. 784.

[2.] *Ibid.,* p. 785.

[3.] *Ibid.,* p. 785.

[4.] Memorandum from Donald Clemmer to Staff, subject: Meritorious Good Time, dated 9-15-48, on file in D.C. Department of Corrections Museum, Lorton, Virginia under file: Procedures for Submitting Meritorious Good Time.

CHAPTER 14

SHAPING THE DEPARTMENT OF CORRECTIONS

As first Director of the newly created Department of Corrections, Donald L. Clemmer faced the formidable task of reorganizing the District's penal institutions to conform with the concepts of modern penology. This new philosophy emphasized rehabilitation through a balanced program for the inmates. A balanced program is interpreted to mean a program which does not stress one particular phase over another. "That is, while custody and discipline may be regarded as of importance, so also is training of inmates wherever possible, as well as their proper feeding, clothing, and medical care."[1] To assist the employees in understanding the meaning of rehabilitation, and the course he wished the Department to take, Clemmer wrote the following statement of philosophy in 1946; and that philosophy applied throughout his years as Director:

> 1. The Department of Corrections exists to protect the communities it serves, first, by maintaining a close custody over its wards until they are released by due process of law and, second by preparing as many of them as possible for a socialized life upon release. Thus, as policy, custody and treatment go hand in hand.
>
> 2. The Department of Corrections views its wards as men and women who have made mistakes, and who are the natural products of their heredity and environment, and not as inherently wicked or depraved. The Department recognizes that some of its wards, by reason of their psychopathy, may be unpredictable and they should be handled accordingly and with patience. The Department refutes, however, the 'mad dog' type of penology. The Department believes and practices kindness, mercy and forgiveness, consistent with orderliness and fairness, in institutional operation.
>
> 3. It is the policy of the Department of Corrections to emphasize for its inmates a full day's work to be willingly done, and the opportunity for varied forms of education and improvement in skills and character, and the opportunity to live a healthy life in clean, safe and wholesome surroundings.[2]

One of the goals of the new Department was the desire to develop a staff of employees that would work in unity to accomplish the mission specified in the philosophy. For that reason, employee participation in matters of the Department was encouraged. One of the first such projects was upgrading the Personnel Enterprize policy, the authority for which was approved by the Auditor of the District of Columbia, May 12, 1948, and became effective July first of that year. Under the supervision of a manager, this policy made available to the Department's employees, commodities and services such as cigarette and soft drink machines for their convenience. The funds realized from this operation were used in part for expenses incurred in restocking and rental of the machines. The remainder was used to cover the expenses incurred by three annual social functions (two dances and a picnic) sponsored by the Department for its employees; for supplies needed to publish the Department's newsletter, known as "Personnel News;" and to purchase athletic equipment for use by the employees.

An additional source of revenue for Personnel Enterprizes was derived from barber shops located in all of the male institutions. The Women's Reformatory operated a beauty shop. Those shops provided vocational training for the inmates and were a convenience for employees of the Department and their families. The program operated through a ticket system, in which the employee purchased a ticket for a haircut, and, in turn, presented it to the inmate barber performing the work. The inmate received a commission on each ticket he submitted to the manager of Personnel Enterprizes at the end of the month.

Another early project involving employee participation was development of the Department seal or emblem. Employees of the Department were asked to submit drawings that would be symbolically appropriate for use as the Department seal. Sixty-seven employees entered the contest which was judged by a committee made up of Department employees. The committee considered the sixty-seven entries and eliminated all but seven. From those finalists, the design submitted by Margaret McGuire was chosen, and became the Department's official seal in May 1948. Each symbol in the design represents a part of the history of the District's penal system.

Seal of the D.C. Department of Corrections

The three stars represent the three commissioners who were in charge of the District government at that time; the two bars were adopted from the District's flag, the book is symbolic of education in prison, the torch represents truth and knowledge, the crossed keys represent prison security, the cog represents the role of industry in prison, and the Bible with the cross on the cover denotes the important role religion has played in the history of penal institutions.

Prior to creation of the Department of Corrections, regulations regarding personnel policies of the penal institutions were the responsibility of the Board of Public Welfare. Under the reorganization, however, personnel policies were established along the lines of those of the Federal Bureau of Prisons. Job descriptions were rewritten to conform with the Federal Bureau, and the training program for employees was intensified. By 1949, a revised handbook for employees had been printed and distributed. The reorganization allowed the new Department's employees to enjoy the same benefits as Federal employees under the Civil Service Commission, with regard to the Federal Retirement Act.

A ruling by the Attorney General of the United States in 1953 determined that the Department of Corrections came within the purview of the Federal Civil Service Act and, therefore, it was subject to the rules and regulations established by the Civil Service Commission in all matters relating to personnel operation. This ruling enabled Department personnel to enjoy such benefits as the Federal Employees Group Life Insurance Act, Federal Employees Health Benefits Act, and the Merit Promotion Plan. By 1960, the Department of Corrections (except the office of the Director) was one of six of the District's 37 Departments under the "...U.S. Civil Service system,"[3] and entitled to the same competitive status as Federal employees.

The American Federation of Government Employees union, Local 1550, was chartered in 1953, and has represented the Department's employees since tht date. "Lodge 1550 aided materially in the establishment of a Federal Credit Union of employees of the Department, and purchased the first $500 block of shares in order that the Credit Union might start immediately to serve personnel with small loans for provident purposes."[4]

The District continued its ties with the Federal Civil Service policies until January 1, 1980, when it began developing its own personnel policies and procedures.

In order to implement the programs that were planned for the new Department, it was necessary for the institutions and operations to undergo a complete reorganization. The reorganization divided the penal institutions and their operations into nine divisions. The rationale for this type of structuring took into account five factors: "The sex and type of inmate, variety and types of care and treatment for inmates; the economy of operation, the space and place factors; and the qualification factors of personnel applying those five considerations..."[5] Under the new set-up, the nine divisions fell into the following: Jail, Reformatory, Workhouse, Women's Reformatory, Agriculture, Industries, Engineering, Business, and Transportation.

In addition to the nine divisions, there were five services, which were defined as "...performance of more or less similar work, regardless of the division for which it may be performed."[6] Those were: the custodial service, the culinary service, the medical service, the classification service, and the religious service. Finally, there were two components known as the office of the Director and the office of Personnel. Each of the nine divisions was broken down into units. It is noted that a number of reorganizations have taken place since 1946, and the original structure has changed somewhat over the years.

The decade following the creation of the Department was spent in shaping the new operational structure into the foundation for a well-organized penal system. It was an era of phenomenal growth and change for the Department. The following several chapters are devoted to noting the major changes that shaped the foundation from which the present Department of Corrections evolved.

Simultaneously with the step forward to modern penology, several new and complex social problems began to appear, as a result of our Nation's society entering a more complex era. One of the most serious problems was the rise in juvenile delinquency at the close of World War II. An article appearing in the September 8, 1948 edition of the <u>Times Herald</u> newspaper reads as follows: "Washington's penal system is beginning to harvest the crop of juvenile delinquents sowed during the war years, Donald Clemmer, corrections chief, reported to the District commissioners yesterday."[7] The article continued: "Among many of the offenders admitted during 1948,...there are a number of very unstable, rebellious young men with antisocial grudges or personal attitudes and values so confused that to predict their future adjustment either in or out of confinement is to forecast ominous and tragic endings."[8] Clemmer further described the delinquents as being "...in a sense, the casualties of World War II."[9] The Federal Youth Corrections Act of 1950 attempted to deal with the young offender. (See Chapter 23 entitled "The Youth Center.")

The incidence of drug abuse began to rise during the 1950s, and, of course, the ongoing problem of alcoholism in the

Workhouse and the Women's Division presented a challenge to the administration.

In addition to the problems that hampered the implementation of the new rehabilitative program, the inmate populations in all of the Department's institutions doubled over the first 10 years of it operation, making it necessary for the District government to appoint a commission to investigate the matter. (The investigation is explained in detail in Chapter 21.)

SOURCES

[1.] Personnel Handbook, Department of Corrections, District Government, 1949, Industrial Division, Reformatory, p. 39.

[2.] _Ibid.,_ p. 40.

[3.] Personnel Handbook, Department of Corrections, 1960, Industrial Division, Reformatory, p. 280.

[4.] _Ibid.,_ p. 331.

[5.] Personnel Handbook, Department of Corrections, District Government, 1949, Industrial Division, Reformatory, p. 39.

[6.] _Ibid.,_ p. 31.

[7.] _Times Herald Newspaper,_ September 8, 1948, Washington, D.C., Clipping File: 1925-1950, D.C. Department of Corrections Museum, Lorton, Virginia.

[8.] _Ibid._

[9.] _Ibid._

CHAPTER 15

THE JAIL DIVISION 1947 - 1960

Under the direction of Superintendent Curtis Reid, the Jail continued to function much as it did prior to creation of the Department of Corrections, as noted in the Personnel Handbook issued in 1949:

> ...The District of Columbia Jail is a maximum security institution charged with the safekeeping and care of the inmates committed to it. It serves as the clearing house institution for the Department of Corrections and, to some degree, for the Federal Bureau of Prisons. Its wards include those persons who await trial as well as those serving short sentences and those due for transfer to other institutions. Additionally, it served as a medical transfer point for other institutional Divisions and as the legal place for executions.[1]

In the wake of the mass escapes from the Jail in 1945 and early 1946, attention of the new administration was focused on renovation of the physical plant and improving security measures. In 1947, an additional 76 employees were hired for the Jail, most of whom were security officers. An important security measure was completion of two towers to guard the East and West entrances. In 1948, two Cyclone fences surrounding the Jail were completed, providing even more security. During the same year, the administrative segregation range for condemned prisoners was established in Cell Block #1, removing them from previously less satisfactory quarters. In 1947, the first motion picture projector (16 mm.) was installed in the Women's Department of the Jail, and in 1950, the public address system, which also carried radio programs, was installed, along with the pneumatic tube system.

Other security measures included a new receiving and discharge center, completed in 1948, and the installation of tool-proof detection sashes on 147 windows of the Jail. The results of these changes are reported in the September 8, 1948 edition of the Washington Evening Star newspaper:

> In spite of an all-time record in the number of prisoners committed to the District Jail during the fiscal year ended last June 20, there have been no escapes, the Department of

> Corrections reported to the Commissioners today.
>
> There were no escapes at the jail in the previous fiscal year, either, which gives the institution a clean record for 24 months.
>
> This is a marked change from 1946 when 12 prisoners escaped...
>
> * * *
>
> The report showed that a total of 18,543 persons were admitted to the District Jail during the 12 months and the average daily population was 730, the largest on record, being 60 above the average daily population for the previous year.[2]

The inmate population at the Jail, and throughout the Department, continued to increase, as shown by the annual report for 1951:

> Fiscal year 1951 has been a significant year in a number of important ways. It has seen a sad parade of 23,989 commitments from the Courts to the Jail Division, the largest number ever received in a twelve month period. Relatedly, the average daily population of the Department's four institutions, at 3,309, shows the second highest resident population in a decade, exceeded only in 1942 when the average number of inmates was 3,419 per day...As an emergency measure during the year, due to the crowding in the Reformatory at Lorton, the Jail Division has been used to hold sentenced felons and has taken on features of a penitentiary, with a penitentiary program in addition to its conventional ones as a detention center and clearing house...[3]

The increase in inmate population in the Department's institutions continued throughout the succeeding years, and by the end of fiscal year 1956, the average daily population of the combined institutions was 4,393. An indication of the steady increase can be seen by looking at the daily average population of 1946, which was 2,094. Over the ten year period, the population had doubled. Despite the severe overcrowding, the Department continued to maintain an excellent escape record. The annual report for 1956 comments: "The institutions continued their enviable record of security, with but one escape, and that from the unfenced Workhouse Division where an unstable inmate with but two days remaining, walked off the Reservation."[4]

With the added responsibility of housing sentenced felons, in September 1951, educational classes were offered to the inmates in residence at the Jail. In addition, daily recreation, library facilities, weekly movies, religious services, a counseling program, supervised visits and letter writing privileges were offered. Inmates received some occupational training through a full work program.

Over the years, the D.C. Jail has been the temporary quarters for Federal prisoners who were brought to Washington to testify before Congress or to stand trial, as in the case of the Nazi spies noted earlier. One such prisoner was Joseph Valachi, the Mafia figure who was confined in the D.C. Jail in 1963 while he appeared before a Senate Subcommittee and the Federal Grand Jury. Valachi, who was serving a life sentence in the federal prison at Atlanta, was housed in a private cell at the D.C. Jail away from the other prisoners. He posed quite a problem for the Federal Prison System, as noted in an article appearing in the October 4, 1963 issue of the Washington Star:

> Joseph Valachi, the talkative mobster, is posing a dilemma for federal officials--where to hide him when he stops talking.
>
> They must find a secluded nook in their prison system where the 60-year old informer can live out his days in safety from vengeful underworld killers who reportedly have placed a $100,000 bounty on his head for spilling the secrets of organized crime.
>
> A Bureau of Prisons official admitted today: 'If we had to take custody of Valachi today, we honestly wouldn't know where to put him.'
>
> For a while anyway, Valachi will continue to stay at the District of Columbia Jail, in a private cell away from other prisoners, with a television set for company. One guard keeps an eye on him.

* * *

The Bureau of Prisons is scrutinizing its high-security institutions in a search for the ideal spot--one where Valachi can be isolated from other prisoners while not being placed in solitary confinement.

* * *

'But every time he names a name in those hearings, it becomes harder to find a place for him,' the Bureau of Prisons said. 'We've got a lot of these celebrities in prisons all across the country. And we sure don't want to put him in the middle of people who want him dead the most.'[5]

Some of the personal items used by Valachi during his stay in the D.C. Jail, including a spaghetti pot and hot plate, will be on display in the Department's Museum at the Lorton Reservation when it opens.

SOURCES

[1.] Personnel Handbook, Department of Corrections, June 1949, on file D.C. Department of Corrections Museum, Lorton, Virginia, p. 29.

[2.] Washington Star Newspaper, September 8, 1948 edition, Clipping File: 1925-1950, D.C. Department of Corrections Museum, Lorton, Virginia.

[3.] Annual Report D.C. Department of Corrections, 1951, on file D.C. Department of Corrections Museum, File: Annual Reports 1946-1956, Lorton, Virginia.

[4.] Annual Report D.C. Department of Corrections, 1956, on file D.C. Department of Corrections Museum, File: Annual Reports 1946-1956, Lorton, Virginia.

[5.] Washington Star Newspaper, October 4, 1963, D.C. Department of Corrections Museum, Clipping File: 1951-1975, Lorton, Virginia.

CHAPTER 16

THE END OF CAPITAL PUNISHMENT IN THE DISTRICT OF COLUMBIA

The Jail was the scene of 15 executions during its first 10 years of operation under the new Department of Corrections. The first occurred July 19, 1946, just 10 days after the Department was created. On that day, Earl J. McFarland was electrocuted for the murder of Dorothy M. Perrum. The weapon used by McFarland was a "snood" (a net used to keep a woman's hair in place). The last of the four triple executions in the District took place on December 2, 1946, when William Copeland, Julius Fisher, and Joseph D. Medley were electrocuted for three unrelated murders. The official in charge at all 15 executions was Superintendent Reid. The 15th execution and the last to be carried out in the District of Columbia was that of Robert E. Carter on April 26, 1957, for the murder of a police officer. The murder occurred July 11, 1953, and Carter was sentenced to death by electrocution in March 1954. He spent three years and one month on death row before being executed. An article written by William Burden, Staff Reporter, in the April 27, 1957 edition of the Washington Post describes Carter's execution as follows:

> Robert E. Carter, 28 died in the electric chair at District Jail yesterday for slaying an unarmed, off-duty Washington policeman four years ago.
>
> Carter was convicted in February 1954, of fatally shooting Pvt. George W. Cassels, 27, of the Third Precinct, on July 11, 1953.
>
> Cassels was felled by a single shot fired from a German Luger pistol by Carter as Cassels was chasing him from the scene of a $115 holdup in a dry cleaning shop at 1637 P St. N.W.
>
> Carter walked calmly to his death with a prayer on his lips. He smiler (sic) briefly at Rev. Carl J. Breitfeller, Corrections Department chaplain, who baptized him as a Catholic on Christmas Day, 1954, but showed no other emotion.
>
> On his bared chest, Carter wore a religious metal given him on the day of his baptism.

> Carter, a construction laborer, had been permitted to see his mother, wife and three small children Thursday, the first time he had seen his 4-year-old son.[1]

* * *

Doctor William E. Carr, Chief Psychological Services Center, D.C. Department of Corrections, retired, was on duty in the Jail on the night of Carter's execution, and recalls the following details in an interview with the author in August 1985:

> In general, as I recall, I was on the number one shift at the Jail back in 1957. I was on duty in the rotunda and things were as quiet as a church mouse. The atmosphere was charged with tensions, people passing by each other were very edgy, very sensitive. Everybody in the prison knew what was going to take place, especially because Bobby Carter was a very intelligent man and very handsome, a very personable type of individual. He confessed to the crime of shooting a police officer who was in pursuit of him for having committed some type of robbery. He was known throughout the city, a kind of celebrity in a negative sort of way. There he was in prison. I talked with him on death row on many occasions and the thing that impressed me was his show of bravado. The kind of man who let it appear that he was ready and able to take whatever happened. He never admitted, and I somehow believe this is true, he never admitted that he set out to deliberately kill a police officer.
>
> On the night he was to be executed, his grandmother and his two small children came into the Jail a few hours before the execution. I can't remember the name of the Assistant Superintendent, but the conference was held in his office. Since I was the officer on duty in the rotunda, I let them in. It was my responsibility to check them in and send them into the Assistant Superintendent's office. I will never forget the look on his grandmother's face. If stares could kill, I would have been dead. The children were playing around. They must have been under five years, and that touched me very much because I had some

youngsters about the same ages at that time. They all went in to the Assistant Superintendent's office, and Bobby was brought down to have his last talk with his kids. I was not permitted to go inside. They stayed in there for about an hour. When his grandmother left, she was in tears and the kids did not really understand what was going on, but they left. Still the place was in the tight most kind of tension. He went back to his cell, and that must have been a couple of hours before the execution.

Some of the officers, I can't recall who all of the officers were on duty at that time and the captain that was on duty, asked me if I wanted to come up and watch the execution. I said, 'I have no desire to do that.' But the edginess of all concerned, and I can't overemphasize here what was going on, but when Bobby came down the last walk and they opened the door, I stood there thinking, you would have thought he was going down to watch a parade or something - no bitterness - just that confident. His uniform was immaculately pressed, he was clean-shaven, and if someone, some casual observer had come in and looked at him, and found out that there is a man who is going to the electric chair, he would have said, 'you have to be crazy.' He looked like he was going out on a little recreational stroll or something like that. So he walked through and the feeling that I had at that time was one of depression, nausea, anger, and misgivings. Here is a man in the prime of life who had just said goodbye to his family and is moving off to his execution. I never quite sorted out all that feeling of misgiving. Why does this have to happen? Well, he went and the story that I got, and I should put this in, when executions took place at the Jail, this is the only one which I experienced, the inmates were pretty quiet, and they were very quiet that evening, especially up on death row, where there was usually a lot of noise, there wasn't any noise that evening, everything was subdued. So when he went up to his execution, the story that I got, he walked in and sat in the chair and gave the impression, let's get it over with, and that was it. There wasn't any speech

> made - there wasn't any emotion shown. I thought about that in the aftermath and that is the same kind of Bobby Carter I talked with, week after week. I could never crack that exterior.
>
> Now, there were some other people up there on death row, about a half-dozen. One of them eventually was released. This person's crime was one of the brutal crimes of the times committed in the early 50's. He went into a package store which was owned by a family who had had it for a long period of time. He went in the store to rob, got the money, got the material goods that he wanted, then in gangland style, assassination style, he killed one or both of the proprietors. As I recall, his first name was Willie. I said to him, 'after you had everything you wanted, why did you kill, were they threatening you? Did they have weapons?' 'No, as a matter of fact,' he stated, 'they begged me not to kill them.' He was a nervous type, very fidgety, even while he was talking to me, he was rolling down his sweater. I could see where he was building up to the crescendo where he would say, 'I had what I wanted, they could have identified me and I had to kill them.' He could have walked out of the store scot-free. Nobody threatened him, except the fear and the paranoia that they know me so I have got to kill them. As I say, I talked to both of those people and my respect, my feeling of concern was far more weighted on the part of Bobby Carter than it was on the other person. I have a feeling that if Bobby Carter could have lasted another year, his sentence would have been commuted.[2]

Robert Carter was the last prisoner to be executed in the District of Columbia in over a quarter of a century. As noted by Carr, there were others on death row at the time of Carter's execution, but their sentences were eventually commuted to life terms. The fact that capital punishment has been a controversial issue for many years could explain the absence of executions in the District of Columbia in recent years. It will be recalled that during the first 50 years the District was in existence, there were only three executions. Then, around 1850 the mood began to change, and a more conservative attitude developed. Capital punishment was used with greater frequency for the next 100 years. During the 1960s and early 1970s, a more liberal attitude prevailed, and capital punishment was not popular; executions throughout the country were almost unheard of. In the late 1970s and beginning of the 1980s, as a more conservative attitude towards punishment of criminals began to sweep the country, capital punishment has regained some popularity, with a number of states reinstituting the death penalty. By contrast, however, the death penalty was repealed in the District of Columbia, February 26, 1981, by D.C. Law 3-113, Sec. 2,27, DCR 5624, as follows:

> § 22-2404. Penalty for murder in first and second degrees.
>
> (a) The punishment of murder in the first degree shall be life imprisonment.
>
> (b) Notwithstanding any other provision of law, a person convicted of first-degree murder and upon whom a sentence of life imprisonment is imposed shall be eligible for parole only after the expiration of 20 years from the date he commences to serve his sentence.
>
> (c) Whoever is guilty of murder in the second degree shall be imprisoned for life or not less than 20 years.[3]

Since 1863, when official record keeping was begun, there have been 108 executions in the District of Columbia government; 62 by hanging and 46 by electrocution. Of interest is that all 108 of those executed were men. It is noted that while Mary Surratt was executed in the District for her part in the President Lincoln assassination plot, it was conducted by Federal authorities. Some additional interesting statistics in relation to the 108 executions of record indicate that 102 of the charges were for murder, five for rape, and one for carnal knowledge. The weapons used in the homicides varied considerably with the most frequently used being the handgun. Other weapons used were knives, hatchet, cleaver, push broom, strangulation, scarves, snood, club, brick, razors, stones, axe, and bare hands. Of further interest, 23 of the offenders were White, 81 were Black and the race of four is unknown. The oldest offender was 59 years of age and the youngest was 17 years. Among the victims there were listed 40 women, five of whom were wives of the offenders, two little girls, ages eight and nine, five police officers, and one President of the United States (James A. Garfield). The remainder of the victims were either men or unknown.

With the 1981 repeal of capital punishment, the District of Columbia has traveled forward from the gallows, a journey that took 181 years to complete.

SOURCES

[1.] William Burden, "Carter Dies in Chair for 1953 Slaying." Washington Post Newspaper, April 27, 1957 edition.

[2.] Interview of August 1985 with William E. Carr, PhD, Chief, Psychological Services Center, D.C. Department of Corrections, Retired, edited (originial tape on file, D.C. Department of Corrections Museum, Lorton, Virginia).

[3.] District of Columbia Code, Annotated, 1981 edition, Vol. 5 (Charlottesville, Virginia: The Michie Company, 1981), p. 547.

CHAPTER 17

THE REFORMATORY FOR MEN (1947 - 1960)

Because the majority of its inmates were confined for long periods of time, the Reformatory for Men was well suited to adopt the philosophy of rehabilitation through academic education and vocational training. The transition from its industrial orientation to that new concept in penology required much planning and preparation.

Very little in the way of academic and vocational training classes existed at the Reformatory prior to creation of the Department of Corrections. The records indicate that, for the most part, inmates conducted the academic classes. The annual report for fiscal year ending June 30, 1946, noted an average of 57 inmates who were enrolled in academic classes and 73 in vocational training, from a population of 1,049. Howard B. Gill, the last General Superintendent of the penal institutions, tried to upgrade the academic and vocational training program at the Reformatory, but his efforts failed. An article appearing in the August 14, 1946 edition of the Washington Daily News notes the following: "When Howard B. Gill became superintendent of District penal institutions he made provision for education of inmates at Lorton reformatory. The Commissioners and Board of Public Welfare gave him...$800 a year. He could get no one from Civil Service list to take the job for the money he could pay."[1] He finally interested Thomas Yahkub in the work. "The latter accepted appointment as a wartime emergency guard at $1900 a year and assignment to a job that should have paid not less than $5000. He rented one of the small Distict-owned houses at Lorton for $15 a month, the rental regularly charged."[2] The article noted that Yahkub was born in Malabar, India, and had been a resident of the United States since 1928. His credentials, according to the article, were quite impressive: "...a graduate of Middleburg College and Harvard Divinity School, founder of India House in Boston, Massachusetts, for five years researcher in the Norfolk, Massachusetts prison colony under a Rockefeller Foundation grant, pupil of Tagore and Ghandi, friend of Pearl Buck, lecturer at many American universities on Indian culture."[3] Of his work at the Reformatory, the article states: "He went to work on a worthless library and expanded it to usefulness. He started classes for illiterate prisoners. He organized extension courses to supplement the shopwork in the prison's industrial department. He earned the confidence of the prison staff and inmates and praise from many prominent visitors, some of whom, including Mrs. Buck, helped with donations of books and ideas."[4] When the Department was created, Yahkub was required to give up his house, and was made to understand that if he stayed on at the reformatory, "...it would be as subordinate to a yet unnamed educational chief. So he closed that phase of his work with a resignation."[5]

At the end of fiscal year 1947, there were 264 inmates enrolled in academic courses and 111 in vocational training at the Reformatory. The courses available to the inmates as well as the enrollment, continued to expand. The following excerpt from the 1947 annual report notes the introduction of classes in social education:

> A series of classes for inmates at the reformatory taught by top-ranking members of the department, including the director, superintendents, business manager, assistant superintendents, psychologist, and others, covers what has been called social education. This department has been among the very first of the progressive correctional institutions in the country to inaugurate this sort of training. The fields of learning covered include: "Principals (sic) of Human Behavior," "Marriage and the Family," "Child Guidance," "Personal Budgeting," "Theories in Leisure Time," "Community Organizations," and other studies of a similar sort. The effort has been to interpret to classes of about 20 men, the fundamental significance in the fields reviewed. Thus, inmates who are fathers, as many of them are, have with careful selection been placed in the class known as "Principles of Child Guidance." Men who have had marital difficulties and whose difficulties seemed causative of their incarceration have been assigned to the class, "Marriage and the Family." ...During the 2 quarters in which the social education curricula has been in operation, 204 inmates at the reformatory participated.[6]

Despite the continued growth of academic and vocational training at the Reformatory, Clemmer had been able to employ only two professional instructors for the education program. Determined to increase the teaching staff, Clemmer offered to exchange two guard positions at the Reformatory for two vocational instructors. An article appearing in the Washington Post, September 20, 1949, notes: "'Though the two custodial positions recommended for abolishment cannot easily be spared,' Clemmer told the city heads, 'the need for teaching personnel is so paramount that the department is willing to assume the risk in order to modernize and dignify its penological approach.'"[7]

In 1949, the addition of Business English, Clerical Workshop, Typing I and II, Shorthand, and Commercial Art had been added to the academic curriculum, along with fundamentals in Music, a Dramatic Club, Art Club, Science and Health, and Spanish. In addition, correspondence courses were offered through the International Correspondence Schools and by the Pennsylvania State College. The vocational training had been formalized and a wide selection of trades training courses were available to the inmates, including auto mechanics, barbering, fireman, janitorial, landscaping, masonry, painting, refrigeration, steel working, drafting, foundry, laundry, machine shop, patternmaking, printing, clothing, and welding. By 1951, the groundwork for a substantial educational program at the Reformatory had been laid.

Aside from the routine maintenance of the utilities at the Reformatory, the Engineering Division (presently known as Facilities Management), completed a number of construction projects at the Reformatory over the first ten years the Department was in operation. The first major construction began in 1949 with the building of a modern deep freeze unit at a cost of $68,000. Completed around 1954, the new plant was capable of storing 500,000 pounds of frozen food. Although the freezing unit was physically located on the Lorton reservation, it was set up to provide safe food storage for the entire Department. In 1950, work was begun on the fence that encloses the Reformatory (presently Central and Maximum Security Facilities). The fence was completed in 1952, and a lighting system for it was installed in 1953. Other major construction included a large building to serve as a control center, which when completed, provided space for 220 beds by releasing space that had been used for control functions, mail distribution, visits, inmate discipline, classification and so forth. It is interesting to note that in estimating the cost of contruction of the control building, Clemmer commented: "...this building, sought for the past 30 years, would cost $400,000 if done on a contract basis with outside labor. But since inmates will do most of the work as well as make the bricks, he estimated the entire job will ultimately cost only $180,000."[8]

Along with the new control center, work was begun on an administration building but was temporarily postponed due to a steel strike. Work was later resumed and the building was completed in 1954.

Along with the many other changes under the new Department was the development of a landscaping program, which was also under the engineering division. Much time and emphasis was placed on beautifying the grounds of the Reformatory. In fact, mention is made in the annual report for 1953 that, during the year, 120,000 plants were propagated, 96 additional shade trees were planted and 72 acres of lawn and several thousand square feet of flower beds were maintained on the Lorton reservation. It has been said that the beautiful grounds of the reservation were admired by many who visited the institutions or those just passing by.

The employees of the Department were saddened by the death in 1953 of Superintendent Welch. He had served as Superintendent of the Reformatory for 13 years and had been an employee of the District of Columbia for 34 years. An article from the July 3, 1950 edition of the Washington Star newspaper contains the following quote by Mr. Welch on the occasion of his 30th anniversary with the District Government: "I'm just a practical guy - no degrees, or anything...Running a prison is a give and take proposition. We're dealing with human beings, ones with the same problems as I have. I don't believe in kicking men around." The article continues: "Mr. Welch knows many of the names of his 1,338 long-term prisoners. 'They call me the old man -- and a lot of other things,' he chuckled. He calls them 'son.'"[9]

H.M. Lindsay was chosen to fill the position of Superintendent, and served in that capacity until 1955, at which time he became Superintendent of the Industries Division. Paul F. Peglow, who had served as Assistant Superintendent of the Reformatory, became Superintendent and served until his death in 1963.

Overcrowding, as a result of a steady increase in inmate population, was more severe at the Reformatory than any of the other three institutions. The average daily population in that institution at the close of fiscal year 1946 was 1,049, compared to 1,857 at the close of fiscal year 1956. The capacity of the institution at that time was 1,350. (These figures include the penitentiary division.)

The overcrowded conditions at the Reformatory prompted an increase in rule violations for minor infractions such as stealing food, stealing clothing, gambling, and sleeping late. In addition, the balanced program for the inmates which included a full day's work along with recreation and academic and vocational training was affected because of idleness created by the overcrowded conditions. Every effort was made, however, to assign all able-bodied inmates to a work or school unit of some kind.

Development of the security system for the Reformatory as well as the other institutions of the Department stressed escape prevention and inmate adjustment. Much credit for the success in maintaining discipline and preventing escapes was given to the training custodial employees received, as noted in the annual report for 1949.

> ...It is believed that, in part, the outstanding escape prevention record and the lack of disciplinary trouble among inmates results from the training programs. Training has not only been instrumental in giving the supervisory personnel information as to major department policy, but even the rank and file employees have been made conversant with objectives.[10]

Another factor in the prevention of escapes was the bloodhounds. At the creation of the Department, the Reformatory had a pack of 16 dogs. One of Clemmer's early budget requests was for $500 to purchase a male and a female English bloodhound. The September 30, 1949 issue of the Washington Post noted: "One corrections official explained the bloodhound item this way. 'The dog people around town tell us that we need fresh blood in our pack; that we have been doing too much inbreeding and consequently some of our hound dogs are losing the keen sense of smell necessary to stay on the trail of an escapee.'"[11] It is easily understood that the bloodhounds would play an important role in the security of the institutions, since the area surrounding the Reformatory and Workhouse was still densely wooded during the 1940s and 1950s, and the dogs performed a valuable service not only to the Department but to the community as well. An example is found in the annual report for 1947: "Assistance was requested by the Virginia State Penal System, Camp No. 13, Fairfax, Virginia on two occasions in the apprehension of escaped prisoners and by Fort Belvoir, Virginia, Army Provost Marshal's office on two occasions for the same purposes. The bloodhounds were dispatched and assisted in the apprehension."[12] Similar requests were noted in other annual reports of that period. Although no documentation could be found, it has been said that on at least one occasion the bloodhounds were used to rescue a child who had become lost in the woods near the Reformatory.

In addition to the routine medical services provided at the Reformatory, a variety of other medical undertakings were carried out during the early 1950s. One such activity was collection of blood among the inmate population for use by Gallinger Hospital. It is noted that for the year 1953, over 3,500 pints were collected. Participation by inmates in antibiotic studies conducted at the Jail indicated that an average of 29 inmates took part in the experiments each five-day week. An average of $110.85 for the year was paid to each participant for an average of 19.7 tests. Later scientific tests were conducted at the Reformatory by the National Institutes of Health.

In addition to the ongoing problem created by the large number of alcoholics in the inmate population, particularly the Workhouse, narcotic offenders were also becoming a problem. There were about 300 known narcotic addicts in the Reformatory population. Transfers to the Narcotic Hospital at Lexington, Kentucky, for treatment reached 219 in the year 1953. The annual report of the Washington Criminal Justice Association for 1955, entitled "Crime in the Nation's Capital," explains the reason for the increase in drug addicts in the inmate population:

> ...This increase in drug offenders has resulted primarily from the longer sentences given under the Boggs Act, the return of addicts originally committed to Lexington, and the somewhat more rigid policy as to retaining addicts with prior criminal records in the penal population rather than transferring them to Federal narcotic farms. The long terms under which narcotic offenders are serving by virtue of the Boggs Act, while in the best interests of society, add serious operating problems for the prison authorities. The Department did an unusual thing when it invited two Assistant District Attorneys to meet in a group session with Boggs Act offenders to explain to them the nature of, and reasons for the law. (The Boggs Act created mandatory minimum and maximum sentences for second and third time narcotics offenders.)[13]

Athletic programs for the inmate population of the Reformatory were expanded during the Department's first ten years of operation. Field sports, including football, baseball, softball, basketball, volleyball, track, and horseshoes as well as boxing were offered for leisure time activities. Various local teams from the community participated in the games. In fact, many local citizens remember participating in sports events at the Reformatory and Workhouse. Other leisure time activities included motion pictures in both the Reformatory and Penitentiary division.

The annual report for fiscal year 1947-1948 notes: "On July 4, 1947, for the first time since the institution was established, a picnic was given to the entire inmate body on the recreation field. The day was given over to boxing matches between boxers from the District of Columbia and inmates of the institution, track events, and various other athletic activities. A box lunch was served on the field and it was a day where the men enjoyed as complete freedom as possible."[14]

The inmate firefighting unit, organized during World War II, continued to provide a valuable service to the community as noted in the annual report for 1947: "The inmate firefighting unit has responded to numerous calls both on and off the reservation, and the men composing this unit are sincerely interested in the work, cooperative and volunteer for any emergency work. They are to be commended for their spirit of loyalty."[15]

While very little information is available in the annual reports and other records regarding the development of the culinary services, mention is made, however, that the four culinary units, especially the Reformatory, played an important role in providing vocational training for the inmates in cooking, baking, and meat cutting, employing about 400 department-wide. The cost of food per man per day during the first 10 years of the Department's operation averaged 67 cents.

In keeping with the trend toward progressive prison administration set by the Industrial Farm experiment era, the Department's first 10 years of experimentation with the balanced program, laid the foundation for continued progressive penology at the Reformatory as well as the other three institutions under it jurisdiction. Prison administrators, both from this country and abroad, continued to visit the District's penal institutions seeking information which could be applied to their correctional systems. Among the foreign visitors seeking ideas and information were representatives of criminal justice departments from China, Peru, India, France, and Australia.

The year 1956 is outstanding in the history of the Department of Corrections as the date its first research component was created. The need for scientific research in the field of corrections had been recognized by the administration of the Department for some time. It was believed that through the study of all facets of inmate behavior, a greater insight into human behavior could be achieved, and with this knowledge many of the serious problems confronting penologists could be solved. Simultaneously with creation of the research unit, an advisory council was named by the D.C. Commissioners to provide guidance and advice to the researchers. The council was made up of a number of persons from the Metropolitan Washington area who had distinguished themselves in the field of Criminal Justice. Sociology professors from several of the local universities joined in the research, "...and the Department...opened its doors to qualified students and graduates of nearby universities to pursue the study of the variety of correctional practices, the personality traits of offenders, and where possible, the additional comprehension of the causes of crime."[16]

From its opening in 1916, the major activity of the Reformatory for Men had revolved around industry, and it continued to play a vital role in the rehabilitation process under the newly created Department by providing a framework for much of the vocational training that was planned for all three institutions on the reservation. In addition, the industrial shops continued to produce goods and services for the Department and other government agencies at a modest cost. The major change to occur in the operation of the industries division under the new Department was passage of Public Law 493, July 9, 1946. In essence, the law rescinded the yearly appropriated working capital fund created in 1929 and established a permanent revolving fund. This permitted the industries division to generate its own working capital, and "pay its own way," so to speak, independent of appropriations.

While the permanent fund placed full financial responsibility on the industries division for its operation, it also gave it greater freedom to expand and experiment with new industries. One such experiment was a commercial fishing venture which began in 1947. As noted in the annual report for 1949:

> A commercial fishing industry was undertaken and while not a complete failure has neither been much of a success. Catches 50 percent less than anticipated has made the operation a dubious one financially and it has been abandoned as a full time project during the year. The limited catch of fish by the Industries Division was shared by commercial fisheries in the Potomac and Chesapeake Bay, and this fact is well known to all informed people. The dollar value of fish caught was $3,331.[17]

The 1953 annual report adds: "The deep freeze operation continued suspended pending the solution of several operating and marketing problems. The total deep freeze situation continues to be the Department's major industrial problem.[18]

An indication of the overall success of the industries division under the permanent revolving fund is shown by its financial statement for 1956 when for the first time ever in the history of its operation it reached a production figure of $1,083,629.

All institutions in the Department continued to be overcrowded, especially the Reformatory for men, which had a rated capacity of 1,218 and a population of 1,900 by the year 1959. It was the severe overcrowding and lack of sufficient personnel to properly man all post assignments that were partially to blame for the death of the first Correctional Officer in the history of the Reformatory to be killed in the line of duty.

On February 13, 1958, Correctional Officer Michael G. Hughes was brutally murdered while on duty in the day room of Dormatory 13 at the Reformatory for men. He had attempted to separate two inmates who were fighting. The inmates turned on Officer Hughes with a chair, knife, and razor. They were later charged and found guilty of second degree murder in the U.S. Court for the Eastern District of Virginia, and both received life sentences.

SOURCES

[1.] Washington Daily News, August 14, 1946, Clipping File: "Corrections Dept. 1946-1959", Washingtoniana Room, Martin Luther King Library, Washington, D.C.

[2.] Ibid.

[3.] Ibid.

[4.] Ibid.

[5.] Ibid.

[6.] Annual Report of the D.C. Department of Corrections, 1949, File: Annual Reports 1946-1956, D.C. Department of Corrections Museum, Lorton, Virginia.

[7.] Washington Post Newspaper, September 30, 1949, Clipping File: Corrections Dept. 1946-1959, Washingtoniana Room, Martin Luther King Library, Washington, D.C.

[8.] Ibid.

[9.] Washington Star Newspaper, July 3, 1950 ed., Newspaper Clipping File 1950-1975, D.C. Department of Corrections Museum, Lorton, Virginia.

[10.] Annual Report of the D.C. Department of Corrections, 1949, File: Annual Reports 1946-1956, D.C. Department of Corrections Museum, Lorton, Virginia.

[11.] Washington Post Newspaper, September 30, 1949, File: Corrections Dept. 1946-1959, Washingtoniana Room, Martin Luther King Library, Washington, D.C.

[12.] Annual Report of the D.C. Department of Corrections, 1947, File: Annual Reports 1946-1956, D.C. Department of Corrections Museum, Lorton, Virginia.

[13.] Washington Criminal Justice Association, "Crime in the Nation's Capital," 20th Annual Report (1955), D.C. Department of Corrections Museum, Lorton, Virginia, pp. 17-18.

[14.] Annual Report of the D.C. Department of Corrections, 1947-1948, File: Annual Reports 1946-1956, D.C. Department of Corrections Museum, Lorton, Virginia.

[15.] Ibid.

[16.] Ibid.

[17.] Annual Report of the Government of the District of Columbia, 1949 (Washington, D.C.: U.S. Government Printing Office, 1950), p. 203.

[18.] Annual Report of the D.C. Department of Corrections, 1953, File: Annual Reports 1946-1956, D.C. Department of Corrections Museum, Lorton, Virginia.

CHAPTER 18

THE WORKHOUSE AND AGRICULTURE DIVISIONS (1947 - 1960)

Although two separate divisions, the Workhouse and the agriculture operation were primarily affiliated with each other under the newly created Department. The Workhouse as an "open institution" confined less serious offenders, providing a work force for the Agriculture Division. The Agriculture Division was charged "...with the scientific development of the farm areas, so that they economically and penologically..." contributed to the welfare of the inmates through training and by producing food for the culinary services "...at a modest cost."[1] Under the administration of W.F. Fleming, Resident Superintendent, the farm activity at the Workhouse included approximately 1,000 acres of land, of which 300 acres comprised the orchard. An article appearing in the July 3, 1950 edition of the Washington Star provides insight into the routine under which Flemming operated the institution:

* * *

> 'I've seen a lot of men come and go,' Mr. Fleming says of his division which receives and discharges an average of 10,000 in a year. 'A man who was on the first load that came here still is coming back.'
>
> On Saturday mornings, Mr. Fleming holds interviews with the 'young boys' of the 950 to 1,050 population. He tries to find out why they got into trouble, listens to their problems.
>
> 'How much good it does, I don't know,' he says. 'But occasionally I'll get a letter from a former inmate telling me he's going straight. That makes me feel awful good.'
>
> After more than 37 years in prison work, which includes service at the Virginia farm near Richmond, Mr. Fleming has a sense of humor. Looking at the Workhouse ball diamond, the 'best one south of Clark Griffith's,' he laughed.
>
> 'My recreational director tells me we are short a good pitcher and catcher. Maybe the judge will send a couple down.'[2]

One of the most significant changes effected at the Workhouse under the new Department was the upgrading of farm equipment. A request for $15,635 was granted in the 1950 budget for mechanized farm equipment. The new machinery made the farm 95 percent mechanized and eliminated 20 of the 37 draft horses that had previously been used in the farm operation. The Agriculture Division continued to produce much of the food for feeding the inmate population of the entire Department. For example, the 1953 harvest enabled the canning factory to conserve 109,652 number 10 cans of fruit and vegetables. During the same year, the lumber and forestry unit cut and sawed 112,000 board feet of lumber, most of which was used for construction of a new swine ranch. The total agriculture operation, including the dairy products, meat, and produce had a total wholesale value of $262,770.

Perhaps the most innovative change occurring at the Workhouse during the first 10 years of the Department's operation was an attempt to cope with the continuing alcoholic problem in the inmate population. Clemmer organized a consultation service made up of Department employees to study the individual cases, collect data on alcoholism and to give advice and counseling. The annual report for 1950 notes: "...the Department calls attention again to the almost utter futility now employed in the handling of conventional alcoholics, and recommends a thorough restudy of this problem by all District law enforcement agencies and representative citizens in order to find some more intelligent and ingenious method to improve the management of this complicated community problem."[3] The annual report for 1949 states: "The alcoholic consultation services at the Workhouse has endeavored to help some 200 inmates during the 2 years of its existence. The Washington chapter of Alcoholics Anonymous sends representatives each week where between 100 and 175 alcoholic inmates voluntarily attend the meetings."[4] This early attempt to alert the public to the fact that the alcoholic needed special treatment which could not be provided by the prison system was instrumental in the eventual removal of those cases from the District's penal institutions.

The Workhouse population showed a steady escalation over the first 10 years of the Department's operation, rising from 530 at the close of 1946 to 1,329 by the end of 1956. With an official capacity of 1,000, it was necessary to house as many as 180 inmates in dormitories designed to accommodate 100. Despite the overcrowded conditions, the escape record was excellent. An article from the July 20, 1954 edition of the Washington Star, reads as follows:

> The District Workhouse for prisoners at Occoquan, Va., today established a record by completing a full year without an escape.
>
> Donald Clemmer, director of the Department of Corrections, hailed the record in a statement praising Supt. William F. Fleming and his entire staff.
>
> Mr. Clemmer said the record is remarkable because there are no walls and no fences at the Workhouse, which admitted 17,622 prisoners in the last fiscal year. The average daily population was 1,213.
>
> The director noted, for purposes of contrast, that an average of 30 escapes are reported each month at a similar institution in Detroit.
>
> The last escape from Occoquan occurred July 19, 1953, when a prisoner being treated for tuberculosis crawled away from the hospital.[5]

Because of the short sentences of the majority of Workhouse inmates, attempts at rehabilitation programs were confined to trying to help the alcoholics which comprised about 60 percent of the entire population. The institution, however, began classes in social education in 1949, under the titles of: "The Nature of Man," the "Nature of Society," and "Marriage and the Family." In addition, training was available in culinary arts, electrical maintenance, and heating plant operations. A small library was maintained, along with religious services, a well developed evening recreational program, similar to the one at the Reformatory for Men, weekly movies, and a rudimentary classification procedure.

SOURCES

[1.] Personnel Handbook, The Department of Corrections, Government, D.C., Industrial Division, D.C. Department of Corrections Reformatory, June 1949, p. 31.

[2.] Washington Star Newspaper, July 3, 1950 edition, Newspaper Clipping File 1950-1975, D.C. Department of Corrections Museum, Lorton, Virginia.

[3.] Report of the Government of the District of Columbia, 1950 (Washington, D.C.: U.S. Government Printing Office, 1951), p. 220.

[4.] Report of the Government of the District of Columbia, 1949 (Washington, D.C.: U.S. Government Printing Office, 1951), p. 201.

[5.] Washington Star Newspaper, July 20, 1954, Clipping File: 1950-1975, D.C. Department of Corrections Museum, Lorton, Virginia.

CHAPTER 19

THE WOMEN'S REFORMATORY (1947 - 1960)

Smallest of the District's four penal institutions, the Women's Reformatory was unique because of its dual role in confining both long- and short-term offenders in an open type facility. For that reason, the program needs of the felony offenders differed considerably from those of the short-term misdemeanants. For some years before the Department was created, the staff of that institution recognized the necessity for academic and vocational programs, conducted by professional instructors, to prepare the women with lengthy sentences for return to the community. Funds to support such programs, however, were never appropriated, and very little in the way of organized educational programs existed prior to 1946.

In the absence of professional instructors, the administrative and custodial staffs at the Reformatory devoted as much time as their regularly scheduled activities would permit in teaching the illiterate to read, write, and spell. A member of the custodial staff who had experience in social work prepared case histories of long-term inmates, and served on the classification committee along with the institutional nurse, the chief principal guard, and the resident superintendent.

The two principal industries, sewing and laundry work, continued to function at the Women's Reformatory. The annual report for 1946 noted: "The laundry employs some thirty-five women. This is good training for the colored women as they can always secure employment in domestic or commercial laundries after release. This department pays from $1.00 to $3.00 per month and the women are given the opportunity to earn industrial good time here."[1] The report further commented that the same wages and industrial good time were given the women who worked in the sewing industry, noting: "Sewing is done for the women in the division, some for the men's division, and other District welfare institutions. Contracts for the Army and Navy and for the Federal Indian Bureau were filled."[2] The women also made arts and crafts articles which were sold through the Department, and were given a 25 percent commission on the sale price of the articles.

By 1949, the educational activities had expanded somewhat to include practical nursing, millinary, typing, beauty culture (personal hygiene), nurse's aide training, waitress training (table and table service), and ethics on how to live. In the years that followed more academic courses were added, along with professional instructors. At the time the Reformatory was closed in 1966, courses in algebra, statistics, shorthand, history, and courses in employment readiness were being offered to the inmates.

Major construction projects at the Women's Reformatory over the Department's first ten years of operation included a new 25-bed hospital to replace the old frame one described in the 1949 annual report as "...the shack-like frame building which has been used for many years and constitutes the worst fire and custodial hazard in the Department."[3] Work has also begun on a dormitory at that institution in 1956.

A unique service provided by the women in the institution was the laboratory work where they conducted milk and water analysis, blood counts, and blood chemistry, G.C. smears, urinalysis, and tuberculosis sputum examinations.

Leisure time and recreation activities included a recreation field with facilities for baseball, croquet, basketball, volleyball, horseshoe ground, and swings. There were weekly movies, plays, picnics, dances, etc. A canteen for the inmates was opened in 1946.

One innovative special project worthy of note was the "little theatre," described in the 1946 annual report as follows: "Beginning in October of 1945 and practically finishing in June of 1946, we developed our special project--a little theatre. A stage was constructed in our Movie Hall, stage screens and scenery made and decorated, new window curtains were provided and the walls of the room painted and decorated. This will add much to our future entertainments and the development of dramatics."[4] In connection with leisure time activities and entertainment, an inmate choir of trained voices provided special music for the religious holidays.

With the retirement of Blanche LaDu in 1950, Lillian E. Hafer became Superintendent of the Women's Division and served in that capacity until 1953. At that time, Sam Anderson became the first male Superintendent, since the days of William Whitaker of that institution.

As with the other three institutions, the inmate population at the Women's Reformatory nearly doubled during the first ten years under the Department, increasing steadily from 114 at the end of 1946 to 204 in 1956. While the proportion of women who were incarcerated was small compared to the number of men, what was significant, however, was that "...in May of 1956, 54% of the Women's Reformatory population serving time for felonies were either narcotic law violators, addicts, or both."[5] In addition, the incidence of alcohol related sentences among the misdemeanants in the institution was extremely high, averaging 63 percent. Treatment for the women was similar to that received by the men. Women with drug problems were sent to the Narcotic Hospital in Lexington, Kentucky. The alcoholic problem was overwhelming and there was no effective rehabilitaton program in the Women's Reformatory or the Workhouse. The alcoholic offenders returned to the institution time and time again, making the recidivism rate extremely high.

SOURCES

[1.] Annual Report of the D.C. Department of Corrections, 1946, File: Annual Reports 1946-1956, D.C. Department of Corrections Museum, Lorton, Virginia.

[2.] Ibid.

[3.] Annual Report of the D.C. Department of Corrections, 1949, File: Annual Reports 1946-1956, D.C. Department of Corrections Museum, Lorton, Virginia.

[4.] Annual Report of the D.C. Department of Corrections, 1946.

[5.] Washington Criminal Justice Association, 21st Annual Report, 1956, "Crime in the Nation's Capital," D.C. Department of Corrections Museum, Lorton, Virginia, pp. 26-27.

CHAPTER 20

INTEGRATING RELIGION INTO THE PENOLOGICAL PROGRAM

Although religion had not been a part of the District's penological program prior to 1954, clergy from the local churches and other religious based community organizations provided the inmates of the penal institutions with spiritual guidance. From the early days of the 19th century, the clergy voluntarily brought religion to the inmates, conducting divine worship services, teaching the illiterate to read, counseling those who sought guidance, and even walking the "last mile" with the condemned. As the inmate population of the institutions grew, so did the demand for religious guidance. Recognizing this growing need, the Washington Federation of Churches, in 1940, began sponsoring a full-time Protestant chaplain to serve the four penal institutions. The first to fill this position was the Reverend Leonard Edmonds. At the time the Department was created, however, the chaplain was the Reverend Dan Potter. An indication of the duties he performed in that capacity is related in the annual report of 1946:

* * *

> There are ten phases of the religious program: preaching and the sacraments, teaching, special programs, counseling, pastoral calling within the institution, pastoral calling outside the institution, interpretive lectures to church and business groups, sponsorship program inter-departmental cooperation, and the clinical pastoral training of ministerial interns.

* * *

> One of the most important functions of the Chaplain is that of counseling. In this individual man-to-man relationship, the Chaplain has an opportunity not only of releasing the emotional tensions of the inmate by hearing his difficulty and life's story, but also an opportunity to give him helpful suggestions when they are desired.
>
> The Chaplain tries to see every incoming inmate at the Reformatory during the quarantine period. In this interview, rapport is developed, the inmate's problems are discussed

> and the religious facilities of the institution are outlined. Resulting from this contact, reports are prepared and submitted to the brochure for classification. After the quarantine period, the inmate may see the Chaplain by request or by referral of staff members.
>
> Nearly every type of problem is brought to the Chaplain's study: social and economic needs of the family while the inmate is confined; legal and parole problems; marital and extra-marital relationships, family relationships; problems of adjustment to society, to prison officials, to other prisoners, to one's self, to one's past and to his future. The question of attitude, habit, ideals, purposes and potentialities are discussed...[1]

Aside from the religious programs, a unique project known as "Opportunity Sunday" was started by the Rev. Potter in 1947:

> Starting in April of this year, we began an experiment of having a talent program one Sunday each month as part of the regular church service at the Reformatory. ...those wishing to participate submit their requests at least one week in advance. The talent consists of essays, musical and vocal solos, quartets, readings, poems, original prayers, choir numbers, congregational singing, and a sermonette. This is now our most popular service.[2]

After nine years of providing chaplain services for the four penal institutions, in 1949, the Federation of Churches had reached a point where it felt that the District government should assume financial responsibility for the religious program in the penal institutions. According to an article appearing in the November 9, 1949 edition of the Washington Post, the request to the District Commissioners, was turned down on the advice of the Budget Officer, Walter L. Fowler, who said, his office did not consider the service a function of local government. He added, the physical welfare of "...inmates is the responsibility of the District...and the spiritual welfare that of the churches of the community, and should be administered on a voluntary basis."[3] The article continued, saying: "The federation pointed out that the Federal Government supports such programs at St. Elizabeths Hospital and in Federal prisons. Fowler said the Federal Bureau of Prisons 'with its Nationwide responsibilities' can't be compared with the 'purely local Department of Corrections.'"[4]

The Federation of Churches continued to provide chaplain service to the Department of Corrections until 1953, when it was found that its budget could no longer sponsor the program. The Federation again renewed its pleas to the District Commissioners for their support, stressing the fact that a "'very detrimental affect in the morale and spiritual welfare of the inmates' would accompany the withdrawal of the Chaplain. They urged the Commissioners that this service should be continued at all costs."[5] In addition, "to accentuate their position, Dr. Frederick E. Reissig, Executive Secretary of the Washington Federation of Churches, enlisted the avid supprt of the then Commissioner, Honorable Renah F. Camalier; Honorable Joel T. Broyhill, Representative of Virginia (10th Dist.,); Senator Francis Case (S. Dak.); and Donald Clemmer, Director of the Department of Corrections..."[6] Finally, "through the indefatigable work of Dr. Reissig and his supporters, the first District of Columbia sponsored chaplaincy was founded in June of 1954..."[7] The chaplain representing the Protestant Community at this time was the Reverend S. Knox Kreutzer.

Father David O'Conner provided religious services and counseling for inmates of the Catholic faith on a voluntary basis for a number of years prior to the time the District government assumed financial responsibility for the chaplaincy program. The first Roman Catholic chaplain to be employed by the District was Father Carl J. Breitfeller, in 1955.

Chapel facilities at the Reformatory for men were very poor:

> Prior to the year 1955, the chapel facilities at the Lorton Reformatory were very poor and there was little hope or even talk of improvement. The auditorium, used for plays, movies, band practice and other types of entertainment, was also used as a chapel for the nearly two thousand inmates. On Saturday night a double feature movie would be shown and on Sunday morning the theatre atmosphere would prevail for religious services. Not only were the provisions for Catholic and Protestant services miserable, but the office facilities in which the chaplains were expected to fulfill their pastoral care of souls were worse. A desk, makeshift file cabinets, and an old

typewriter were all that occupied the small cubicles called the Chaplain's Offices."[8]

As early as 1944, Reverend Potter, Father O'Connor and Dr. Reissig had discussed the possibility of building a chapel at the Reformatory but it seemed a dream that was completely out of reach at that time. By 1955, however, when the District was establishing a permanent chaplaincy for the penal institutions the construction of a chapel at the Reformatory was under advisement in "...what was known as 'The Ten-Year Plan.'"[9] Reverend Kreutzer and Father Breitfeller decided to reduce the "ten" to "now." This was the beginning of a three year struggle to secure funds for construction of the chapel. The first step in their plan was to find an architect to design the building. While the credentials of the architect selected by Father Breitfeller were not impressive, the design he eventually produced was truly a masterpiece.

THOMAS, FARMER C. Born 2/26/26, male married. Sentenced 7/8/55 to serve 5 years 8 months to 17 years for: Conspiracy, Forgery, Uttering, Counterfitting, Transportation of Stolen Motor Vehicle. ...two detainers from other jursidictions. Attempted suicide in D.C. Jail. Attempted escape from Alexandria Jail.

Learning that Thomas had experience in architectural engineering which he acquired while serving a previous sentence in San Quentin prison, Fr. Breitfeller asked him to prepare a sketch of a prison chapel. Thomas' answer was, 'Fine, Father Breitfeller, but I've never seen the inside of a Church.' ...In several weeks he had sketched a beautiful building but it only fulfilled the requirements of most non-sectarian chapels in that it was traditional in design, looked nice, but was entirely useless and would become just another white elephant. He was given the order that no one cared how the chapel looked, just so long as it was completely functional and would serve the purposes of religion integrated into the prison setting.

By the spring of 1956 everyone connected with the project had a pretty good idea of what the chapel would look like. Through the

> drawing of fifteen different sets of blueprints, the idea was developed and taking shape -- a set of prints would be drawn and Rev. Kreutzer and Fr. Breitfeller would add to or subtract and Thomas would spend endless hours preparing another set to be butchered.[10]

The final set of plans produced a chapel "...so designed that three religious services may be held simultaneously, each with a seating capacity of 400 to 500. With the ease of opening a door, any one service may be expanded to a capacity of over 800, or further, even to well over 1,200."[11] In addition, "...When the Chapel is opened for these larger accommodations and the main altar is used, the smaller altars are easily moved into a niche provided for that purpose. The Chapel floor is graduated every 20 feet, thus providing a perfect view for everyone."[12] The plan further provided ample office space for the chaplains, "...for sacristies, reception areas, libraries, classrooms, etc., the Chapel becomes an entire plant for religious activities."[13]

Working untiringly, the two chaplains, with the help of the Director of the Department and the avid support of many of the District's churches, convinced the District Commissioners and the Congress that the chapel would not only fill an urgent need for the inmates population, but the inmates themselves would "...do the excavation, the laying of brick, and the general overall construction. Rehabilitation was also stressed and the idea took hold."[14] Congress allocated $192,000 needed to build the prison chapel in the budget for the fiscal year of 1957-1958. A year later the site was selected by the chaplains with the aid of the Director and the Superintendent of the Reformatory, Paul F. Peglow.

> During the time when the funds became available and actual construction began (July 1957 - August 1958) two distinctly impressive things happened. One was that Reverend Robert Bruce Robey entered the Department of Corrections as its Protestant Chaplain. Enthused over the prospect of entering the prison chaplaincy when such ambitious efforts were being launched, he became an excellent working-partner in the project with Fr. Brietfeller. The other event, though a seriously regrettable accident at the time, actually lended itself to the circumstances as a spur to get construction rolling. The auditorium, in which religious services had

> been held, burned in the night from the roof to the ground due to a shortage in the wiring of the organ. This expedited ground-breaking considerably. A set of construction drawings were also completed during this year by the District firm of Mills, Petticord and Mills, so when ground was broken, the only thing remaining to do was build the chapel.
>
> Construction--excavating, cement and foundation pouring, bricklaying, the erection of bulky steel girders--all proceeded at a noticeable rate. All of the labor and construction was executed by prisoners at the reformatory. From the time of the initial idea's inception, in October of 1956, to the day of the Chapel's dedication, September 14, 1961, the physical and mental contributions of hundreds of prisoners went into getting the Chapel built, men whose identity is indicated only in their having prison numbers ranging within the low number of 2507 in 1955 to 20700 in 1961. The entire construction was controlled and administered by the Engineering Division of the Department of Corrections, and implemented by Mr. Roland M. Uhler, General Foreman, Construction.
>
> * * *
>
> At this time, also, Pope John XXIII, at the request of Fr. Breitfeller, granted the Apostolic Blessing for all who actively participate in the attainment, construction and furnishing of the Prison Chapel.[15]

Several outstanding features express in symbols the sincerity of thought contributed by the chaplains and inmates alike in making the chapel unique among churches.

"On Good Friday, April 15, 1960, a pure white, reinforsed concrete cross was erected as the frontal piece for the Chapel. Towering ten feet high, and framed in red, open-set brickwork, it shows to all who enter the main gate of the prison the dominant place that religion holds in the rehabilitative program at the Lorton Reformatory."[16] Since the chapel is inter-denominational, its general title is simply "The Chapel." The chapel on the left of the foyer which is used predominately for Protestant services "...bears the title, 'Crossroad.' The spiritual connotation of this title is its reference to the turning point in life. A much needed message in its prison setting."[17] The chapel to the right of the foyer which is used for Catholic services is dedicated to "Christ the Prisoner." "Since Christ voluntarily chose arrest and imprisonment, it is only fitting that He be held as a model and protector of prisoners."[18]

> In planning the Chapel, an emphasis was put on window space in the hopes that the Chapel would lose its instititutional identity. One entire wall of each Chapel is made up of windows, affording light and a commanding view. The remaining Chapel walls contain ten large windows. These five feet wide by thirteen feet high windows portray The Ten Commandments in original stained-glass process. Sketches for these windows were prepared by two inmates, Herbert H. Hall, and Williston Knorl. The scenes depicting The Ten Commandments were adapted from the Old and New Testaments, and will serve as a constant reminder of the dignity of the law.
>
> The process of staining clear glass windows was the result of trial and error by Mr. Herbert H. Hall. The process was developed and applied by Mr. Hall during the summer of 1961. The effect is one of stained-glass, rather than merely painted glass, in a modern design.
>
> The Catholic Crucifix. Elevated over the alter and dominating the Catholic Chapel, is a life-sized and life-like crucifix of Christ the Prisoner. It is the work of an inmate sculptor, Williston Knorl, and an inmate painter, Herbert Hall. The head of the figure was sculptured in clay and cast in stone. The body was cast in a unique fashion. Plaster of Paris casts were made of an inmate's body, selected for this purpose because he at one time awaited execution. These molds were then filled with cast stone.
>
> The cross upon which the figure is attached was carved by the above two inmates from seasoned oak logs. Above the head of Christ there is an inscription in the three languages ordered by Pilate.

> One outstanding feature of this magnificent crucifix must be noted. The traditional wound in the side of Christ is missing, indicating that He is still alive and therefore still a prisoner. Thus, the crucifix vividly portrays the significance of the title of the Catholic Chapel.
>
> The Choir Loft. With function as a dominant factor, the inmate architect designed the choir loft so that it may be used in any one or in all three chapels. The organ donated by Mrs. E. J. Galway through Fr. Nicholas R. Reid, O.P., to the Department of Corrections is wired to the speakers placed in the ceilings of each chapel. In this way, its rich tones may be heard in any one or all chapels.
>
> The first religious service of any type was held on July 1, 1961, on which occasion 17 men were Baptized into the Catholic Church by Fr. Nicholas R. Reid, O.P.
>
> In the summer of 1961, a former inmate, Mr. Ronald Couch, interested Mr. J. Toshiyuki Maeda, a landscape architect, in doing a master plan so that the Chapel would have a proper setting...[19]

Rev. Robey was joined by Rev. Rea V. Kleinfeldt in 1960 and Rev. David Turner, Jr. in 1961, and together the three Chaplains laid the ground work for the Protestant religious program throughout the Department. Both Chaplains Kleinfeldt and Turner remained with the Department for over twenty years. Fathers Nicholas R. Reid, O.P. and Donald F. Sheehy, O.P. joined Father Breitfeller during the early years of integrating religion into the penological program of the Department.

Aside from Father Breitfeller's efforts in securing the much needed chapel for the Reformatory for Men, and his work in organizing a religious program for inmates of the Catholic faith, he was instrumental in bringing entertainment to the Reformatory in the form of "Annual Jazz Festivals," during the late 1950s and early 1960s. The following is an excerpt from a copy of a press release dated July 20, 1960:

> Since the gates of the prison were first opened to the entertainment field, for one day a year the men of Lorton have listened to such performers as Louis Armstrong, Jack Teagarden,

> Art Blakey's Jazz Messengers, the Hi-Lo's, Charlie Byrd and his Trio and the Kai Winding Septet. Last year, Ella Fitzgerald, the Oscar Peterson Trio, Stuff Smith and the Charlie Byrd Trio came and conquered! Felix Grant of Station WMAL in Washington has been the m.c. for the program since its inception and his greeting to the men on his last appearance, 'it's great to be back,' more than typifies the feeling that exists between entertainer and convict on these occasions.
>
> * * *
>
> ...each performer who passes through the gates of the Lorton Reformatory does so knowing that no gratuity whatsoever is offered -- only applause, cheers and prayers. This is charity with a capital 'C'!
>
> The philosophy behind this venture is simple. It demonstrates to the men confined in prison that while they are removed from society, they are still, nonetheless, thought of as part of the human race. Disciplinary problems are reduced considerably and a good spirit exists among the men. These are the things that money cannot buy, so it's only fitting that they not be obtained with money...rather, through the large and generous heart of JAZZ![20]

Another popular source of entertainment during the 1950s and 1960s was the Protestant Choirs from both the Women's and Men's Reformatory. Those groups not only entertained their fellow inmates, but performed at various activities outside the institutions, including the Summer Watergate Concerts in Washington. On many occasions the two choirs performed together.

SOURCES

[1.] Annual Report of the Chaplain, 1946, File: Annual Reports 1946-1956, D.C. Department of Corrections Museum, Lorton, Virginia.

[2.] _Ibid._

[3.] _Washington Post Newspaper,_ November 9, 1949 edition, Clipping File 1925-1950, D.C. Department of Corrections Museum, Lorton, Virginia.

[4.] _Ibid._

[5.] "The Crossroads Chapel," pamphlet, Refty. Div., Department of Corrections Industries Div., 1962, on file D.C. Department of Corrections Museum, Lorton, Virginia, p. 2.

[6.] _Ibid.,_ pp. 2-3.

[7.] _Ibid.,_ p. 3.

[8.] "The Chapel," pamphlet, Refty, Div., on file D.C. Department of Corrections Museum, Lorton, Virginia, p. 1.

[9.] _Ibid.,_ pp. 2-3.

[10.] _Ibid.,_ p. 8.

[11.] _Ibid.,_ p. 8.

[12.] _Ibid.,_ p. 10.

[13.] _Ibid.,_ p. 5.

[14.] _Ibid.,_ pp. 5-6.

[15.] _Ibid.,_ p. 9.

[16.] _Ibid.,_ p. 9.

[17.] _Ibid.,_ p. 10.

[18.] _Ibid.,_ pp. 7-10.

[19.] _Ibid.,_ pp. 7-8.

[20.] Protestant Religious Activities File 1959-1960, D.C. Department of Corrections Museum, Lorton, Virginia.

CHAPTER 21

THE KARRICK COMMITTEE (1957)

As previously noted, the Department's inmate population doubled during the period between 1946 and 1956. By contrast, the crime rate indicated a constant decline in the same period. This unusual situation prompted the D.C. Commissioners to appoint a committee to conduct an intensive study of the matter and report its findings and recommendations. The official report of the committee is entitled "Prisons, Probation, and Parole in the District of Columbia," however, it is most often referred to as the "Karrick Report," so named because D.C. Commissioner, David B. Karrick was chairman of the group.

> The aim of the inquiry was to determine whether the District of Columbia must inevitably make huge capital expenditures to construct an additional prison or, as a practical alternative, whether this could be averted in whole or in part by increased utilization of expanded probation and parole programs. The Commissioners were particularly anxious to determine whether certain categories of offenders, such as intoxication, non-support and traffic cases, as well as carefully selected felony offenders might not be corrected and rehabilitated more effectively by some method other than incarceration and, thereby, more readily returned to productive self-respect in the community.
>
> The task was assigned to a Committee on Prisons, Probation and Parole, selected and appointed by the Commissioners, whose job it was to 'oversee and exercise policy direction' in the conduct of this important study. The Committee is composed of Honorable David B. Karrick, Commissioner of the District of Columbia, Chairman; Honorable Bolitha J. Laws, Chief Judge, United States District Court; Honorable Leonard P. Walsh, Chief Judge, Municipal Court; Honorable Edith H. Cockrill, Judge, Juvenile Court; Colonel Campbell C. Hohnson, Chairman Board of Parole; Honorable Robert V. Murray, Chief of Police, Metropolitan Police Department; Honorable Donald Clemmer, Director, Department of Corrections; Mr. Edward W. Garrett, Chief Probation Officer, United

States District Court; Mr. Irving Cooper, Director of Probation, Municipal Court; and Mr. John Larkin, Director of Social Work, Juvenile Court. Special Counsel to the Committee is Mr. C. Aubrey Gasque, a General Counsel of the United States Senate.

The Committee recognized at the onset that the study has a special significance, first, because nowhere else in the United States do the prison authorities of one governmental unit — whether state, county or municipal — have the responsibility of dealing with the whole complex problem of adult offenders, from common drunks to professional murderers, as well as felony offenders who elsewhere would be handled by the Federal Bureau of Prisons.

Second, the problem of the misdemeanant -- the petty offender — which has been so neglected in this country, is very serious in Washington.

Finally, the District of Columbia correctional system, as well as probation and parole programs, should take leading roles in the development of enlightened and progressive policies in the United States. The Committee does not consider it imperative that our prisons be models in terms of brick and mortar, but we do insist that they and probation and parole should be models in terms of quality of program, policies, and personnel.

* * *

The Committee obtained the expert assistance of Mr. Will G. Turnbladh, Executive Director of the National Probation and Parole Association, a nationally recognized authority; and Dr. E. Preston Sharp, President of the American Correctional Association. These experts came individually to Washington, visited our institutions and offices, studies our statistics and other data, held important conferences with our officials, and filed reports containing their respective views. Their contributions to the Committee's work are invaluable.[1]

In April 1957, the Committee issued its findings, along with 44 recommendations for improvement in all levels of law enforcement in the District. The Committee found the imbalance between the over population in the institutions and the decline in crime to be due primarily to: "(1) the Metropolitan Police solving more major crimes than any other comparable metropolitan city in the United States; (2) the imposition of longer sentences in recent years; (3) probation and parole services having been utilized in a limited way."[2]

An in-depth study was conducted by the Committee on the overwhelming problem of alcoholism in the District. Statistics in the study indicated that approximately 79 percent of all commitments to the Workhouse were for charges of intoxication. Almost the same percentage held true for the Women's Reformatory where 69 percent of the offenses were intoxication charges. Several case studies were made of inmates with high arrest records for intoxication. One of interest was that of a 54 year old man who had spent 25 years of his life in prison for intoxication, serving the time in sentences of five to 300 days at a time. His arrest record revealed that he had been incarcerated 285 times for intoxication for a total of 9,396 days.

The report noted:

> More than 90 percent of the 16,267 persons committed to the District Jail for intoxication during fiscal 1956 had served prior prison terms for the same offense. Many who were discharged from the Workhouse on Monday, reappeared for another term before the week was up. The Committee believes that anything more futile than this process of getting drunk, being arrested, receiving 10, 15 or 30-day sentences, going to the Jail and to the Workhouse, serving time, going out and getting drunk again, can scarcely be imagined. The rate of recidivism moreover, is the best evidence that existing procedures are failing to rehabilitate the alcoholic.[3]

Among the sixteen recommendations made by the committee to combat the alcohol problem in the District was legislation for an indeterminate sentence of one day to one year for the offense of intoxication to insure more effective treatment and rehabilitation of the chronic alcoholic; that funds be appropriated to continue the treatment of alcoholics at D.C. General Hospital; "That appropriate action be taken by the Chief of Police to encourage the policeman on patrol to make a more determined effort to send persons who are simply intoxicated to their homes, and avoid where possible, arrest and detention."[4] One other important recommendation stated that the "...Board of Commissioners authorize and direct the Chief of Police to select a Committee, including at least one representative of the Corporation Counsel, to study and report to the Commissioners ways and means for better handling the first offender intoxicant, particularly with a view to his release without a formal charge of intoxication."[5] Despite the recommendations and action taken by the criminal justice system as a whole, the problem of the alcoholic offender persisted for almost another decade.

Nine of the forty-four recommendations of the Karrick Committee dealt specifically with the Department of Corrections. Recommendations were made for construction of additional dormitories at the Workhouse and Women's Reformatory to accommodate the rising population; that several buildings at the Reformatory be remodeled to provide extra bed space; and a badly needed medical facility be constructed that would include conventional hospital wards and space for outpatient treatment.

The Committee further recommended that the Department implement a pilot program for intensive treatment of hardened criminals. In accepting this proposal, the Congress appropriated $44,000 for the project. The program, officially known as the Psychological Service Center, began at the Reformatory in 1958 with a staff of six members made up of four psychologists, a sociologist, and a case worker. The center provided psychological diagnosis and intensive individual and group therapy to 57 inmates during the initial six months of operation. While the use of psychiatry and psychology was not new to the Department, this was the first operation with sufficient staff to provide services for a significant portion of the inmate population. From this pilot project, the Department expanded its psychological services to include all of its institutions.

The Karrick Committee concluded its report as follows:

> In summary, the Committee does not believe that probation and parole by themselves can solve our prison problem, but we do believe that (1) increased housing in low-cost dormitories, (2) an increased reliance on probation and parole, (3) new methods of handling intoxicants, and (4) improving ways of handling traffic violators, non-supports, and other petty offenders, can all combine to prevent the outlay of huge expenditures for

> additional prison facilities and, at the same time, offenders will be successfully supervised and rehabilitated in a normal environment -- their homes and community.[6]

Although some progress was made during 1959 in terms of decreasing overcrowding, especially in the Reformatory for Men, as a result of the Karrick Committee recommendations, the annual report for that year describes the following conditions:

> Whereas the crowding factor is the most difficult obstacle to improved operation, related to it is the fact that, especially among the adult male felons, the degree of criminality seems higher among those admitted during the last year. Actually, while it can be demonstrated that a large majority of the men and women conduct themselves quite acceptably, there still is a hard core of four or five percent of our inmates who are dangerous and unstable and unpredictable. It is from this hard core that serious conduct problems arise within the institutions; it is this segment of the inmates which contribute most seriously to growth of crime in the community when their sentences have been completed and they are released. To the credit of 95 percent of our inmates, the Department is able to register but one escape during 1959; an escape of a misdemeanant offender who walked away from the unfenced Workhouse Division and who was recaptured within a few hours. Whereas there have been expected fights among the men, thefts of food, gambling, some disrespect to employees, poor sanitation of quarters and other infractions, no serious or major difficulties were experienced. There were seven attempted suicides during 1959 with but one actual death.[7]

The Karrick Committee defined the major problems confronting the Department during the 1950s. The remedial measures it recommended, however, were somewhat obscured by major changes in the organizational structures of the Department as well as many new, more complex, problems that began to develop in the 1960s.

SOURCES

[1.] Prison, Probation and Parole in the District of Columbia, April 7, 1957, Bureau of Rehabilitation, National Capital Area, Washington, D.C., pp. 1-4.

[2.] _Ibid.,_ p. 13.

[3.] _Ibid.,_ p. 102.

[4.] _Ibid.,_ p. 132.

[5.] _Ibid.,_ p. 132.

[6.] _Ibid.,_ p. 180.

[7.] Annual Report of the Government of the District of Columbia, 1959 (Washington, D.C.: U.S. Government Printing Office), p. 121.

PART IV
1960 - 1982

CHAPTER 22

INTRODUCTION TO AN ERA OF RAPID CHANGE FOR THE DEPARTMENT OF CORRECTIONS (1960 - 1982)

The decade of the 1960s prefaced an era in which the Department's problems became increasingly more complex and changes in organizational structure and treatment techniques occurred more rapidly than at any previous time in its history. The 1960s is remembered as a time of unrest among various groups in our society. Throughout the decade there were countless demonstrations and rioting in the streets; beginning with the Civil Rights Movement, followed by student protests regarding many social issues, especially the Vietnam War. The tempo of unrest in the community was reflected in the District's penal institutions, and by the close of the decade the Department had experienced inmate rioting for the first time in its history.

Within the Department, the leadership changed three times during the decade of the 1960s, beginning with the untimely death of Donald L. Clemmer, in September 1965, after having served as the first Director for 20 years. Thomas Sard whose career with the Department spanned 35 years, became the second director and served until his retirement in December 1966. Kenneth L. Hardy, also a career employee of the Department, became the third director in January 1967. It is noted that Hardy holds the distinction of being the first Black director of a correctional system in the United States. A change in the District's government known as Reorganization Plan No. 3 (H. Doc. 132), occurred in 1967, abolishing the Board of Commissioners, and replacing it with a single commissioner, an assistant to the commissioner, and a nine-member council - all appointed by the President of the United States.

Other changes of great consequence to the Department resulted from the "President's Commission on Crime in the District of Columbia," organized in 1965, and the "Easter Decision" in 1966 (the test case that determined alcoholism a disease rather than a misdemeanant offense in the District of Columbia). Occurring almost simultaneously, those two events were responsible for reshaping the Department's organizational structure.

The Department, like many other correctional systems throughout the nation, had high hopes for the success of the rehabilitation movement, and the decade of the 1960s was a time of experimentation with new ideas in modern penology. Creation of the Law Enforcement Assistance Agency (LEAA), under the Department of Justice in 1965, provided funding for many innovative pilot programs in the field of corrections that otherwise would not have been possible under regular appropriations. The Department was able to introduce a number of new programs into its institutions as a result of LEAA grants. The move toward community corrections and work release in the early 1960s was a major step forward in the Department's endeavor to remain among the more progressive penal systems in the nation.

The increase in drug abuse to epidemic proportions in the District, and throughout the nation as well, placed an added burden on the entire criminal justice system. Drug abuse was especially difficult for the Department, since it created a need for special treatment programs for the users, and the introduction of contraband drugs into the institutions placed an additional burden on security.

The rapid pace with which change occurred during the 1960s carried over into the 1970s. The inmate population continued to rise and remained high throughout the decade. Escapes from the Department's institutions reached an all-time high during the early years of the decade of the 1970s. Inmate unrest continued to be a major problem for the Department's administrative staff, resulting in several disturbances. Morale among the correctional officers became extremely low as a result of the conflict between the more traditional methods of handling the prisoners and the new, more liberal, concepts that were introduced as part of the reforms of the 1960s.

A further shift in the racial makeup of the Department's inmate population took place in the 1970s. In addressing the 32nd Annual Conference of the Middle Atlantic States Conference on Corrections, Kenneth L. Hardy noted:

* * *

> 'Already 70% of Americans live on only 1% of the land. By 1986, our cities will swell by the equivalent of five more New York Cities. While most urban whites can flee the cities for the suburbs, most urban Blacks are trapped in their ghettos by circumstances or social rejection. Black populations in cities have risen rapidly -- from 6 1/2 million in 1950 to 12 million in 1966. Projections of suburban populations indicate that between 1960 and 1980, the increase will be over 40 million -- and 98% of suburban growth between 1960 and 1966 was white.'

> To us in corrections this means we are going to continue to get, at an increasingly rapid rate, larger numbers of young offenders, most of them Black, unschooled, and without significant work experience. And, tragically, many with hostile, militant attitudes against society.[1]

* * *

By the close of the 1970s, approximately 98 percent of the inmate population was Black. A dramatic change also occurred in the racial makeup of the Department's staff. At the end of the 1960s, 26% of the Department's staff was Black, and by the close of the 1970s it had shifted to approximately 55%.

The turnover in administrative personnel, especially in the Adult Services Division (Minimum, Maximum, and Central Facilities at Lorton), was rapid during the early 1970s, creating an additional hardship on efforts to formulate and carry out policies and procedures for those institutions. For example, in the years between 1969 and 1973, six superintendents of adult services served as follows: Allen Avery, who was appointed to the post of Superintendent temporarily to replace Dr. D.J. Sheehy; Claude Burgin (acting), John O. Boone, James Freeman (acting), Delbert C. Jackson, and Lawrence Swain, each serving one year or less. In November 1973, Marion D. Strickland became Superintendent of Adult Services and served until November 1980. At that time, a change in the organizational structure of the Department placed both Adult Services and Youth Centers I and II under the supervision of an Assistant Director of Correctional Services. James A. Freeman was named to that post, and served in that capacity until 1986.

A change in leadership of the Department occurred in 1973 with the retirement of Kenneth L. Hardy from his post as Director of the Department. Delbert C. Jackson became the fourth Director of the Department at that time. Jackson began his career with the Department in July of 1964, and served in several administrative positions prior to being named Director.

Jackson assumed leadership of the Department in the midst of the penal reform which had begun in the 1960s. The following brief excerpt from his Statement of Philosophy and Goals for the Department of Corrections provides insight into his commitment to continue the reform movement.

> The winds of change which swept the country after World War II have blown away many long-standing preconceptions. There has been a

genuine effort to deal with the causative factors and not merely with their symptoms. Reformation, long a goal of far-sighted leaders, received increased emphasis but little support. Efforts, though all too limited, have been extended to make prisons more humane places. Society has been asked to assume some of the corrections burden through community programs. These advances have not been without trauma, confrontation, and conflict. Against a backdrop of generally unsettled social conditions, they have been accompanied by riots, court actions, and, in many cases, public sacrifices of correctional personnel who sought to do the right thing.

We are still in the midst of this era of change. The public does not articulate what it wants from its corrections systems. Correctional administrators have offered limited guidance. Little effort has been made to look at the causes of crime which, if corrected, could preclude the existence of large prison systems. It is small wonder, then, that there is confusion as to correctional goals and philosophies. A formerly simplistic philosophical base has been fragmented, and the answers to new directions are sophisticated and complex.

* * *

It is mandatory that today's penologists exhibit those qualities of leadership, compassion, and strength compatible with the concept of "directing by leading." Correctional system personnel must be cognizant that the policy of this Department is management by objectives and is concomitantly goal-oriented. Correctional system personnel must be aware that "our business" is dealing with those peope who, in the past, and in some cases presently, have according to law, exhibited anti-social or deviant behavior and are in dire need of stimuli for self-motivation, treatment, psychological, academic and vocational training, and above all, the inculcation of that humanist concept: "I am."[2]

* * *

The constant turmoil created by the large number of escapes and the disturbances within the Department's institutions prompted a considerable amount of adverse criticism by the news media, which led to several investigations into operations at the Lorton reservation. Unfortunately, the notoriety received by the Department caused irreparable damage to its relationship with the local citizens of southern Fairfax County which over the years had been one of friendship and cooperation.

Despite the many obstacles it faced, the Department's administration was intent upon expanding the community corrections program, building the new detention center and improving the facilities at the Lorton reservation, in addition to developing new academic and vocational programs.

By the end of the 1970s, the enthusiasm for the rehabilitation movement that sparked the 1960s was beginning to fade, and a more conservative approach to the treatment of offenders began to emerge in correctional systems throughout the country. This swing to a more conservative movement in the field of corrections signaled the end of an era, and the beginning of a search for a new philosophy in penology. For this reason, I have chosen to end this chronology with the year 1982.

The 1980s began on a sad note for the Department with the death of Delbert C. Jackson, March 10, 1982. Throughout his tenure as Director of the Department Jackson was a firm believer in the rehabilitation movement. It is an interesting coincident that his death occurred at a time when the rehabilitaton era was coming to a close. For the remainder of 1982 the directorship of the Department was filled by rotation of the three Assistant Directors in an acting capacity as follows: Patricia Taylor, George Holland, and William Golightly. In January 1983, James F. Palmer became the Department's fifth Director, and he is currently serving in that capacity.

The following chapters chronicle in greater detail the events outlined in this introduction to more fully define their impression on the history of the Department.

SOURCES

[1.] Kenneth L. Hardy, "Corrections - Thoughts for the '70's," speech delivered at 32nd Annual Conference Middle Atlantic States Conference on Corrections, Statler-Hilton Hotel, Baltimore, Maryland, on file D.C. Department of Corrections Museum, Lorton, Virginia.

[2.] Delbert C. Jackson, Statement of "Philosophy and Goals," March 28, 1975, unpublished, on file D.C. Department of Corrections Museum, Lorton, Virginia, pp. 1, 2, 10.

CHAPTER 23

YOUTH CENTER I

The Federal Youth Corrections Act of 1950 was created by Congress in the belief that many young offenders, both men and women, between the ages of 18 and 22 years could be rehabilitated through treatment and training geared to their age level. The need for such a program was especially necessary in the District where the incidence of crime among young adult males was particularly high. The Act was amended April 8, 1952, to make its provisions applicable to the District of Columbia, with specified limitations set forth in Section 5025, Title 18, U.S. Code Annotated:

> The District of Columbia is authorized either to provide its own facilities and personnel or to contract with the Director for treatment and rehabilitation of committed youth offenders convicted of offenses under any law of the United States applicable exclusively to the District. Wherever undergoing treatment such committed youth offenders shall be subject to all provisions of this chapter as though convicted of offenses not applicable exclusively to the District. (Added April 8, 1952, Ch. 163, Sec. 3 (a), 66 Stat. 46).[1]

The Act provided an indeterminate parole date and was designed to allow judges flexibility in sentencing by providing several sentencing alternatives, as well as segregation of the youths from adult offenders. In addition, the Youth Act required mandatory classification and treatment as well as a mandatory period of parole supervision.

As early as 1954, initial plans were under consideration for construction of a medium security institution for young males of the District, sentenced under the Federal Youth Corrections Act, to be located on about 50 acres of land at the Lorton reservation. The Youth Act limited capacity of the institution to approximately 340 inmates. The architectural design of the institution was a departure from the type of structure ordinarily associated with correctional facilities of the 1950s. Instead, the buildings and grounds were designed to resemble a college campus, to permit considerable freedom of movement by the inmate population inside the 12 foot fence enclosing the compound. A diagnostic unit was included in the overall operation for the purpose of conducting presentence studies of the Youth Act cases for the District of Columbia courts.

In planning the program for the young men who would be incarcerated there, emphasis was placed on creating an environment that would offer every opportunity for resocialization, through a wide variety of educational programs, both academic and vocational, professional counseling and guidance, and social and recreational activities. In addition, the housing was designed to provide each inmate with his own room, and each housing unit contained a dayroom for television viewing and game activities.

Officially known as "The Youth Center," the new institution opened in September 1960, and "...it became the first institution constructed to implement the Youth Corrections Act of 1950."[2] The initial administrative staff chosen to implement the new concepts in rehabilitation at the Youth Center included Joseph H. Havener, Superintendent; Elwood Nelson, Assistant Superintendent for Programs; Holton C. Rogers, Assistant Superintendent Operations; and Anthony J. Del Popolo, Assistant Superintendent of Education.

The mission of the Youth Center as interpreted by the Department at the time of its opening was to provide individual treatment of the offender through a "team" approach." An innovative concept in the treatment of offenders for that era, it was described as follows:

> At the vital core of the treatment team is the key three, the classification and parole officer, the psychologist, and correctional officer assigned to each case.
>
> The key three act preceptorially in analyzing the new case and developing a feasible program of treatment. As the program is commenced the treatment team expands its membership to include chaplains, teachers, work squad supervisors, dormitory officers, athletic coaches and others.[3]

The following excerpt from a booklet entitled "So We All Understand," issued by the administration to inmates upon entering the Youth Center is a further indication of the new philosophy in the treatment of the youthful offenders:

> We have got to talk together a lot. All of us. The Registrar first, then your Counselor, -- the Officers, Chaplains, Psychologists, Officials, -- everybody. We will talk problems out.

> Every man has strengths on which to build. Sometimes they are hidden. We need to know them and you need to know them. So you will be interviewed and questioned. But keep in mind, we do all this for your ultimate benefit. That is, for your better life ahead.
>
> As to your offense, -- that is in the past. It's spilled milk. You come here clean. As behavioral scientists we won't hold past mistakes against you. We know that many people flocking into institutions have been sinned against as much, in some cases, as they have defaulted. Our interest in the offense is historical only, and to seek answers to the question. 'Why.'
>
> We can help you to help yourself only as we get to understand you. Please keep this in mind especially during your early days here.[4]

It is noted that the relatively few young female offenders sentenced under the Federal Youth Corrections Act were first confined in cottage type housing on the grounds of the Women's Reformatory. Later, the practice of designating the female Youth Act offenders to Federal institutions for service of sentence was initiated.

Despite the efforts to create an environment that would be conducive to the resocialization process of the youthful offenders, just three years after the Youth Center opened, the following appeared in the Annual Report for 1963:

> The year 1963 will be remembered primarily as the only year thus far since the Department was created in 1946 when there has been a serious inmate disturbance. Late in July and early in August, at the Youth Center, a group of some fifty young inmates professing adherence in various degrees to the Black Muslim faith conspired and engaged in riotous behavior in posing their will to authority. Control was maintained after some $7,000 of property damage to the Youth Center, but without injury of any kind to inmates or personnel. Throughout the year the agitation of Muslim inmates tended to upset the good order of not only the Youth Center, but also the Reformatory Division, and to some degree, the Jail Division. Except for the minor riot

> mentioned, however, there was no other rebellion, though a constant flow of court petitions criticizing the District of Columbia Government and the prison administration was another unusual feature of 1963.[5]

The feeling of unrest persisted, although there were no further disturbances at the Youth Center until 1968.

Through a contract between the Secretary of Labor and the National Committee for Children and Youth (NCCY), in May 1966, the Youth Center was given an experimental and demonstration project in which the inmates were given multioccupational training, counseling, employment, and community support. This project was noted in the 1967 Annual report as follows: "During the past year, the National Committee for Children and Youth established a vocational training program in seven trades, in which trained workers are needed in the Washington metropolitan area. VISTA volunteers were also utilized in this promising endeavor."[6]

Originally, the Federal Parole Board was responsible for all Youth Act parolees. In 1967, however, legislation was passed that placed those cases under the jurisdiction of the District of Columbia Board of Parole. A Youth Services Division was created in the Department, September 1969, with the merging of Youth Parole, Youth Center I, and the Community Treatment Center for Youths.

SOURCES

[1.] Federal Youth Corrections Act, Sec. 5025, Title 18, U.S. Code.

[2.] The Youth Center Story, Brochure, undated (Rockville, Maryland: Studio Printing, Inc.), on file D.C. Department of Corrections Museum, Lorton, Virginia, not numbered.

[3.] <u>Ibid.</u>

[4.] "So We All Understand," pamphlet, issued by Administrative Staff, Youth Center, undated, on file D.C. Department of Corrections Museum, Lorton, Virginia, p. 4.

[5.] Annual Report of the Government of the District of Columbia, 1963 (Washington, D.C.: U.S. Government Printing Office), p. 5-14.

[6.] Annual Report of the D.C. Department of Corrections, 1967, on file in the D.C. Department of Corrections Museum, Lorton, Virginia, p. 7.

CHAPTER 24

EARLY COMMUNITY CORRECTIONS

The opening in 1964 of the first halfway house in the District of Columbia by the Bureau of Rehabilitation of the National Capital Area, was an important milestone in the history of the Department of Corrections. It signaled the beginning of a new trend known as "community corrections."

The Bureau had for many years worked closely with the Department in assisting offenders and their families in prerelease planning and follow-up casework. The Bureau recognized, as did the Department, that the first few months following release from prison are crucial to the offender's adjustment in the community. A demonstration research study conducted by the Bureau during 1961-1963 revealed that "...attempts to reach releases once they entered the community were only partially successful and that recidivism was at its highest point during the first few months following release."[1] As a result of the study, the Bureau decided to establish a halfway house for a limited number of releases from the Department's institutions, to provide additional support during early adjustment in the community. The project was supported by a grant from the National Institute of Mental Health, The Public Welfare Foundation, The Eugene and Agnes E. Meyer Foundation, and the Shaw Foundation. In March 1964, the project was approved and the first resident was received in the house July 1, 1964.

The house located at 1770 Park Road, N.W., was named Shaw Residence, in honor of G. Howland Shaw, a former president of the Bureau of Rehabilitation, and who had devoted much of his life to assisting prisoners and ex-offenders. In fact, the first progress report on Shaw Residence, issued in September 1965, was dedicated to G. Howland Shaw and Donald Clemmer "who worked to give meaning to the administration of justice and the rehabilitation of offenders."[2]

While the number of residents the house could accommodate was limited, it offered a program of service that included employment development, individual and group counseling, recreation, room and board as well as referrals to community resources. Of greater significance was the fact that the District now had a facility to bridge the gap between the institution and the community.

The opening of Shaw Residence was followed by enactment of the Prisoner Rehabilitation Act in 1965 (P.L. 89-176) which authorized prerelease employment of sentenced felons in the community and specified permissable housing procedures. The Misdemeanant Work Release Act of 1966 (P.L. 89-803) and the D.C. Bail Reform Act of 1966 (P.L. 09-465) provided further legal sanction to community based treatment programs in the District by extending work release privileges to misdemeanants at the time of sentencing and to persons awaiting final court decision. In addition:

> By an Act of Congress approved September 10, 1965 (18 USC 4082, 79 Stat. 674), the fundamental custody-authority of the Attorney General was amended to provide for furloughs and the establishment of residential community treatment centers, or so-called half-way houses, as correctional 'facilities.' The Attorney General delegated his authority under the Act to the Board of Commissioners or their authorized representatives over such prisoners as may be in their custody or supervision, by Order No. 352-66, dated January 13, 1966.[3]

The Department immediately began planning its first work release program. Known as the Prerelease Employment Program (PREP), it was implemented in April 1966 at the Reformatory for Men. In the beginning, the participants were bused to their employment sites in the Metropolitan area daily. In December 1967, however, the program was transferred to the D.C. Jail.

The advent of work release and halfway houses (officially known as Community Correctional Centers) added a new dimension to the Department's treatment programs. The practice of providing the inmate with a suit of clothes and $50.00 in cash upon his release from the institution was fast becoming a thing of the past. The concept of community corrections provided an opportunity for the inmate to test his readiness for return to the community by actually working in the community for several months prior to his actual release on parole. Further, it was now possible for the inmate to earn money to help care for his family, or to save for use when he reentered the community. For those inmates with no strong family ties or those who would benefit from gradual reentry into the community, the halfway house filled an urgent need.

SOURCES

[1.] Shaw Residence, The Bureau of Rehabilitation, Progress Report, March 1964 - September 1965, on file D.C. Department of Corrections Museum, Lorton, Virginia, p. 6.

[2.] Ibid., p. not numbered.

[3.] C. Francis Murphy, Corportion Counsel, D.C. Memorandum to Kenneth L. Hardy, Director of D.C. Department of Corrections, Washington, D.C., April 11, 1972, Subject: The Role of the District of Columbia Council in the Operation of the Department of Corrections, on file in the D.C. Department of Corrections Museum, Lorton, Virginia, p. 2.

CHAPTER 25

THE PRESIDENT'S COMMISSION ON CRIME IN THE DISTRICT OF COLUMBIA

By Executive Order issued July 6, 1965, President Lyndon B. Johnson established a commission on crime which included all three branches of the criminal justice system in the District of Columbia. The President appointed a team of experts in the field of criminal justice to study the city's law enforcement, corrections, and the courts, and to recommend methods of making the Nation's Capital a model for other criminal justice systems throughout the nation to follow.

Under Section Two of the President's Order, "Functions of the Commission," the following areas of inquiry pertaining to the Department of Corrections:

> (3) The correction and rehabilitation of offenders, particularly first offenders.
>
> (6) Improving the methods used in the correction and rehabilitation of offenders.[1]

Section Three, "Liaison and Coordination," stated:

> The Attorney General, the Secretary of the Treasury, the Secretary of Health, Education, and Welfare, the Director of the Office of Economic Opportunity, and the Board of Commissioners of the District of Columbia each shall designate a representative to serve with the Commission as liaison. All departments and agencies of the Federal Government and the District of Columbia shall cooperate with the Commission and furnish it such information and assistance, not inconsistent with law, as it may require in the performance of its functions and duties. The Commission shall establish liaison and cooperate with any similar body constituted to study law enforcement and the administration of justice throughout the Nation, and shall consult, as may be appropriate, with members of the federal and District of Columbia judiciary and their assistants concerning matters of common interest.[2]

The Department's institutions were surveyed by the American Correctional Association as part of the Commission's study.

The Crime Commission presented its report to the President on December 15, 1966. "The President endorsed the Report and urged immediate action to implement its recommendations."[3] The Board of Commissioners of the District of Columbia designated the Department of General Administration to "...monitor and report on the efforts of all agencies, public and private, involved in carrying out those recommendations."[4] There were 262 numbered recommendations in the Crime Commission Report, "...as well as many additional proposals and suggestions made throughout the text of the Report,"[5] Some of the recommendations involved details only, but others were more complex and required legislative action to authorize the proposed changes or budget increases to provide the necessary funds. Of the 262 recommendations of the Crime Commission, 26 were specifically directed to reorganization of the Department of Corrections. Kenneth L. Hardy, who assumed directorship of the Department in January 1967, took on the monumental task of evaluating and implementing the changes contained in the Crime Commission's recommendations.

Consolidation of parole and probation services within the Department was one of the major recommendations and called for reorganization in the structure of the Department, as follows:

> The Department of Corrections should be reorganized and renamed the Department of Correctional Services, and should be consolidated with the probation and parole services now under the D.C. Court of General Sessions and the D.C. Parole Board respectively.
>
> For all practical purposes the District of Columbia is similar to most states in general operation of its total correctional system. The Department, therefore, should have two large line subdivisions, each headed by a deputy director: one for management of the five institutions, the other for administration of probation and parole services and a variety of community-based programs.[6]

Although the Crime Commission recommended that both probation and parole services become a part of the correctional services, probation remained under the jurisdiction of the courts. Parole services, however, was placed under the Department of Corrections in February 1967. With the reorganization, the institutional parole office located in the Men's Reformatory, whose staff prepared applications for parole, counseled inmates on parole matters, and prepared memoranda for Parole Board Hearings, was dissolved. The duties of the institutional parole office staff were combined with those of the Department's classification officers, creating a new type of counselor known as "classification and parole officer." The parole officers who supervised parolees in the community, along with the institutional parole office staff, were placed under the jurisdiction of the Department of Corrections by a Civil Service process known as "blanketing in." The Department then became responsible for preparation of all hearing memoranda for the Parole Board as well as for establishing a parole service unit to meet the needs of the parolees. The major advantage of placing the parole services under the Department, it was felt, was the reduction in duplication of effort in collecting data relating to inmate case history, in addition to providing a greater continuity of service by having just one counselor work with the inmate in the institution. The Parole Board, along with a small administrative staff, remained under the jurisdiction of the D.C. Commissioners.

Additional recommendations of the Crime Commission relating to parole and community-based rehabilitation programs included increasing the number of parole officers in order to reduce the size of the caseloads and upgrading parole officers' salaries and providing them with in-service training programs. Other recommendations of the Crime Commission included expanding work release and expanding community correctional centers. In order to comply with those recommendations, the Department created a Community Services Division which included three units: parole supervision, community correctional centers, and employment development. Allan Avery became the first Associate Director in charge of the new division.

The President's Crime Commission emphasized that the work furlough be utilized to a much greater extent, pointing out that community-based programs are less costly to operate than institutions. In addition, it was suggested that a diagnostic and outpatient clinic, staffed by psychiatrists, psychologists, and other clinical specialists, be established to serve parolees, probationers, and their families. While this type of facility would have aided the parolees and probationers in their adjustment to the community, plans were never completed to provide such a service.

A major research and evaluation program was recommended by the Crime Commission to improve the effectiveness and efficiency of all components of the correctional process. In addition, a further recommendation suggested the eventual installation of an automatic data processing unit, and stated:

> In the immediate future we may expect great stress to be placed on the need for even broader scientific technology, such as electronic devices and applications in information storage and retrieval, over the continuum of the entire system of criminal justice. In particular, crime and arrest statistics, and offender characteristics in such detail as necessary to become a criminal career history are needed for better understanding and planning.[7]

Plans were immediately carried out to establish a research unit to replace the Institute for Criminological Research established by the Department in 1956. The new research unit was originally located on the grounds of the Reformatory for Men. Officially known as the Office of Planning and Research, it became operational February 1967, headed by Doctor Donald Stewart.

The Commission's recommendation for an automatic data processing unit did not become a reality until 1968. Since automated recordkeeping was a rarity in correctional systems throughout the United States at that time, the Department's Data Processing unit earned the distinction of being among the first of its kind in the nation. The new automated system was designed to provide the Department with records on all inmates in all stages of incarceration, making it possible to maintain inmate records with a fraction of the paperwork that was required prior to its implementation.

With regard to the Crime Commission's recommendation for a treatment program for prisoners with drinking problems, the Department responded as follows:

> The alcoholic was removed from the jurisdiction of the Department by the Easter decision. A similar task has been accomplished with the narcotic offender, who continues to be a problem for the Department as well as for the District. The nation's first methadone maintenance program to be established by a department of corrections was implemented by the Department in September 1969.[8]

In making its recommendation requiring long-range plans for construction of a detention center to replace precinct lockups and the D.C. Jail, the Crime Commission commented that these facilities were antiquated in their physical plants as well as their programs and functions. "Funds for planning the facility were requested in four successive budgets and approval was obtained in the 1970 budget."[9] Planning was begun as soon as the funds became available.

In a message to Congress March 8, 1965, President Johnson proposed that the Attorney General be provided with authority to establish a program of technical assistance as well as grants to enable state, local, and private groups to increase their efforts in developing and testing new methods of crime control. As a result, Congress passed the Omnibus Crime Control and Safe Streets Act of 1968, (Public Law 90-351), creating the Law Enforcement Assistance Administration (LEAA), to be administered by the Department of Justice. Funding by the LEAA enabled the Department to implement a number of the Crime Commission's recommendations. One such grant funded program was the development of a Warrant Squad for the Department.

Over the years, a backlog of outstanding warrants had accumulated and it was believed that parole violators were committing a "...significant number of crimes while evading parole violations apprehension."[10] The Crime Commission strongly recommended that those violators be found and returned to custody. At that time, the U.S. Marshals were assuming the primary responsibility of serving Parole Board warrants. That agency was severely understaffed and could not devote the time and personnel required to keep the service of parole warrants current. For that reason, a demonstration project establishing a warrant squad within the Department was funded by LEAA, to strengthen "...both the safety of the public and the effective operation of the parole system in the District."[11] It was further hoped that the Warrant Squad would improve "...the efficiency of the administration of criminal justice and deter potential violation of parole conditions."[12] The operation proved to be effective in accomplishing its objective, and when the LEAA funds expired, it was made a permanent unit of the Department.

The Crime Commission recommended that the Department of Corrections establish a correctional training academy to train correctional officers as well as employees and representatives of the courts, juvenile institutions, and related private agencies. "Planning for the Academy was accomplished in April 1969 with the aid of a Law Enforcement Assistance grant. The Academy was staffed in early 1969..."[13] In connection with training, LEAA grants were available for educational purposes, and many of the Department's employees took advantage of the opportunity to receive higher education by enrolling in specialized training in correctional science courses offered by local colleges and universities. That training did much to enhance the professionalism of the Department.

A regional training academy was established in 1970 as a result of a grant proposal submitted to LEAA by the District of Columbia and endorsed by the States of Maryland and Virginia. The plan for this project represented the joint effort of those three jurisdictions to pool as much information as possible in the areas of corrections, probation and parole, and to share ideas and methods of improving operations.

Two national studies were used in developing the training course: The President's Commission on Law Enforcement and Administration of Justice and the Joint Commission on Correctional Manpower and Training. The training was conducted at the Department of Corrections' Training Academy at Lorton. It was funded for a one year period, during which time 39 seminars were to have been conducted and training offered to approximately 775 managers, supervisor trainees, and some other personnel. At the end of the year, however, 44 seminars had been conducted and more than 900 persons had been given some type of training. Unfortunately, the Regional Academy was not funded for a second year and plans to establish it on a permanent basis did not materialize. In addition to the fact that LEAA saw fit not to fund it after the end of the first year, the States of Virginia and Maryland had begun to develop their own training programs. Although the academy was discontinued, the project made it possible for all concerned to benefit from a far greater amount of resource material than would have been possible had it not been established.

In compliance with the Crime Commission's recommendation that the educational program at the Reformatory should be expanded, additional teachers at the grade and high school levels were employed, and proposals were submitted to the Labor Department and Office of Education for increasing the scope of the vocational training. The expansion, however, went beyond the high school level to include the inauguration of a prison college program in May 1969. While the idea of a college program within a prison was not unique for that era, the Department was among the first prison systems in the nation to experiment with that type of training.

It was believed that among the prison population there were inmates who possessed high intellectual ability and that they should be given an opportunity to pursue college level training. It was hoped that once these inmates had attained the education, they could provide leadership within the prison population as well as in the District's inner city area.

The Community Education Department of Federal City College provided the instructional staff. Initial funding for the first two quarters was provided by D.C. Department of Vocational Rehabilitation and Sears, Roebuck Foundation. The LEAA provided funding through 1972. At that point, the project was well established and appeared to have a promising future, and funding for its operation became part of the Department's appropriation.

In the beginning, a limited number of freshman college subjects were offered, however, as the project progressed additional subjects were offered and eventually inmates who had completed the required number of courses at the Reformatory, had maintained a certain average, and were eligible to receive educational furloughs, were bused to the campus of Federal City College.

Another recommendation by the Crime Commission suggested that "The Department's industries should be operated by the Federal Bureau of Prisons."[14] That recommendation was not implemented. Instead, "Two Bureau surveys were made of the DCDC industries and their operating problems. At the end of the second survey, it was decided that the Bureau should serve the Department of Corrections in an advisory consultative role."[15]

Implementation of the Crime Commission's recommendations, together with the changes necessitated by the Easter Decision were incorporated with the reorganization of the Department's institutions early in 1968.

SOURCES

[1.] U.S. President, Executive Order, Establishing the President's Commission on Crime in the District of Columbia, July 16, 1965, on file in the D.C. Department of Corrections Museum, Lorton, Virginia, pp. 1-2.

[2.] _Ibid.,_ p. 2.

[3.] D.C. Crime Report Team, Summary Statement of Action Taken on Recommendations of the D.C. Crime Commission, June 28, 1967, on file in the D.C. Department of Corrections Museum, Lorton, Virginia, p. 1.

[4.] _Ibid._

[5.] _Ibid.,_ p. 1.

[6.] Report, President's Commission on Crime in D.C., on file D.C. Department of Corrections Museum, Lorton, Virginia.

[7.] _Ibid._

[8.] Planning and Research Report, "Implementation of President's Crime Commission Recommendations by the D.C. Department of Corrections," December 3, 1969, D.C. Department of Corrections Museum, Lorton, Virginia, p. 6.

[9.] _Ibid.,_ p. 1.

[10.] Office of Criminal Justice Planning Report, "Comprehensive Plan for Justice in the District of Columbia," June, 1969, p. C-29.

[11.] _Ibid.,_ p. C-29.

[12.] _Ibid.,_ p. C-29.

[13.] Planning and Research Report, "Implementation of the President's Crime Commission Recommendation for the D.C. Department of Corrections," December 3, 1969, D.C. Department of Corrections Museum, Lorton, Virginia, p. 2.

[14.] _Ibid.,_ p. 2.

[15.] _Ibid.,_ p. 2.

CHAPTER 26

THE EASTER DECISION AND ITS IMPACT ON THE WOMEN'S REFORMATORY AND THE WORKHOUSE

A March 31, 1966 ruling in the United States Court of Appeals, known as the Easter Decision, because it was based on the test case of DeW. Easter v. District of Columbia, "...held that chronic alcoholism is an acceptable defense to the charge of public intoxication,"[1] and it should be treated as a public health problem rather than a criminal offense. In this case, expert medical and psychiatric evidence established that a person charged with public intoxication is a chronic alcoholic who lost control over his use of alcoholic beverages.

While the Easter Decision was hailed by the Department's Director and staff, who for many years had tried to cope with intoxicaton as a misdemeanant offense, the ruling called for the immediate release of all inmates serving sentences for that type of offense. The Annual Report for 1967 illustrates the impact of the Decision on the inmate population of the Workhouse: "As of June 30, 1967, the population was 420. This figure represents a drastic decline in population which was primarily occasioned by the Easter Decision...,"[2] accountng for "...more than a 60 percent reduction in the Workhouse population."[3] An indication of the decline in the Workhouse population, once the alcoholics were removed, is seen when the average daily population of 1,518, reported for the second quarter of fiscal year 1966 is compared with the 420 noted in the 1967 annual report. A similar decline occurred in the population of the Women's Reformatory, where a "...drop from 148 on July 1, 1966, to 72 on July 1, 1967,"[4] was noted. The Department could not justify retention of the two institutions, therefore, a major reorganization was undertaken in an effort to provide suitable housing for the small number of remaining inmates.

Once the alcoholic cases were removed from the Women's Reformatory, the District Commissioners ordered the Department to relinquish the buildings and grounds to the Department of Public Health by November 7, 1966, for use as an alcoholic rehabilitation center. Initially, the Women's Reformatory was transferred to Cellblock Four of the D.C. Jail, which was renovated to provide the necessary security, and space for inmate activities as well as office space for staff. Hallie C. Massey, Superintendent noted the following in her annual report to the Director of the Department for 1967:

> ...This move was certainly a very unsettling and anxious period for both inmates and staff. Many rumors were abroad for several

> months before the decision was finally made to give up the Reformatory for Women at Occoquan...
>
> * * *
>
> Work Release in the Women's Reformatory has been a unique experience. Our first inmate was placed in the program during late November 1966, and to this date fourteen women have been placed. Of this number four were under the Misdemeanant Work Release Act. Of the ten involved in PREP, five were removed for cause, the other five remained on the job until release. Of the four Misdemeanants, two have been removed for cause, one of whom was subsequently tried and sentenced to an additional ninety days for smuggling heroin into the institution.
>
> * * *
>
> Morale of both inmates and officers has been greatly impaired in these last months because of the Reorganization Plans for the Department which greatly affect the Reformatory for Women. Plans which have been formulated are at a standstill since we must await Congressional approval of budgetary requests - however, this explanation has done very little to allay the fears and anxieties of those to whom it is given. It does appear that in the near future we will be able to effect the long term inmates who have been designated to Alderson, West Virginia.[5]

A far cry from the open institution and well landscaped grounds of the Women's Reformatory at Occoquan, Cellblock Four at the Jail was cramped and heavily secured. That situation prompted Mrs. Massey to close her annual report with the following: "'Stone walls may not a prison make, nor iron bars a cage' but they definitely <u>do not</u> make a Women's Reformatory - not even a reasonable facsimile, thereof."[6]

In the meantime, a facility known as the Women's Bureau of the Metropolitan Police Department, located at 1010 North Capital Street, N.W., Washington, D.C. was acquired and renovated to meet the specifications of a detention center. It is noted that the building was shared with the Women's Bureau until 1968, at which time the women under the jurisdiction of

Corrections acquired the entire building. Known officially as "The Women's Detention Center," the new facility opened November 2, 1966, with Anna Roach-Hardy serving as its first Administrator. The Center originally functioned as a holding facility for pre-trial detainees, its role was expanded.

> In September, the Women's Reformatory was dissolved and its staff and prisoners were transferred to the Women's Detention Center. Also, on September 27, 1969, the Women's Detention Center assumed from the Police Department, responsibility for booking and total processing of all female arrests. This added responsibility has presented quite a challenge to our staff inasmuch as it requires learning police and court procedures, fingerprint classification and a variety of knowledge not known to us in the past.[7]

When the Women's Reformatory was dissolved, the long-term felony prisoners were transferred to the United States Penitentiary for Women, Alderson, West Virginia, for service of sentence, and that the practice of using Federal facilities to house D.C. women prisoners is still in use today. The Detention Center, however, continued to serve as a holding facility for the women awaiting transfer to the Federal Penitentiary as well as a facility for confining misdemeanant offenders for service of sentence. It is of interest to note that Cellblock Four was converted into a work release unit for felony and misdemeanant males when project PREP was transferred to the D.C. Jail.

With approximately 60 percent of the population removed, as a result of the Easter Decision, M.C. Pfalzgraf, Superintendent of the Workhouse noted the following in his first quarterly report for fiscal year 1966-67:

> The definite change in the type and character of the inmate body at this institution has greatly affected the overall operation, and will cause very definite changes in the programs and planning for the future. For the first time in over 15 years, we are not over-crowded. This factor, itself, has helped the morale and attitude of the inmates.
>
> * * *
>
> The greatest change and improvement of our operations has been the installation of the four-place tables and chairs in the inmate

> dining room. This was well received by inmates and personnel. It has reduced tension and improved morale of all concerned.
>
> * * *
>
> Because of the reduced population, the double-deck beds have been removed from all dormitories and the number of beds in each dormitory has been reduced to comply with A.C.A. standards.
>
> The overall appearance of the institution is not as good as desired. A study is being made to enable us to reappraise our assignment of inmates in order to give the proper priority to the basic operations. Maintenance and repairs have, by necessity, been curtailed in comparison with inmate manpower availability.
>
> * * *
>
> The drastic changes in the population of this institution has caused much concern to all personnel. All areas are being reevaluated to determine the most desirable steps to take to up-date our programs to better serve those in our custody.[8]

The farm manager also noted the following in his report for the same period: "Cannery production is down 90% and will probably be phased out of our operation in the near future."[9] With the major portion of the work force removed from the Workhouse, farm operations such as the orchard and the swine ranch could no longer exist, and the production of farm produce was gradually limited to hay and corn for use in feeding the dairy and beef cattle.

After 55 years of operation, the brick yard was phased out in 1966. Its closing was due in part to lack of inmate labor and in part to the decline in demand for bricks. The brick yard remained just as it was the day it closed with bricks still in the kilns until 1982 when the Northern Virginia Park Authority, through an agreement with the Department of Corrections, developed a park on the site. Today, all that remains of the brick yard is one kiln which has been left standing to remind visitors to the park that once prisoners produced the bricks with which they built their own prisons.

Further decline in population to 259 inmates prompted the official closing of the Workhouse February 17, 1968. The major portion of the buildings and grounds were turned over to the Department of Public Health for use as an Alcoholic Rehabilitation Center. The Department, however, retained two dormitories which were used to create a minimum security institution.

SOURCES

[1.] The District of Columbia Department of Corrections 1967 Annual Report, on file in the D.C. Department of Corrections Museum, Lorton, Virginia, p. 6.

[2.] _Ibid.,_ p. 6.

[3.] _Ibid.,_ p. 6.

[4.] Annual Report of the Reformatory for Women, Fiscal Year 1966-1967, Memorandum to Director Department of Corrections, on file in the D.C. Department of Corrections Museum, Lorton, Virginia.

[5.] _Ibid._

[6.] _Ibid._

[7.] Aiken, Olivia D., Dissertation, "History of the Women's Detention Center," unpublished, on file in the D.C. Department of Corrections Museum, Lorton, Virginia.

[8.] Quarterly Report of Superintendent of the Workhouse, 1966-1967 (First Quarter), on file in the D.C. Department of Corrections Museum, Lorton, Virginia.

[9.] Quarterly Report of Farm Manager, First Quarter 1967, on file in the D.C. Department of Corrections Museum, Lorton, Virginia.

CHAPTER 27

REORGANIZATION OF THE DEPARTMENT OF CORRECTIONS - 1968

Implementation of the many recommendations proposed by the Crime Commission, together with the changes required under the Easter Decision, necessitated a reevaluation of the Department's resources in order to make maximum utilization of its facilities and personnel. As a result, a restructuring of the Department's institutions was undertaken February 17, 1968.

The two dormitories at the Workhouse site, retained by the Department when that institution was transferred to the Department of Public Health, were used to establish a minimum security institution to provide "...additional facilities and an expansion potential for minimum custody type male offenders."[1] In addition, the population of that institution "...would also provide a work force for the Department's extensive agricultural and dairy operations, and to operate a...sewage treatment plant, water purification plant, railroad and landscape force."[2] Designed to operate as an open facility, with a capacity of 225, for housing short-term prisoners as well as long-term prisoners who were good security risks, the new facility was originally considered to be a temporary arrangement. Although it consists of only two dormitories and mobile home type trailers which serve as offices for the staff, the Minimum Security Facility was in operation until 1985 when a new facility was opened with a 400 bed capacity. Over the years, it provided housing for inmates involved in a work training program as well as for participants in the Prison College Program.

The Men's Reformatory was deactivated and at its site the Department established a Correctional Complex and a Penitentiary. The Complex (later renamed the Central Facility) had a capacity of 935 and originally housed both misdemeanants and felons. Having a capacity of 325, the Penitentiary (later renamed Maximum Security Facility) was located in the walled area of the former Reformatory. Under the reorganization, the Penitentiary became a separate entity from the Complex and housed those inmates considered to be: "intractable, overt homosexuals, inmates dangerous to the well-being of the staff and general population, and severe disciplinary transfers from other institutions."[3]

In the memorandum to Thomas E. Fletcher, Deputy Mayor of the District of Columbia, dated February 26, 1968, Director Kenneth L. Hardy expressed the dilemma involved with the reorganization:

At the time the Department recommended the deactivation of the D. C. Workhouse, it was felt that we would negotiate with the Department of Public Health and offer them the expanded facilities of the Workhouse (capacity 1200) for the former Women's Reformatory (capacity 400), now the Rehabilitation Center for Alcoholics. This facility was transferred from this Department to Public Health as an expedient to temporarily house alcoholics, as a result of the "Easter Decision" in November 1966. We anticipated ready concurrence of this plan by the Health Department since it would enable them to expand their present facilities three-fold.

We have discussed these matters with the Department of Public Health and have not reached a mutual agreement since they are intent on acquiring both institutions, with the exception of two dormitories at the site of the Workhouse which we have temporarily retained. We can appreciate their concern for providing treatment facilities for the alcoholic, however, we are concerned here not with their responsibility, nor with ours, but the overall responsibility of the District Government.

Attention is invited to the following factors which could cause grave concern both to this Department and the District Government.

a. The recent steadily increasing inmate population of the department.

(1) The D. C. Jail has a capacity of 592 and the population is presently 955. We are in the process of reviewing the cases to determine whether or not some of these unsentenced prisoners can be transferred to our Lorton complex.

(2) The Complex and Penitentiary have a combined capacity of 935 and the present population is 1100.

(3) The temporary site of the Minimum Security Institution has a capacity of 225 and its present population is 125.

(4) The above figures reveal that these institutions have a combined capacity of 1752 and a current population of 2186. These figures, of course, do not include the Women's Detention Center, Youth Center, or our Community Treatment and Work Release Centers which are not directly related to the matters discussed herein since these institutions house inmates other than male adult misdemeanants and felons. As can be readily seen, these figures preclude any appreciable expansion which could conceivably pose problems, especially with the steady increase in population. The Department's population has increased by over 200 in the past month.

b. The problems the Department has encountered with the confinement of demonstrators in recent months have revealed that additional facilities should be available to preclude dual treatment standards within the confines of the D.C. Jail and the Correctional Complex.

c. The possibility of demonstrations, not to mention civil disturbances, would certainly place the Department and the District Government in an embarassing position of being able to house only a limited number of persons committed for safekeeping or sentencing by the Courts.[4]

Although minor changes have since occurred, the 1968 reorganization was the last major restructuring within the Department.

SOURCES

[1.] Memorandum, Subject: Restructuring of the Department of Corrections, February 26, 1968, from Director Kenneth L. Hardy to Deputy Mayor Thomas E. Fletcher, on file with the D.C. Department of Corrections Museum, Lorton, Virginia, p. 2.

[2.] Ibid., p. 2.

[3.] Ibid., p. 2.

[4.] Ibid., pp. 2-4

CHAPTER 28

INMATE DISTURBANCES OF THE 1960S

Beginning with the 1963 disturbance created by the Muslim Group at the Youth Center (noted in Chapter 23), a climate of unrest prevailed throughout the inmate population of the Department's institutions, gradually escalating into what the news media termed a "guard riot" at the Reformatory for Men, November 18, 1968. Official reports of the investigations cited overcrowding in the institutions, racial prejudice, insufficient correctional staff, and the resistance to authority by the young Black militants from the District's ghettos as the dominating factors responsible for the unrest and violent behavior exhibited by the prisoners. Other less obvious factors included the growing awareness of the prisoners of their Constitutional rights, brought to light by the civil rights movement, and the general unrest in the community at large. The following excerpts from official investigations provide insight into the attempts by the staff to cope with three disturbances occurring during the period of September 21, 1968 to November 18, 1968.

The incident of September 21, 1968, occurred at the D.C. Jail, when 260 inmates in the northeast wing set fires and destroyed furniture in the recreation area. There were no injuries as a result of the disturbance, however, the inmates voiced a number of complaints, including: "Poor food, overcrowded, dirty cells which attract vermin, visiting rules which allow only two half-hour visits by friends or relatives weekly, refusal of jail officials to allow maximum security and homosexual prisoners the use of recreation areas, brutality and abuse by guards, poor recreational facilities."[1]

A correctional advisory council was appointed to investigate the incident and report its findings. The summary of that report reads as follows:

> The evaluation of the disturbance at the D.C. Jail made by the Correctional Advisory Committee concurs with previous investigations. The D.C. Jail is obsolete and the personnel is inadequate to do the job. Overcrowding, understaffing, and lax court action have created an explosive situation. The current incident, superficially touched off by the interruption of television viewing, has far deeper causes.
>
> Staff and inmates have generally agreed that morale is low, attitudes are depressed.

> The lack of understanding between inmates and staff, between upper and lower echelon staff, mitigates against cooperation and coordination. In addition, overcrowding, vermin, poor food, inadequate showering and visiting privileges increase frustration and hostility. Any rehabilitative process is notably missing as is true constructive administrative process.
>
> It should be noted that there has been improvement in many of the conditions noted above under the tenure of Mr. Kenneth Hardy, Director, Department of Corrections. The Committee agrees with previously made investigations that there is a need for a new jail.
>
> The Committee also questions the cuts made in the realistic Department of Corrections budget request. It believes that the cuts made within the District Government should be seriously questioned. A meaningful, realistic budget would enable the Department of Corrections to correct many of the problems faced in the D.C. Jail.[2]

The second disturbance occurred October 22, 1968 at the Youth Center. A Board of Inquiry was appointed to assess the problems and events leading up to the incident. The following is quoted from the findings of that Board:

> Until the head count at 9:15 p.m., there was no awareness among the Youth Center staff that October 22, 1968 was an unusual day. The daytime activities had proceeded without incident. The evening meal was served and regular Tuesday visiting from 7:00 to 9:00 p.m. was uneventful. The gym, which had been closed for several weeks to refinish the floor, was to reopen after the 9:15 p.m. count was cleared.
>
> At 9:15 p.m., following the end of visiting, the inmates assembled in their dormitories for the usual count. By 9:20 the Control Center at the Youth Center received reports that inmates were missing from the Reception Building. Then each living area in turn reported absences. Eleven inmates were missing. This was puzzling and highly

> unusual...A unit was dispatched to search the fence-line for evidence of escapes...[3]

It was discovered that a hole had been cut through the inner and outer fence lines at Tower Number Six. "There was no sign of anyone in the area. It was concluded that the eleven missing men had escaped. Search parties were stopped inside the institution and two patrol units, each with two men, were sent out of the institution."[4] The report further relates:

> Following the clearing of the Count, the officers were very concerned about the mass escape. The inmates quickly learned of the escapes and a mood of excited tension and uncertainty dominated both inmates and staff. Both groups thought and talked actively about the unprecedented escapes and the possible immediate and long-range effects it might have. The gym did not open as planned...Milling groups of inmates congregated unsupervised and talked of 'the eleven dudes who made it.'
>
> Although it is possible that the disturbance was planned to inhibit search efforts for the escapees, there is no direct evidence to support this. The only evidence of any kind which does support this hypothesis is the following: 1) the disturbance did in fact inhibit the search since it effectively brought back all patrols and other available staff to the Youth Center, and 2) the escape was clearly well planned and executed suggesting that the escapees had the capacity for careful and effective planning. However, it is difficult to understand why it took nearly an hour for the disturbance to start after the Count was cleared. It certainly is possible to understand the disturbance and its relationship to the escapes without assuming any premeditation.
>
> * * *
>
> ...There was strikingly little anti-staff behavior and many people present commented on the fact that if the inmates had wanted to hurt the staff members they had ample opportunity to do it with little likelihood that they would be caught. From 10:30 p.m. to 12:15 a.m., when effective force was mobilized and entered

> through the gate at Number One Tower, there was no direct control exerted by the staff inside the perimeter of the Youth Center.
>
> The actual disturbance lasted an hour and 45 minutes and was a period of considerable confusion for all. Fires were reported in many buildings, masses of inmates roamed the compound, and the sound of breaking glass mixed with the smoke. Officers were removed to the Control Center or to the perimeter towers. The local fire department was called at 11:04 p.m. and waited outside the Number One Tower until 12:15 a.m. due to fear that the firemen would not be safe inside the institution...
>
> How many men were actually involved in the destruction cannot be determined. Inmates reported later that not more than 30 to 50 inmates were actively involved during the disturbance. Of course, virtually all the 350 inmates were 'passive' participants.[5]

The direct costs of the disturbance and escapes amounted to $53,903, which included damaged equipment, damage to buildings and utilities, and overtime pay for correctional officers.

The Board of Inquiry cited 17 recommendations to improve conditions at the Youth Center, pointing out that "the single most important factor contributing to the escapes and disturbance was understaffing..."[6] The report further noted:

> ...On October 22, 1968, the Youth Center was crowded as it has been in recent months. The climate of rebellion against traditional authority which is sweeping urban America -- which includes the inmates of the institutions of the Department of Corrections -- was a potent force contributing both to the escapes and the disturbance. Staff, which was adequate six years ago, or even one year ago, is no longer adequate to maintain meaningful control. We, therefore, recommend considerable increases in the correctional force at the Youth Center.[7]

Among the other recommendations was tool control. "The bolt cutters apparently used in the escape were assigned to the Engineering Division, but no specific responsibility for them can be assigned."[8] The need for planning for de-escalation of disturbances was noted as well as incorporation of review and alteration of disturbance and escape plans as part of the meetings of the Associate Director for Institutions and the Superintendents. Other recommendations included a reduction of idleness, the use of group and individual activities for the prisoners, and a review of the education program at the Youth Center, since that appeared to be a major complaint of the inmates, administrators, and teachers alike. A systematic orientation of each new commitment to the Youth Center was also recommended by the Board, "...to encourage pro-social behavior and to foster maximum constructive use of the Youth Center's programs."[9]

The most serious of the three disturbances occurred on November 18, 1968. As early as April 1968 a feeling of unrest became apparent among the inmate population of the Reformatory for Men. This was construed to be due in part to a carry over of tensions resulting from rioting in the community after the assassination of the Reverend Martin Luther King, Jr., and in part to the agitation of about 64 militant inmates who were considered troublemakers. Throughout the Summer of 1968 minor disturbances were frequent occurrences causing tension to mount among both the staff and inmate population of the institution. The situation culminated in what was referred to by the news media as a "guard riot," so named because the correctional officers removed the troublemakers by force with the use of firearms during a planned operation known as "operation sweep." A number of minor injuries were sustained among the inmate population and one inmate was accidentally wounded.

The details of the operation are outlined in a report by a special Committee appointed by the Mayor Walter Washington, of the District to investigate the incident:

> By 5:00 p.m. on November 18, 1968, a brief but severe rainstorm that had deluged the Lorton Reformatory's rolling acres of green had ceased. The rainstorm's end signaled the start of 'Operation Sweep' -- a maneuver of armed men designated to remove 60 of the 1100 inmates housed in open dormitories of the D.C. Correctional Complex.
>
> At the command of the Reformatory's Superintendent, the electrically-controlled wire gates of the institution opened to admit a force of approximately 120 correctional officers equipped with shotguns, revolvers, modified pickax handles, tear gas, paraphenalia, and riot-control equipment.

Another force of about 80 Metropolitan Police Officers, specially-trained for civil disturbance control, backed them up.

The armed units advanced into the compound to seal off the dormitories. Squads of men, some firing their shotguns and revolvers, moved to predesignated positions and secured the institution. Clusters of inmates, milling outside of the dormitories, scrambled inside.

Then, once it became clear that the initial squads had secured the compound, two special squads moved into the complex to begin the sweep.

Their instructions were to march from dormitory to dormitory, to enter each unit and to remove specifically identified inmates -- prisoners who, in the opinion of their custodians, were hard-core troublemakers and whose removal from the general prisoner population was necessary if order and security were to be maintained in the institution.

The pick-up squads moved briskly through the prison complex. They hand-cuffed the selected inmates and hurried them to waiting vehicles for transfer to maximum security.

Shortly after the first inmates were handcuffed and removed, the injured began to appear at the reformatory hospital -- head wounds, a severely mashed finger, cuts and bruises, and one victim of a gunshot.

The entire sweep operation was over in about 2 hours. By 10:00 p.m. the Metropolitan Police units had returned to the District, and all inmates had been accounted for.

Then, several days later, press accounts began to appear which cast doubt on staff reports of a successful transfer at Lorton. Details of injuries to inmates, of the use of firearms, of the massive character of the sweep, began to emerge. At the same time it was obvious that there was a lack of precise information on the part of officials as to exactly what had occurred that night.

These emerging factors led to a need for a thorough investigation into the incident of November 18. Accordingly, the Mayor's special committee was formed on December 6 to investigate the incident. This report is the result of that investigation.[10]

In its Statement of Purpose, the Committee noted the following:

> The Mayor's Ad Hoc Committee was appointed to establish — to the extent possible — exactly what happened at the Lorton Reformatory on November 18, 1968. The Committee has tried to discover what led up to the sweep on that date — and whether the sweep itself was properly handled.
>
> There have been numerous disturbances at the Lorton Reformatory in recent months. This report does not attempt to study these incidents — or, indeed, to analyze the Lorton situation in great detail. The Committee is concerned with one specific incident -- and past situations are relevant only as they enable a better understanding of the sweep.
>
> The Committee has purposefully refrained from any attempts to examine or analyze the overall problems of the Department of Corrections with respect to its needs for additional personnel and facilities. These needs have been under study by a team of penologists of the Federal Bureau of Prisons whose expertise is essential for a detailed evaluation of the broader problem areas. The Committee, however, has noted the serious need for impovements within the Department and the continued efforts being made to achieve such improvements.[11]

After an intensive investigation that included interviews with staff and inmates alike, who were present during "operation sweep", the Committee issued the following findings:

> The Committee believes that the sweep operation was poorly conceived, poorly planned, and poorly executed. This is most clearly illustrated by the entire approach to the guards' use of firearms.

> It is simply a stroke of fortune that no one was killed during the sweep and that more people were not shot or seriously wounded. Many of the guards showed complete indifference to the welfare of the inmates. And there was a grave lack of control over the guards.
>
> This lack of supervision left open the possibility that the guards might not be able to control their resentments once they entered the Complex, and this apparently is exactly what happened. Some guards were striking back at defenseless inmates -- whom they hated and feared.
>
> This attitude of the guards was astonishingly evident when a group of them battered down the doors of the Psychological Testing Center -- a place where the inmates receive professional counseling -- on the pretext that an inmate might be hiding there, although some of the doors of the Center are glass so that the interior of the room was clearly visible. The Center is a place where the new theories of rehabilitation are actually put into practice -- and consequently is disliked by many of the guard force.
>
> After the pick up was completed, the guards let loose with a volly of firing to signal the completion of "their" sweep. This points up the attitude of the guards, and the lack of supervision over them.[12]

There was one dissenting member on the Committee who did not concur entirely with his fellow members, and he expressed his views as follows:

> Although I am in agreement with the majority's basic conclusions that, on November 18, some guards at Lorton acted completely irresponsibly and, in some instances, caused injuries without provocation, I nevertheless must disassociate myself from the majority's statement that in certain cases the guards' conduct amounted to a 'guard riot.'
>
> This characterization is so inexplicit -- yet containing a strong emotional connotation -- that its use results in an unfair and

> inaccurate overall picture of the Lorton correctional force. The broad brush stroke of a sensational label does not stand up under close scrutiny in what is an otherwise carefully considered report.
>
> Further, in my view, the report does not sufficiently reflect an underlying factor prevalent at the Lorton institution which is significant in understanding the unfortunate development of resentments and frustrations on the part of the conflicting forces. That factor was the presence within this medium-security facility of a group of intractable inmates, whose conduct and attitudes required their removal from the general inmate population. They were not removed for various reasons -- lack of facilities in the maximum security unit, lack of personnel, lack of space in Federal institutions where incorrigible Lorton inmates are frequently sent. Despite the reasons for their continued presence within the Complex, the fact remains that there were enough troublemakers to cause problems and they should not have been in such a medium-security facility.
>
> All levels within the Department administration agreed that there was need for a transfer of troublemakers. With the continued failure to find a solution and act on the removal, the atmosphere at the institution remained tense...But the lack of forceful, positive, and effective leadership at all levels of the Department administration was a contributing cause to the events of November 18.[13]

Mayor Washington further requested an assessment of the D.C. Department of Corrections by the Federal Bureau of Prisons, in an effort to identify some of the problem areas. The group directed its attention to four specific areas: management, personnel, facilities, and inmates. The summary of their findings follows:

> In summary, some perspective is necessary. The incredibly complex and intense conflicts that regularly attend attempts to move from correctional obsolescence to correctional

> progress and efficiency have been documented in the social science literature for years now. In that sense, the problems of the Lorton Reformatory are strictly old hat. This is the first time, in the knowledge of this writer, that the change attempt has been so inexorably intertwined with the overlying boundaries of community and national social change. And this is possibly the first time when the inmate group was so tied together in terms of community of origin, with previous bonds of friendship and kinship and race; and during an era when social activism and collective confrontation techniques have gained ascendance.
>
> Both officers and inmates are in a situation of injustice: officers because they were not prepared for or involved in the change; and inmates because of the consequences of having their status position in a tiny society where managerial failure from a long time ago has come to haunt and frustrate a staff so that staff vents its fury upon the inmates. At the same time, it should be recognized that there has been grave administrative recalcitrance at the institutional level. Any new administrative policy and administrative actors will first have to rearrange existing priorities to build a viable organization, and it will be a Herculean task. It will need both new and renovated facilities as well as new administrative insight to do the job. Changing the reformatory in this era will be a first order social experiment.[14]

Finally, Mayor Washington appointed a task force, February 3, 1969, to seek solutions to the many problems confronting the Department. In the introduction to its report to the Mayor, the task force reflected further on the disturbance of November 18, 1968:

> The 'Lorton incident' of November 18, 1968, used the language of violence and near tragedy to tell us that we are failing in our attempts to cope with the twin problems of crime and the rehabilitation of the criminal. The incident pointed up the terrible complexity of the task of restoring the offender to a

state of useful functioning in the community at large. It informed us that the Department of Corrections is torn between conflicting philosophies of harsh treatment and rehabilitation, between crowded, inadequate facilities, and the requirements of physical and mental health; between the militant attitudes of young black men from the troubled ghetto and the conservative philosophies of the white staff members from the rural and suburban communities.

* * *

The present report addresses itself to two tasks. First, it outlines a number of immediate actions that must be taken if troubles of even greater dimensions are to be averted in our jails and prisons. Second, it develops a plan for constructive long-range actions in our correctional agency and our criminal justice system.[15]

In outlining the remedial measures necessary to improve conditions within the Department, the Task Force took into consideration the fact that, with the exception of the Youth Center, the Department's physical plants were outdated and inadequate for the inmate population which was on the rise. At the Correctional Complex at Lorton, for example, the daily average population increased from 1066 in 1968, to 1401 in 1969. The racial distribution had changed over the years, and by 1969, black prisoners accounted for 89% of the Department's population, while 26% of the Department's personnel was black. The Task Force defined the Department's most urgent needs as falling into five areas:

(1) Improve and accelerate recruitment, provide effective training and modify social and racial composition of staff.

(2) Upgrading of institutions and structures for effective security, for health and safety, and for improved correctional climate and programs. Tighten security, improve housing and lighting, and decrease overcrowding.

(3) Development of effective programs for correctional rehabilitation: Add 173 officer, 19 counselor and 9 MTA positions;

develop new vocational and academic training programs; and redesign the prison industries program.

(4) Utilization of community resources, extension of correctional programs into the community. Expand the work release program, develop additional community-based programs, and foster self-help and citizen-sponsored activities.

(5) Creation and development of an effective, responsive management organization. Create needed executive positions, revise organizational structure, and clarify lines of communication and responsibility.[16]

The recommendations of the Task Force laid the groundwork for the expansion and organizational changes that would take place during the 1970s.

SOURCES

[1.] Report, Investigation of the D.C. Jail Incident of September 21, 1968, by Correctional Advisory Committee, dated December 10, 1968, on file in the D.C. Department of Corrections Museum, Lorton, Virginia, p. 1.

[2.] Ibid., pp. 8-9.

[3.] Report, Board of Inquiry of the Escapes and Disturbances at the Youth Center, dated October 22, 1968, pp. 6-7.

[4.] Ibid., p. 7.

[5.] Ibid., p. 10-15.

[6.] Ibid., p. 20.

[7.] Ibid., pp. 20-21.

[8.] Ibid., p. 22.

[9.] Ibid., p. 28.

[10.] Report on the Lorton Complex Incident, November 18, 1968, by the Mayor Commissioner's Temporary Committee to Investigate Activities at the Lorton Correctional Complex, on file in the D.C. Department of Corrections Museum, Lorton, Virginia, p. 1-2.

[11.] Ibid., p. 3.

[12.] Ibid., p. 60.

[13.] Ibid., (Appendix).

[14.] Federal Bureau of Prisons Report, "An Assessment of the D.C. Department of Corrections," December 18, 1968, on file in the D.C. Department of Corrections Museum, Lorton, Virginia, p. 12.

[15.] Hearings before the Committee on Business, Commerce, and the Judiciary of the Committee on the District of Columbia U. S. Senate, 92nd Congress, First Session, June 16-17, 1971, p. 216.

[16.] Ibid., p. 217.

CHAPTER 29

IMPACT OF COURT REFORM ACT ON THE CORRECTIONAL SYSTEM

The Court Reform and Criminal Procedure Act of 1970 was the result of the President's Crime Commission's recommendation for increasing the efficiency of the District Courts and the Police Department. Recognizing the effect the Act could have on the Department's inmate population, the Senate Sub-Committee on the District of Columbia held oversight hearings June 16-17, 1971, entitled "Court Reform Act Impact on Correctional System." Appearing before the Committee, Herbert J. Miller, former Chairman, President's Commission on Crime, testified as follows:

> ...The content of the Commission and the whole philosophy behind it tried to ascertain factually a study in which the administration of criminal justice operated in the District of Columbia. In too many instances decisions were made on surmised assumptions rather than hard facts.
>
> * * *
>
> We think the main result which came out of the Crime Commission in its objective study was the knowledge that any time you take steps to improve a part of the system you must at the same time look to the balance of the system because if it does not operate as a cohesive whole you are losing the advantage of the improvement that you tried to impose on a part of the system.
>
> We have hence seen in the District of Columbia a substantial increase in the number of police officers. We have seen a substantial reorganization of the police force. We have seen increases in the number of prosecutors assigned to the U.S. Attorney's office.
>
> Now, under the present format, we have seen a substantial increase in the availability of individual manpower and support personnel for the courts. The new superior court, in turn, has and will engender a substantial increase in the number of individuals going through the system.

The question which this committee has readily posed upon is: What steps have been taken, what steps can be taken, and what should be done with respect to the correctional system and all the outshoots thereof? We all know sitting here that there is going to be a substantial increase in the number of individuals who are convicted in the District of Columbia.

We can further assume, and I think properly assume, that there will be a substantial increase in the number of inmates in Lorton and other places of incarceration...The correctional system in conjunction with the other elements of the District of Columbia, have concluded on the basis of projections...that facilities at Lorton which have a rated capacity of 1384, by the end of fiscal 1972 may well have inmates in the numbers of 2300 or 2400; and an obvious problem with overcrowding.

The same thing we would find in respect to the Youth Center at Lorton which has a rated capacity of 324 and it is suggested that there would be from 495 to 618 inmates there by the end of fiscal 1972.

* * *

I am informed that right now there is a problem with the Youth Center. There are currently individuals who are waiting in the District of Columbia jail for transfer to the Youth Center. Judges will sentence individuals, they think under the Youth Corrections Act and because of the fact that there are insufficient facilities they remain in the local jail until such time there is a slot available at the Youth Center.

* * *

...I have read documentation and reports prepared by Mr. Hardy, who knows the work, and I must say if the reports are correct, and I have no reason to disbelieve it, that the correctional system in the District of Columbia has indeed made great strides over the past 2

> or 3 years. I think it is time that the correctional system should no longer be ignored in favor of the police, the prosecution, and the courts. I think it is gratifying the way it is handled in this jurisdiction. We have a correctional system which has moved forward while I think that there is room for improvement, and all I am saying is...on the basis of what I have seen what the correctional system has accomplished. I do think they are faced with a serious problem that greatly needs the help of this Committee. If the overcrowding foreseen comes to pass we are going to have, I think, a breakdown of the rehabilitation process that has been built up in the system and the net result will be an adverse impact on the system...[1]

The Committee heard testimony from the Director as well as other members of the Department's staff regarding the progress that had been made in implementing the President's Crime Commission recommendations as well as plans for coping with the overcrowding problem, expanding community corrections, and new treatment programs that would be introduced during the 1970s.

The Senate Sub-Committee favored expansion of the Community Corrections program as a method of reducing overcrowding in the institutions.

The increase in the inmate population placed a burden on the Department. Since the Workhouse and Women's Reformatory had been relinquished to the Health Department for use as Alcoholic Rehabilitation Centers, space in the remaining institutions was limited. Although plans were under way to build a new detention center to replace the old D.C. Jail, and plans were under consideration for extensive expansion of the Lorton reservation, under a project known as the Lorton Improvement Plan (LIP), it would be several years before construction of the detention center could be completed.

It is noted that the LIP project never materialized, although elaborate plans were made for expanding institutions on the Lorton reservation and money was appropriated. Consequently, the populations at the institutions remained overcrowded during the 1970s causing much unrest and disciplinary problems.

To relieve the overcrowded conditions at Youth Center I in 1972, the Department recovered the Women's Reformatory from the Health Department and converted it into a medium security facility for Youth Act offenders. The new institution could accommodate an inmate population of 225. Officially known as Youth Center II, it opened May 2, 1972. The academic and vocational programs at the new Youth Center were essentially the same as those of Youth Center I.

As part of the reorganization plan that began in 1968, several of the Department's support services that traditionally had been located on the Lorton reservation were relocated in Washington to carry out a centralization plan. The first to be relocated was the personnel and budget offices in 1970, followed by the finance and planning and research offices. The offices were temporarily located on First Street, S.E. in the District and later they were moved to the North Potomac Building, 614 H Street, N.W. which also housed a number of other city agencies.

SOURCES

[1.] U.S. Senate, Committee on the District of Columbia, Impact of the Court Reform and Criminal Procedure Act of 1970 on the Correctional Institutions in the District of Columbia, June 16-17, 1971, 92nd Congress, 1st Session (Washington, D.C.: U. S. Government Printing Office, 1971), pp. 2-5.

CHAPTER 30

THE DEPARTMENT IN CRISIS

"During the summer of 1972, the Department experienced a severe population increase brought about by the impact of the D.C. Court Reform Act. At its peak the population stood at 56% over rated capacity."[1] As a result of the overcrowded conditions, escapes and assaults increased as did general unrest within the inmate population, making the Department the target of adverse criticism by the news media. It was only natural that the notoriety should cause concern among the residents of Fairfax County for their safety. This in turn drew the attention of local Fairfax officials and Virginia authorities, along with Congressman Stanford E. Parris and Senator William L. Scott, both of whom represented Northern Virginia in the United States Congress at that time. Thus began a five-year attempt to close down the Lorton institutions either by take over by the Federal Bureau of Prisons or by removal of the inmate population from Fairfax County soil.

The first attempt to remove the Lorton facilities was an investigation of the Department's operations by a Special Select Committee of the Committee of the District of Columbia, (91st Congress, 2nd Session). The Special Select Committee held its investigation over a period of several months, and its findings were presented to the Honorable John W. McCormack, Speaker of the House, February 23, 1970. The findings cited a lengthy list of deficiencies within the Department, including improper chain of command, lack of prisoner discipline, escapes, narcotics in the institutions, manufacturing and drinking alcoholic beverages by the prisoners, sex perversion, weapons made from eating utensils, prison sanitation, hiring policies, training of personnel, contagious diseases of the prisoners, and visiting policies.

The conclusions reached by the Committee recommended that the Department's institutions located in Fairfax County, Virginia, be placed under the jurisdiction of the Federal Bureau of Prisons, as follows:

> The opportunity presented here to the Federal Bureau of Prisons, to implement their proven penology theories as to corrections, treatment and rehabilitation of prisoners, from first offender to that of recidivist, is fantastic.
>
> There further appears a quite unique bonus for the Federal Bureau of Prisons, in that by

having jurisdiction over the Reformatory at Lorton, Virginia, they will for the first time have jurisdiction over paroled prisoners. They will have a full opportunity to set up the D.C. penal system, as a model for the Nation to observe, from first admission to an institution, through that of parole.

In view of the documented depth of incompetence in the present operation, it is recommended that H.R. 11956, 91st Congress, 1st Session, by the Honorable William L. Scott of Virginia, be enacted into law as reported by the Special Select Subcommittee.[2]

A response to the Special Sub-Committee's allegations was made in the "Statement of Kenneth L. Hardy, Director, District of Columbia Department of Corrections before the Senate District Committee March 23, 1970." The following is an excerpt from that statement:

* * *

How does the proposed transfer stand in relation to professional correctional thought?

Recent studies of the Department of Corrections by the President's Commission on Crime for the District of Columbia, by a Study Group from the Bureau of Prisons, and by the District's Advisory Panel Against Armed Violence have spoken to this point. These distinguished groups all recognized the need for the District of Columbia to improve its correctional process. However, not one person spoke for fragmentation of the system.

The recommendations included changes in policy, shifts in organization, renovated facilities, expansion of community correctional processes, reduction of parole caseloads, further integration of the total correctional process -- all with the assistance of increased financial resources.

By approving the Department's 1970 budget, Congress has given the Department opportunity to make improvements -- to upgrade its facilities, to enlarge its staff, to increase

> its community programs -- in short, to strive for increased effectiveness in corrections.
>
> * * *
>
> It is fair to say, I think, that we have accomplished much in the past year or two. We have also learned a great deal. We have made careful studies of our effectiveness in rehabilitating prisoners, for example. It has been gratifying to learn that we have a relatively low recidivism rate -- compared with those few states that maintain records on their success and failures.
>
> This relatively good success rate is not, I think, an accident. It probably reflects a combination of sound correctional philosophy, appropriate institutional and community programs, and hard work by a dedicated staff. It comes from teamwork between the institutions at Lorton, the community programs in the District, and a supportive citizenry in the community at large.
>
> These results are now endangered by the proposed Lorton transfer. They are in danger because the transfer is contrary to sound correctional practice.[3]

While the Special Select Committee failed in its attempt to place the Lorton facilities under the Federal Bureau of Prisons, other attacks on the Department were quick to follow.

In a suit filed in the Fairfax County Circuit Court against the District of Columbia on January 4, 1973, Virginia's Attorney General, Andrew P. Miller, asked that the Lorton Correctional Complex be closed unless security at that facility was improved by the District prison officials. Virginia's plea for an injunction to halt operations at Lorton termed the institution "...a public nuisance, posing a threat to the Fairfax residents who live near it and a threat to the surrounding area's future economic development."[4] The suit cited the fact that "...79 Lorton inmates escaped during 1972 and that 39 of the escapees 'physically breached the security perimeter' at Lorton and fled into the surrounding countryside."[5] One specific incident noted was a 21 year old escapee who was arrested and charged with taking part in a bank robbery in December 1972 in which an "...Alexandria detective was shot to death."[6]

The suit brought by Attorney General Miller against the District drew criticism from Virginia's Governor, who stated that it was filed without his knowledge. An article by Harriet Griffiths, Staff Writer, appearing in the January 5, 1973 edition of the Star Newspaper states:

> Virginia Governor Linwood Holton today gave State Attorney General Andrew P. Miller an unprecedented tongue-lashing, calling Miller's lawsuit aimed at tightening security at Lorton Reformatory a 'source of embarrassment,' to the state.
>
> Holton said the suit filed in Fairfax Circuit Court yesterday could be 'most disruptive' to negotiations the governor has initiated to seek solutions to the reformatory's problems.
>
> * * *
>
> Holton said that he is 'totally sympathetic with any effort' to solve the problems of the reformatory, and that his office already had initiated talks with District officials.
>
> The governor also said he 'personally' had consulted with the offices of President Nixon and U.S. Attorney General Richard Kleindienst, according to the Associated Press.
>
> * * *
>
> And Kenneth L. Hardy, director of the D.C. Department of Corrections, charged that criticism of Lorton is often led by interests wanting to get the valuable piece of property away from the District.
>
> * * *
>
> Hardy agreed that security at Lorton was far from ideal, but maintained it was little worse than in the Virginia penal system and better than that in Maryland. While Lorton had 43.58 escapes, per 1000 prisoners in 1972, Virginia had 41.46 and Maryland 52.36, he said. The federal prison ratio was 30.38 during the year.

> The corrections chief also said that another 100 guards are in training for Lorton, bringing the total here to 432. The city's proposed budget for next fiscal year calls for 215 more corrections officers to be assigned to Lorton, he added.[7]

Fairfax County's Board of Supervisors also expressed concern that Attorney General Miller had filed the suit against the District without first notifying its members. At the time Attorney General Miller's suit was filed, the Fairfax County Board of Supervisors were in the process of negotiating with the District in matters regarding the following issues:

> In January 1974, Mayor Washington met with Fairfax officials to discuss problems such as fire protection services, sewage treatment, and which jurisdiction has legal-judicial authority over Youth Center One. At this meeting the Mayor shared with Fairfax County the proposal for improving the Lorton facilities.
>
> Further meetings were held in January and subsequent months to resolve such matters as modifying the water lines at Lorton so fire-fighting could be effective. Also, the two jurisdictions began preliminary work to establish a service contract for purchase of fire-fighting services.[8]

In time, however, the Fairfax County Board of Supervisors filed a "public nuisance suit" of its own against the District.

Within several weeks, Attorney General Miller's suit against the District had gained support in Virginia's House of Delegates. In a resolution that passed the Virginia Assembly by 97 votes out of the 100 house members, asked to give the Lorton issue "...most expeditious consideration and to take action assuring 'proper administration and security' at the penal institution in southern Fairfax County."[9] In addition the resolution charged that "...D.C. Administrators of the facility 'have responded to local citizen concern in an arrogant and most uncooperative manner.'"[10] In a speech before the Virginia Assembly on January 2, 1973, "...newly elected Delegate James R. Tate, (R-Fairfax) devoted his maiden speech to support of the plea for congressional action to transfer Lorton from the D.C. Department of Corrections to the U.S. Bureau of Prisons. Tate called the escape problem a 'national disgrace' and Lorton itself, 'a disaster waiting to happen.'"[11] The resolution filed by the Virginia Assembly further noted that "...escaped inmates last August broke into a Fairfax home near the complex in the middle of the night and held a family hostage before fleeing in the family's car."[12]

A meeting was held February 2, 1973, at the District Building, in which Attorney General Miller and the Fairfax Board of Supervisors met with a representative of the District's Corporation Counsel and officials from the Department to "...discuss the suit and 'problems in general' at the penal institution in southern Fairfax County."[13] Earlier that same week, the suit was transferred to the Federal District Court in Alexandria, Virginia.

The Department of Corrections' efforts to improve and maintain security at its Lorton facilities finally met with the approval of Attorney General Miller and he decided to drop the case against the District. "This decision was formalized in a March 1, 1975 Court Order, successfully ending months of negotiations by the two jurisdictions. The Order specified twelve security improvements, recommended and endorsed by the Attorney General..."[14] In time, the Fairfax County Suit was also dropped.

Meanwhile, Congressman Parris and Senator Scott introduced legislation "...which would require a federal takeover of the Lorton Correctional Complex..."[15] The January 24, 1973, edition of the Evening Star Newspaper carried an article by Jack Kneece from which the following excerpts are taken:

> Parris said he is coordinating his efforts with Scott in what will be an all-out congressional effort to resolve the issue early in this session of Congress.
>
> * * *
>
> SCOTT YESTERDAY wrote U.S. Attorney General Richard Kleindienst about the security problem at Lorton, asking that the Justice Department take a position. He sent a similar letter to the ranking minority member of the Senate Judiciary Committee...
>
> A spokesman said Scott feels a boost by the Justice Department will enhance chances for the legislation in the Senate.[16]

In addition to the legislation he introduced for the takeover of Lorton in June 1973, Congressman Parris requested an audit of the Department by the General Accounting Office (GAO).

"The purpose of the audit was to look into the Department's security management at its Lorton Complex."[17] After a year long investigation, a report entitled, "Better Management Needed for Tighter Security at Lorton Correctional Installations," (District of Columbia Government B-118638), was issued June 21, 1974. The scope of the audit included the following:

> --Reviewing District records, policies, and procedures and interviewing officials responsible for managing, administering and operating the Department.
>
> --Visiting the facilities at Lorton and interviewing staff responsible for the day-to-day activities.
>
> --Visiting several facilities operated by the Bureau of Prisons of the Department of Justice, and discussing certain operating policies and procedures with its officials.[18]

In general, the GAO report cited as some of the most pressing problems: the large number of escapes by inmates from the Lorton institutions, the steady increase of assaults by inmates on other inmates and on correctional officers; insufficient testing for drug abuse in the inmate population; insufficient restrictions of contraband in the institutions (contraband that could be made into dangerous weapons); excessive granting of rehabilitation furloughs for the community outreach and college programs. In addition, the report suggested remedial measures be taken such as uniform and definitive guidelines be established for the institutions in selecting inmates for rehabilitative furloughs; each release program should be assessed regularly to determine whether it is serving a legitimate purpose; perimeter security should be tightened, as well as security inside the institutions; investigation of all escapes; the District's office of Planning and Management should maintain a close working relationship with the Department, "...to insure that effective corrective action is taken on management problems;"[19] and "...that the Office of Municipal Audit and Inspections periodically review Department operations to help insure that the operations continue to be efficient and effective."[20]

The Department responded to each allegation made in the GAO document, with a 34 page paper which noted: "The Department has taken solid steps to increase its security, steps which have demonstrated some success. With this fear reduced, it is hoped that the Department will in the future be judged on how well it meets its rehabilitation mandate as well as its security obligations."[21] Perimeter escapes at the Central Facility were greatly reduced with such improvements as increasing the number of correctional officers used in that area, routine patrol of the perimeter roads, improved lighting at the fence line. Later in 1976, electronic surveillance equipment was installed on the fence line, permitting the tower officers to observe the fence line area by closed circuit television.

Steps were taken to control the flow of contraband into the institutions by updating entrance regulations. Some of the new features included use of metal detectors, procedures for checking visitors' purses and packages, searching visitors and employees alike, use of ultra-violet light marking for visitors and restricting visitors from wearing blue denim jeans, since it is part of the inmates' dress. In 1974, for the first time ever, women correctional officers were permitted to work in the Department's male institutions. At that time, they were employed to perform search duty of female visitors entering the Department's male institutions, as a part of the effort to reduce contraband being brought into the institutions. Prior to that time, female visitors were not searched upon entering the male institutions, since regulations prohibit male officers from searching females. Originally, the duty post of the women officers was limited to the check point at the entrance of the institutions. In time, however, they were assigned other duties in the male institutions and today, they work side by side with the male officers.

Other remedial measures by the Department included improvement of the urine surveillance program, closer monitoring of the community outreach and college programs by assigning two correctional officers to monitor the inmates who were participating in those activities.

Senator Scott was persistent in his attempts to remove the Department's correctional institutions from Southern Fairfax County. "His first Bill, S. 375, was defeated on July 10, 1973. His later attempt to amend the Home Rule Bill also failed, on January 30, 1974."[22] The third Bill, S. 1243 (1975), designed to move the Lorton prison facility to the District, also failed. The Senate Judiciary Committee's Subcommittee on National Penitentiaries held hearings on Bill S. 1243, which, in effect, would have forced the District of Columbia to move Lorton prison facilities to the District. The Bill provided that $55.4 million of District Capital funds be transferred to the Attorney General of the United States, directing him to sell the Lorton Reservation and use the proceeds, along with the Capital funds to purchase sites and construct penal facilities in the District by 1978. In the event that plan failed, the Bill further provided that the Attorney General transfer the District prisoners to the Federal Bureau of Prisons.

The Department strongly opposed Senator Scott's Bill, and prepared a lengthy paper to defend its position, from which the following is quoted:

> There are a number of problems with the Scott Bill. In the first place, there is no land available in the District. In 1971, in conjunction with site location efforts for the New Detention Center, over 100 parcels were surveyed. These were reduced to eighteen locations and then to nine, on which a detailed study was conducted. One significant difference between the requirements for the New Detention Center and those for a sentencing facility is the size parcel required. In the case of the Detention Center, nine acres were determined sufficient. A sentencing facility will require 35 to 40 acres for programmatic and recreation needs, and to produce the requisite living conditions for those who must remain for an extended period of time. The differing size requirement automatically rules out some of the sites considered in the New Detention Center study.
>
> Recently, these sites were again reviewed, as well as added possible locations. Since seven institutions will be required to reproduce Lorton within the parameters of the Lorton Improvement Plan, the potential exists (including the New Detention Center) for two major correctional facilities in each quadrant of the City. There are no large tracts of land available, and one quickly reaches the conclusion that size is by no means the only problem. In some cases, park land would have to be utilized. In other cases, homes and property would have to be condemned. In all cases, the use would be incompatible with surrounding development, both because of its nature and the proximity which would be required. The net result is that what now exists on 3500 acres in Lorton would be jammed into 300 acres in the District of Columbia.
>
> This leads automatically to the second major problem: It is impossible to reproduce

Lorton anywhere except on a similar tract of land. There are a number of physical and programmatic advantages to the Lorton Reservation. Not the least of these is buffering — the open space separation which exists between the institutions and the surrounding residential uses, and of the institutions, one from the other. This could not be reproduced in the District.

Open space at Lorton also permits an extensive agricultural operation upon which the Department depends for many of its consumable supplies. Prison Industries would have difficulty in finding a suitable location in the District. A number of economies would be lost with the necessary abandonment of central maintenance, warehousing, commissary, garage, and transportation units. Advantageous in the present location is the ability to centralize medical services, and the entire medical services delivery system would have to be reviewed in the event of disbursal. The Lorton institutions have operated as an integrated programmatic unit for a number of years, and the systems of training, rehabilitation, and counseling as they now exist would suffer a breakdown through relocation and would have to be restructured.

A third problem is cost. A conservative estimate on land acquisition alone is $57,000,000. To reproduce the institutions and auxiliary facilities under the Lorton Improvement Plan, design and capacity will require $116,000,000. This totals $173,000,000 against which only $70,000,000 would be available ($55,000,000 in existing Lorton Improvement Plan funds, and an estimated $15,000,000 from the sale of the land at Lorton). This means $103,000,000 additional dollars will have to be found, a fact which is alone sufficient to illustrate the impractibility of the proposal.

The prohibitive cost engendered by the Scott Bill, the unreal time limitations of the Bill, the unpopularity of the facilities in Virginia, and the incompatibility of the proposed land use in the District of Columbia

> all point to the fourth major problem: The net result of the entire transaction will, in all probability, be transfer of prisoners to the Federal system. This means disbursal of D.C. prisoners to a Federal system which is basically unready to receive them. Norman Carlson, the Director of the Federal Bureau of Prisons, has recently testified that the Federal Bureau is currently 20% over capacity. Prisoners who now benefit from proximity to home environment, ready accessibility for visiting purposes, and an extensive community contact and outreach program, would be distributed across the United States. This is an absolute variance with modern penological thinking, where the trend has been to bring prisoners closer to home so that they can benefit from the rehabilitative effects of community ties. This is perhaps the most severe impact of the Bill.
>
> The motivating factors behind the Scott proposal are not clear. A number of suggestions for the use of the property, which almost take on the aspect of a 'want list,' have been made, incorporating recreation, moderate income housing, or even a national cemetary. The interest of real estate developers is unknown, except it has been calculated that a profit of between $7,500,000 and $12,500,000 could be realized on subdivision and improvement alone, without taking into consideration the profit on the sale of homes. A small city of some 15,000 to 25,000 people, depending on density, could be located in the roughly six square miles represented by Lorton. The racial composition of the Department has changed, which could also be a subtle motivating factor.[23]

While the attempts to remove the Department's institutions from Fairfax County were unsuccessful and the law suits and investigations subsided during the latter half of the 1970s, the idea still remains and is used by the local politicians as an issue at election time. Some of the local citizens still voice their fears in having to share their community with penal institutions, even though the Department has effected many improvements in its security and has kept escapes to a minimum since the mid-seventies. The most regrettable aspect of the antagonism that exists on the part of the local citizens of

Fairfax County against the District and the Department is the loss of the spirit of friendship and cooperation that existed between them in the years prior to the 1970s.

SOURCES

[1.] District of Columbia Position Paper on Senate Bill 1234, July 9, 1975, on file in the D.C. Department of Corrections Museum, Lorton, Virginia, p. 51.

[2.] Special Select Subcommittee, Report, "Investigation and Study of the Department of Corrections of the District of Columbia," Committee on the District of Columbia House of Representatives, 91st Congress, Second Session, U.S., (Washington, D.C.: U.S. Government Printing Office, 1970), p. 30.

[3.] Hardy, Kenneth L., Director, District of Columbia Department of Corrections, Statement before the Senate District Committee, March 23, 1970, on file in the D.C. Department of Corrections Museum, Lorton, Virginia.

[4.] Kelly, Brian and Love, Thomas, "Virginia Sues D.C. to Close Lorton," _Evening Star Newspaper,_ January 4, 1973, Clipping file, D.C. Department of Corrections Museum, Lorton, Virginia, p. A1.

[5.] _Ibid.,_ p. A1.

[6.] _Ibid.,_ p. A6.

[7.] Griffiths, Harriet, "Holton Hits Miller for Lorton Lawsuit," _Evening Star Newspaper,_ January 5, 1973, Washington, D. C., p. A1.

[8.] District of Columbia Position Paper on Senate Bill 1243, July 1975, on file in the D.C. Department of Corrections Museum, Lorton, Virginia, pp. 20, 21.

[9.] Bredemeier, Kenneth, "Takeover of Lorton is Urged," _Washington Post Newspaper,_ January 23, 1973, on file in the D.C. Department of Corrections Museum, Lorton, Virginia.

[10.] _Ibid._

[11.] _Evening Star Newspaper,_ January 23, 1973, on file in the D.C. Department of Corrections Museum, Lorton, Virginia.

[12.] Bredemeier, Kenneth, "Take Over of Lorton is Urged," _Washington Post Newspaper,_ January 23, 1973, on file in the D.C. Department of Corrections Museum, Lorton, Virginia.

[13.] "Virginia, D.C. to Meet on Lorton Suit," Evening Star Newspaper, February 1, 1973, Clipping file, D.C. Department of Corrections Museum, Lorton, Virginia.

[14.] District of Columbia Position Paper on Senate Bill 1243, July 9, 1975, on file in the D.C. Department of Corrections Museum, Lorton, Virginia, p. 24.

[15.] Keece, Jack, "U. S. Takeover of Lorton Proposed in Senate Bill," Evening Star Newspaper, January 24, 1973, Clipping file, D.C. Department of Corrections Museum, Lorton, Virginia.

[16.] Ibid.

[17.] Response by D.C. Department of Corrections to Comptroller General's Report to the Honorable Stanford E. Parris (date?), on file in the D.C. Department of Corrections, Office of Planning and Program Analysis, p. 1.

[18.] Comptroller General's Report to Honorable Stanford E. Parris, "Better Management Needed for Tighter Security at Lorton Correctional Institutions, June 21, 1974, on file in the D.C. Department of Corrections, Office of Planning and Program Analysis, p. 42.

[19.] Ibid., p. 5.

[20.] Ibid., p. 5.

[21.] Introduction and Background of Response by D.C. Department of Corrections to Comptroller General's Report to Stanford E. Parris, on file D.C. Department of Corrections, Office of Planning and Program Analysis, p. 3.

[22.] District of Columbia Position Paper on Senate Bill 1243, on file inthe D.C. Department of Corrections Museum, Lorton, Virginia, p. 51.

[23.] Synopsis of Position Paper on Senate Bill 1243, Lorton Transfer Bill, undated, on file in the D.C. Department of Corrections Museum, Lorton, Virginia, pp. 2-5.

CHAPTER 31

EXPANSION OF COMMUNITY CORRECTIONS

Although the Prisoner's Rehabilitation Act of 1965 authorized community correctional centers as alternative housing for inmates involved in work release, the Department did not actually embark upon an expansion plan for such facilities until late in 1969. An important factor in the slow beginning of the program was community resistance to such centers being placed in certain neighborhoods:

> Any community correctional center program is based upon two major premises: that the community has the resources which can help to integrate the offender, and that the community is willing to accept the past offender into its midst and offer its resources. In the District of Columbia the community as represented by groups of neighborhood citizens, local businesses, and police officials has been antagonistic towards the community center program at one time or another.
>
> In the fall of 1969 the Department sought to open a correctional center in a semi-residential neighborhood. Several local residents and business concerns successfully organized against the center and petitioned the Court to issue an injunction against the Department on the grounds that the rooming house license under which the Department sought to operate the halfway house did not cover such buildings. The trial focused upon the definition of rooming houses and whether or not a halfway house met that definition. In March 1970, the U.S. District Court issued a permanent injunction preventng Department use of the site under question as a halfway house.
>
> Organized neighborhood resistance to halfway houses again occurred beginning June 1971 with the opening of a halfway house in Southeast Washington...This time the D.C. Board of Zoning Adjustment initially ruled that the halfway house in question could not claim rooming house status. However, due to pressure from the Mayor and members of the D.C. Zoning Commission which establishes the District's Zoning policy, the Board voted in August 1971

to delay its order pending a Commission draft of rules governing halfway houses. In April 1972, after public notice and hearings as prescribed by law, the District's zoning regulations were amended to include a definition of halfway houses and to permit these facilities in semi-residential or less restricted districts pursuant to certain provisions.

At the same time, in 1971, the neighborhood residents were protesting halfway houses, the District's police department and its Office of Criminal Justice Plans and Analysis began to challenge the Department's administration of its halfway house program. They were particularly critical of the number of halfway house residents who were being arrested, and the Office of Criminal Justice Plans and Analysis recommended a moratorium on halfway houses pending further evaluation. For a time the controversy as played out in the local press threatened to alienate the police department and the correctional system. Proponents of one extreme claimed that an overly permissive Department of Corrections was turning hardened criminals willy nilly into the streets while the other extreme suggested that political pressure and a repressive law-and-order element in highest government levels sought to turn the clock back on community-based corrections.

The controversy resulted in the Department's temporary suspension of halfway house expansion. Subsequent events reduced the tension. As of 1971, once the initial fervor subsided, communication between the police and the Department began to improve, in large part due to the Mayor who in October 1971 pointed out that the whole area of conditional release was a problem and he did not want Corrections singled out for examination. In April 1972 procedures for an outside in-depth three-year program evaluation of the community centers was initiated by the Office of Criminal Justice Plans and Analysis. By the summer of 1972 relations between the police and Corrections had substantially improved...[1]

Much of the credit for the development of community corrections in the District goes to M. Robert Montilla, who served as Deputy Director of the Department from 1969 through 1971. An article appearing in the Evening Star, December 10, 1971, at the time of his resignation from the Department, noted:

> In the brief span of three years, the prison reforms wrought by M. Robert Montilla have created a virtual revolution in the District's corrections system. Its programs of narcotics treatment, halfway houses and other types of prisoner release, for which Montilla as deputy director was chiefly responsible, are thought to be the most innovative in the nation. His resignation this week, while anticipated, leaves an immense gap, which the mayor must fill by seeking a replacement of equal ability from outside the city government.
>
> The furor that led to Montilla's demotion and subsequent resignation centered not so much on the concepts of halfway houses and other community programs as on the manner in which those projects were controlled and administered. Certain policies of prisoner release were challenged strongly by police and District Building officials....
>
> It had been our hope that a solution might be found under which Montilla could remain. But Montilla, for his part, was as intractable in relations with his superiors as he was in commitment to the programs he was defending. And the political in-fighting early in the game reached a point of such bitterness that his continued effectiveness became doubtful if not impossible.
>
> * * *
>
> But the more important consideration, as Montilla noted in his letter of resignation to the mayor, is that 'Only correctional processes which deeply involve the community and the former offender can be expected to restore him to an acceptable new role in the community. We have moved very fast,' he said. 'Yet, I sincerely hope that what is now happening is only a pause to catch our breath before we

> continue both in service to the city and as an important national demonstration.'[2]

The opening in June 1968 of a community treatment center for selected youthful (CTCY) offenders marked the Department's first direct involvement in the administration of halfway houses. "This halfway house originally opened August 1965, on the third floor of the YMCA, under the joint administration of the Federal Bureau of Prisons, the Department of Corrections and the United Planning Organization."[3] The center, with a capacity of 15 men, accepted referrals from the Department's Youth Center, as well as Federal Youth institutions. "The reversion to Department administration resulted in the program moving into a separate building and the center's residents consisting solely of Departmental referrals."[4]

The first halfway house for adult offenders to be administered by the Department opened September 1969. Known as Community Correctional Center Number One, "...It was established to house participants in the Department's Work-Release Program which began in 1966 and originally operated out of a correctional institution. The decision to move the program into halfway houses was based upon the Department's hopes to develop treatment more relevant to the community and the Department's recognition of the limitations and drawbacks of an institutionally operated work-release program"[5]

In an effort to cope with the ever increasing number of heroin addicts within its institutions, in September 1969, the Department established a correctional center with a program specifically designed for those inmates. The center, "...in addition to operating individual and group therapy sessions, providing urine surveillance, and helping with job placement, became the Department's center for the administration of methadone both for daily maintenance and as a withdrawal aid."[5] The center was later transferred to the District's Narcotic Treatment Administration (NTA) which served "...as the umbrella agency in the District's fight against drugs."[6]

"As of November 1972, there were 12 centers which housed approximately 450 individuals or 14 percent of the convicted population."[7] Some of the centers were operated by the Department, while others were administered by private organizations. For example, the Psychiatric Institute Foundation which opened Euclid House, October 1970, was the District's first halfway house to adopt the "therapeutic community" approach to treatment. "In accordance with these principles, the house emphasizes treatment based upon current behavior."[8] the therapeutic community approach "...encourages resident responsibility for treatment and house operations,..."[9] emphasizing group therapy as the mode of treatment.

Another privately operated center was Efforts From Ex-Convicts (EFEC), Inc., which opened in 1970. That particular center was "...run by and for ex-offenders."[10] The method of treatment used by EFEC included "...a trifold program of job development and placement, follow through, and counseling."[11]

Still another privately operated halfway house was Social Educational Research Development, Inc., (SERD) which emphasized educational and vocational training for youthful offenders.

"The first halfway home for women in the District opened in 1968 as a component of the D.C. Health Department's Drug Addiction program, under a contract with the Bureau of Rehabilitation."[12]

Expansion of the halfway house program took a number of different approaches to community corrections. One novel approach was the "Lincoln Heights Project" which began January 25, 1971, and is described in the following press release issued by the Department:

> Next Monday (January 25) a group of inmates from Lorton Reformatory and some ex-offenders will pick up their tools and start rebuilding part of Washington.
>
> The men, 16 of them, will begin the renovation of six 2-bedroom units at the vandalized Lincoln Heights Apartments, operated by the National Capitol Housing Authority (NCHA). It will take an anticipated nine weeks to complete the work and cost the authority $32,780.55.
>
> D.C. Department of Corrections Director Kenneth L. Hardy, who brought up the idea at a recent meeting of Mayor Walter E. Washington's cabinet, said the project is somewhat experimental and that, initially at least, the inmates and ex-offenders would work only on the six apartments. 'We are not, however, adverse to taking on the whole 591 units if this pilot program works out. I am confident our men can and will do a good job, one of which Mayor Washington and the entire city can be proud.'

> Initially, the workers will renovate one or two apartments so they can live in a setting identical to that of other releasees in the Department's 12 Community Correctional Centers (halfway houses) where men participate in work release.
>
> The construction group will meet all the work conditions for the type of work they'll do. They will be paid prevailing wages ranging from $5.16 an hour for the supervisor (an ex-offender) to $3.99 for laborer-trainee.
>
> Claude L. Burgin, supervisory manpower development specialist, will be the project administrator and Robert Goodloe, NCHA training officer, will coordiate the agency's role. They and other Department staff members have worked out a detailed work schedule, and will maintain liaison with interested community, business and union representatives.
>
> During the day, the men will work under the direction of the supervisor, but at night they will be the responsibility of professional staff who will live and work with them.[13]

An article in the Evening Star Newspaper, February 11, 1971, written by Lurma Rackley, noted: "Although the renovating process is in the early stages, the halfway house (the first apartment building to be worked on) is beginning to look like a college dormitory. There is a pool table and TV set and the bedrooms are freshly painted and comfortable."[14] The article further quoted Charles Lindsay, administrator of the halfway house who stated: "We have correctional counselors who supervise the individuals and assist them in budgeting and who help involve the family in the man's return."[15]

One of the most progressive programs in the trend toward community corrections was the Youth Crime Control Project. Established in 1970, it was the first attempt by the Department to establish a program for treating youthful offenders in the community as an alternative to the traditional institutional setting. In addition, it was the first of its kind in the nation.

> The D.C. Department of Corrections in 1970 received approval from the D.C. Government and from Congress to undertake an experimental project in correctional treatment of Youth

> Corrections Act cases. The project was to be based on random assignment of YCA offenders, ages 18-26, to two correctional modalities. Modality No. 1 was the regular practice of the Department with Youth Act cases: incarceration in the D.C. Youth Center, which was a progressive training institution where the young prisoners were exposed to academic and vocational training, plus a variety of psychological and social treatment options, with stays averaging about one year.
>
> Modality No. 2 was to consist of treatment in a community correctional center which was organized as a therapeutic community, with provision for several stages of development, starting with 30 or more days of 24-hour supervision, followed by return to the outside in work-release or study-release status, progressing through graduate and alumni phases, and moving into regular parole status in about 24 months.
>
> * * *
>
> ...Thiry-two delinquent, male youths reside in a 52-room "halfway house" in an inner city residential area in Washington, D.C. The residence provides a minimum security setting in which practically all signs of traditional institutional incarceration have been eliminated. There are no barred windows, locked doors, guards, or uniforms.[16]

Operating as a therapeutic community, the project attempted "...to change not merely the superficial behaviors of the men but rather their deep-seated attitudes, identities, and personal-social orientations."[17]

The project was operated with a staff of 25 members, including professionals, employment specialists, ex-offenders, secretaries, and food service personnel. "All staff were given 60 hours of training in the aspects of a therapeutic community by the Psychiatric Institute Foundation of Washington, D.C."[18]

The students were Black male offenders between the ages of 18 and 26, who had been sentenced under the Federal Youth Corrections Act, and were chosen by random selection from a larger group from the diagnostic unit of the Youth Center. Excluded from the project were men with I.Q.'s below 80, "...or charges of murder, forcible rape or other notorious crimes, or with other charges pending."[19] The control subjects had the same criteria for selection.

The project was to have run as a five-year research demonstration program, however, because of a dispute over its effectiveness and the Department's funding priorities, it was terminated in March 1974, after four years in operation.

Although the community correctional center concept became an integral part of the Department, most of the centers that were opened in the late 1960s and early 1970s have been closed. As of 1982, the Department operates three centers and contracts with the Bureau of Rehabilitation, EFEC, and the Washington Halfway House for Women for three additional ones.

SOURCES

[1.] Halfway Houses for Criminal Offenders in the District of Columbia: A Brief Review of their Origin and Operation, undated, on file in the D.C. Department of Corrections Museum, Lorton, Virginia, p. not numbered.

[2.] "The City's Loss," The Evening Star Newspaper, Friday, December 10, 1971, Clipping file (1951-1975), D.C. Department of Corrections Museum, Lorton, Virginia.

[3.] Halfway Houses for Criminal Offenders in the District of Columbia: A Brief Review of their Origin and Operation, undated, on file in the D.C. Department of Corrections Museum, Lorton, Virginia, p. not numbered.

[4.] Ibid.

[5.] Ibid.

[6.] Ibid.

[7.] Ibid.

[8.] Ibid.

[9.] Ibid.

[10.] Ibid.

[11.] Ibid.

[12.] Ibid.

[13.] Public Information Service, D.C. Department of Corrections, Press Release, January 19, 1971, Re: Lincoln Heights Project, on file in the D.C. Department of Corrections Museum, Lorton, Virginia (Halfway Houses).

[14.] Rackley, Lurma, The Evening Star Newspaper, February 11, 1971, Clipping File (1951-1975), D.C. Department of Corrections Museum, Lorton, Virginia.

[15.] Ibid.

[16.] Auerbach, Anita and Adams, Stewart, "The Youth Crime Control Project, Progress Report No. 1.," June 1971, D. C. Department of Corrections Museum, Lorton, Virginia, pp. 1, 10.

[17.] *Ibid.,* p. 11.

[18.] *Ibid.,* p. 11.

[19.] *Ibid.,* p. 12.

CHAPTER 32

EXPANSION OF INMATE SELF-HELP ORGANIZATIONS

The idea of self-help among the inmate population of the District's penal institutions was not new in the 1970s. In fact, it will be recalled that the first attempt by inmates to organize for the purpose of self-help began at the Workhouse in the early 1920s when the inmates formed the "Inmates' League," an organization that offered friendly support to each other and cooperation with the administration.

Over the years, other self-help groups gradually emerged, beginning with the inmate publication of "Time and Tied," a small newspaper first published in May 1939. The early issues were circulated to other penal institutions throughout the United States and on a small scale to members of the local community. Eventually, the publication became a member of the International Institutional Press Association. A slight change in the name of the publication from "Time and Tied" to "Time and Tide" was made. Over the years, the responsibility for carrying on the tradition of the publication was passed from one group of inmates to another. The Editor and Chief of "Time and Tide in 1977, described the publication as follows:

> Since the birth of this inmate publication, Time and Tide has constantly made improvements in the area of a better structured lay-out format, a wider range of news coverage, improved art work and relative issues pertaining to the changing times. The circulation to the community has increased over the years, there are approximately 800 subscribers on its mailing file, which include community and penal exchange. Time and Tide is free of charge to anyone requesting copies of this publication. From incoming letters from across the country, indicates that Time and Tide is one of the most modern inmate publications throughout the penal system.[1]

Another early self-help group was Alcoholics Anonymous which began around 1946 through the assistance of representatives from the Washington, D.C. chapter of that organization. Alcoholics Anonymous was one of the few programs the Department could rely on for help with the overwhelming problem of alcoholism in the inmate population prior to the Easter Decision.

Self-help expressed in the form of arts and crafts has long been practiced in the Department's institutions. Both men and women prisoners have fashioned crafts such as leather work, jewelry, and needle work as a leisure time activity as well as a means of earning small amounts of money from the sale of such items. Visual arts have also thrived among the inmate population. From time to time, inmate artists have left their mark on the walls of the institutions. One such contribution was the murals that graced the walls of the rotunda of the old D.C. Jail. The hammered brass "Stations of the Cross" which hang on the walls of the Catholic Chapel at the Correctional Complex were fashioned by an accomplished artist who was confined in the Reformatory for men in the early 1960s. The same artist also built a scale model of the Correctional Complex at Lorton. The model is complete in every detail, including every building and the shrubbery as well. The model has been used over the years by the Department's training staff to acquaint new employees with the layout of the Correctional Complex.

Early in 1970, the concept of self-help within the inmate population took on a new dimension. The Department's Adult Services Division at that time was under the supervision of John O. Boone, who introduced a totally new self-help program on a much wider scale than had been practiced by the Department in the past. The new program, "Self-help and Community Outreach," as the name implies, had a twofold purpose: 1) to afford the inmate an opportunity to help himself in the rehabilitation process, and 2) to foster a better understanding between the community and the correctional institution. The community outreach portion of the program was made possible by authority contained in Title 18, U.S.C. 4082, Public Law 89-176 (79 Stat. 674). Under that authority, five types of furloughs were available to the inmate population of the Department, including death bed and funeral visits, employment contacts, medical, community program, and other compelling reasons. Under the category of "other compelling reasons," the Department developed the "evaluative furlough." Its purpose was to permit inmates who met certain criteria to prove their trustworthiness and ability to function in the community for periods of time ranging from 12 to 48 hours. The evaluative furlough provided an opportunity for the inmates to reestablish community ties with families and neighborhoods. The first test of the evaluative furlough was made on Thanksgiving Day 1970, when the Superintendent of Adult Services released 170 inmates to spend the holiday with their families. The inmates were given 12-hour furloughs, and all 170 returned to the institution at the end of the 12 hours. Again, at Christmas of the same year, 250 men were released on a 12-hour furlough to spend the holiday with their families. One inmate absconded from the Christmas furlough. However, there were no known crimes committed by any of the inmates while in the community. The evaluative furlough made it possible for inmates who met the criteria to receive that furlough to participate in community programs on an ongoing basis.

The inmate population responded to this program with considerable enthusiasm, and, within a short period of time, there were approximately 36 self-help groups within the Central Facility. Six of those groups were engaged in community outreach activities on an ongoing basis. For example, one group whose interest was in work-study attended Washington Technical Institute on a half day basis and worked with the profoundly handicapped children the remaining half of the day. The program provided the men with para-professional skills that could be utilized upon their release to the community while providing a one-to-one relationship which the handicapped child might not otherwise experience.

Another group known as the "Youth Guidance Council" worked as tutors with children who were wards of the D.C. Welfare Department at the Laurel, Maryland Center and the D.C. Receiving Home. Still another group known as "Save a Child" provided planned recreation for the children in the Kenilworth area. A group known as the "Intensive Narcotic Group," originally a therapy group under the leadership of Psychologist William Bedanus, participated in narcotic seminars in the community schools, talking to the students regarding drugs and performing psychodrama to dramatize the evils of drug abuse.

One of the most successful self-help groups was known as "Inner Voices," a creative expression dramatic group that wrote its own material and was responsible for its own direction. Directing its efforts toward drug abuse and social injustice, the Inner Voices presented over three hundred performances in the community, performing in many area high schools, colleges, military installations, government and civic organizations and on all of the major television channels in the metropolitan area. In addition, the Inner Voices recorded for the Voice of America, and Radio Free Europe, and participated in a National Conference of the American Red Cross and a conference held by the National Alliance of Business Men. In 1972, the Inner Voices did a one hour film for Public Television using material written by the group's director, entitled "Holidays Hollow Days," depicting Christmas in prison. The film has been shown on Public Television Channels throughout the United States.

In addition to the community outreach programs, several groups organized with affiliation in national organizations such as the Junior Chamber of Commerce and the Toastmaster's

International. Other groups organized along religious lines. For these groups, representatives from the community came to the institution to participate with the inmates in seminars and other forms of interaction that provided an opportunity to foster a better understanding between the prisoner and the community.

A unique inmate group known as the "D.C. Citizens Council for Criminal Justice" was formed as the result of an experimental conference held at Shenandoah College, Winchester, Virginia, and co-sponsored by the Department of Corrections and the National College of State Trial Judges, June 12-20, 1970. The conference brought together participants in every phase of the District's criminal justice system, including judges, policemen, correctional personnel, prosecutors, defense attorneys, probation and parole authorities and private citizens. An added element was the presence of 18 consultants in the field of criminal justice and inmates from the Department's institutons to represent the "consumer" of the criminal justice system.

The workshop was directed by "...the Berkeley Associates: Dr. Richard Korn, a criminologist, Dr. David Fogel, a sociologist, and Douglas Rigg, a public defender; local planning and counsel for the Berkeley Associates and the National College was conducted by Ronald Goldfarb and Linda Singer, Washington Attorneys."[2]

The workshop was devoted to seeking solutions to the many problems that beset the District's criminal justice system. Through psychodrama and role playing, the workings of the police, court, prison and parole were explored. The following is an excerpt from the report on the workshop:

> Whatever their individual conclusions, all the participants left Winchester with the feeling that they had shared a unique and hopeful experience--that something special had happened. We criticized; "told it like it was" on each other and in front of each other; we cajoled and cried and--to some immeasurable degree--we came closer together. Prisoners told policemen what it was like to be arrested; depicted the problems involved in the police breaking up a family fight. Judges justified their sentencing procedures to people they had sentenced; prisoners and guards told of the brutalities that prisoners inflict on one another. There was intensive, no-holds barred interaction among people who had previously

> been strangers or who were so inhibited by the trappings of their official roles that they had been unable to break through their stereotypes and relate to one another on a personal level. The open, frank commuication carried over to informal, prolonged evening sessions, and by the end of the week, no matter what his position, every participant was less ambivalent as to where he stood.
>
> The participants resolved to concentrate their efforts on developing private, unofficial methods of aiding both offender and victims. It was the concensus of the group that the private establishment and the public officials of our city must trust, ally with and support members of the inner-city community, particularly the ex-offenders in an effort to better our criminal justice system; that only together we can do the job.[3]

When the workshop ended, the inmates who participated formed the self-help group known as the D.C. Citizens Council for Criminal Justice, to perpetuate the interest and interaction between the institution and the community that was generated by the workshop.

Another attempt by the Department to encourage participation by community organizations in the rehabilitation process of the prisoners was an agreement with American University Law School in 1967. "The pilot program was offered as part of the A. U. Law School curriculum as a three credit-course for two semesters open to second and third year law students. The program was operated under a grant from the Council on Education in Professional Responsibility of the Association of American Law Schools."[4] The law students were permitted to assist inmates and their families with legal matters involving civil cases. The program was officially entitled LAWCOR, and it was the first legal program of its kind to be engaged in by the Department.

The practice of permitting law students to assist the inmates with legal matters was expanded in the 1970s to include Georgetown Law School students who were permitted to enter the institutions to assist inmates with criminal problems. The Young Lawyers of the D.C. Bar Association were also active in helping inmates with legal matters. The legal program provided an avenue through which the inmates could discuss their legal problems and relieve anxiety and tension.

Since the concept of community outreach was relatively new to the Department, and there were no pre-established criteria to follow, guidelines had to be laid down as the need arose. Thus, mistakes were many. One of the most constant dangers encountered by the program was the inmate who was insincere in his desire for self-betterment or enrichment and who used the program as a means of serving his own selfish interests. This was perhaps the greatest threat to the success of the self-help program. On a number of occasions inmates escaped from community excursions and the results were damaging to the program as well as to the accountability of the administration. Another problem was lack of staff to properly supervise and monitor the self-help groups, especially the activities of the inmates participating in community programs on evaluative furloughs. Finally, by 1974, the Department had experienced much criticism of the community outreach program from the police. That adverse criticism prompted Attorney General W.B. Saxbe, on October 1, 1974, to advise the District's Mayor, Walter E. Washington, of his order to modify and greatly curtail the Department's evaluative furlough program, as follows:

> Dear Mayor Washington:
>
> Recent events involving furloughed prisoners in the District of Columbia have caused me great concern. Since these prisoners are by statute committed to my custody, even though they are supervised by the District of Columbia Department of Corrections, I feel it incumbent upon me to take steps to ensure that furloughs are granted only for compelling reasons consistent with the public interest.
>
> Attached is a copy of an order I have signed today modifying the delegation of authority previously given to you to insure that furloughs of prisoners convicted of certain violent offenses are authorized only in exceptional circumstances and only on the personal approval of the Director of the Department of Corrections. I have also provided that notice be given to you prior to a furlough so that you can continue to monitor the operation of this program.
>
> I hope that this will prove adequate to ensure that the safety of the people of the District of Columbia is not jeopardized by the premature release from custody of dangerous

offenders and will make any further action on my part unnecessary.

Sincerely,

/s/ W. B. Saxbe
Attorney General[5]

The Attorney General's order ended the outreach program. Self-help groups within the institution continued but enthusiasm for the program subsided.

SOURCES

[1.] Carr, Jerry, Editor and Chief, Time and Tide, Memo to Mary H. Oakey, April 6, 1977, on file in the D.C. Department of Corrections Museum, Lorton, Virginia.

[2.] Pinkett, Flaxie, et al, "A Report from Shenandoah", undated, on file in the D.C. Department of Corrections Museum, Lorton, Virginia, p. 1.

[3.] Ibid., p. 3.

[4.] LAWCOR (Lawyers in Corrections and Rehabilitation) Project, Initial Grant Application, August 26, 1969, D.C. Department of Corrections Museum, Lorton, Virginia, pp. 1, 2.

[5.] Saxbe, W.B., Attorney General, U.S., Letter to Honorable Walter E. Washington, Mayor, District of Columbia, October 1, 1974, on file in the D.C. Department of Corrections Museum, Lorton, Virginia.

CHAPTER 33

INMATE UNREST AND VIOLENCE IN THE 1970S

On September 27, 1972, just one year after the uprising by the inmate population of the Attica New York prison, an event took place at the Lorton Correctional Complex that proved to be an alternative to prison rioting. On that day the prison population chose to negotiate with prison officials rather than to riot. An editorial in the Septemer 30, 1972 issue of the Washington Post newspaper entitled, "Lorton: New Dialogues and Directions," said of the unprecedented occurrance:

> ...after months of fairly grim news out of Lorton, the news this week from our local reformatory is exceedingly good. In what some observers are terming a 'first' - a number of humanizing reforms were instituted not in the aftermath and as a result of violence, but rather as a result of civilized dialogue...Both the correctional officials, who showed strength and flexibility in the face of a real challenge, and the inmates, who acted with restraint and discipline, are to be congratulated for a rare show of productive civility in a segment of the world which makes that kind of display extraordinarily rare."[1]

As indicated in the foregoing quotation, the situation at Lorton was indeed grim, and tension was high throughout the prison population. The climate was right for mob rule and violence, however, there were no hostages and no destruction of property. Instead, a sit-down strike was called by the inmates and the work stoppage included the entire inmate work force with the exception of those who were employed in the culinary unit, hospital, and heating plant; functions the inmates deemed critical to the operation of the institution. Anger was held in check while a grievance committee of 47 inmates, representing a population of approximately 1600 men, presented a list of grievances and negotiated with prison officials.

In essence, the demands set forth in the grievances were for better medical treatment, better quality of food, better overall visiting facilities and improved representation in disciplinary actions. The negotiations resembled the usual labor-management bargaining session. The administration represented by Kenneth L. Hardy, Director of the Department of Corrections and his top administrative staff on the one side, and on the other, the inmates represented by the grievance committee, an attorney from the Public Defender's Service,

Washington, D.C., and an ex-offender who, at the time, directed a pretrial release program with the courts of Baltimore, Maryland. Each grievance was thoroughly discussed by both sides over an initial five day period in an effort to reach an amicable agreement on the demands. In a lengthy article entitled "Dignity, Suffering and Kenneth Hardy," appearing in the November 26 1972, issue of the Sunday Magazine, "Potomac" of the Washington Post newspaper, William Claiborne described the final day of the negotiations as follows:

> The visitors' hall at the Lorton Reformatory was filled to capacity on September 29, and several hundred blue-denim-clad inmates pressed forward to hear the conclusion of a marathon negotiating session with top D.C. corrections officials.
>
> The leader of a bitter, week-long work strike waited for silence, and then looked directly into the eyes of Kenneth L. Hardy, Director of Washington's troubled penal system.
>
> 'Because you have established your credibility with us, we do not feel the need for continuing the work strike,' he said, and the room suddenly shook with a standing ovation for Hardy.
>
> Visibly moved, Hardy for the moment was able to summon only a few words: 'Men of Lorton, I want to thank you.' Clearly, it was one of the high moments of Hardy's 15 year career in penology.[2]

The Claiborne article continues, but the scene changes to the D.C. Jail and a group of desperate inmates who were intent upon violence and destruction:

> 12 days later, almost to the hour, Hardy again stood before a group of inmates, this time at the D.C. Jail, with a .38 caliber snub-nosed revolver pressed against his head.
>
> This time, the leader of a 'freedom-or-death' rebellion shouted, 'we have come to the conclusion we are going to die. When this is all over, and the other brothers come along, make it better for them.'

> Another inmate, with a knife close to Hardy, yelled through the cellblock window, 'His head is coming off. You better believe that.'[3]

Housed in Cell Block One of the D.C. Jail, the rioting inmates, about 160 in all, held 11 correctional officers and Director Hardy hostage for a period of 22 hours. One of the hostages who chose to remain anonymous, gave an account of the ordeal of October 11-12, 1972, to William Basham, Staff Writer, Evening Star newspaper.

> I learned from another guard that an 'outsider' threw a gun over the fence into the recreation yard from Independence Avenue on Tuesday afternoon, and that's how the prisoners got it. It was a .38 caliber.
>
> I was on the midnight shift when an inmate in a cell on the third floor of Cell Block One began yelling. It was 1:15 a.m. yesterday. The man complained that his cellmate was suffering from a seizure. Two guards checked with their superior, for permission to check, then responded to the cell.
>
> The guards saw one man lying on the floor of the cell. When they entered the cell to examine him, the other prisoner who yelled suddenly drew a .38 caliber, dark, short-barreled gun with black paper wrapped tightly around the handle. The man with the gun demanded keys and they turned them over.
>
> The prisoners went to the fourth floor, taking the guards with them. Once there, they locked several of us in a cell, then headed down the row of cells, letting other prisoners out.
>
> Several inmates who were let out walked past my cell and asked me if there was anything they could do.
>
> Finally, one of the prisoners agreed to go to a nearby phone and quietly call main control. I was just able to tell him to call as he walked by my cell, I couldn't tell him about the gun. I didn't have time, so when the

other guards arrived to help, they were unprotected.

We were all then herded down to the first floor.

I don't know exactly when Hardy came in, but they got him.

The guy with the gun saw an acetylene torch with a tank on the floor...they are working on the cells on the first floor now and no prisoners are kept there now. Then the guy with the gun looks out the window and seen the guard manning the south tower. He fired a shot at the tower and I don't know if that guard knew he was being fired at.

But the gunman's attention again was drawn to the tank. He had everybody back up and he fired at the acetylene tank twice while it was resting against the wall. They hoped the tank would explode and blow a hole in the wall and get into the recreation yard. But nothing happened.

We were herded to the second floor of the cellblock and they locked us up again. Then they forced Hardy to a window, this also is on the second floor, and he shouted something. I don't know what he said.

The prisoners began to discuss how they would leave the jail. They took the rest of us out of our cells again and said how they were going to break out. They said they would use us as shields.

They pushed Hardy through the block door to the rotunda door. That's the door that opens to the visitors' room.

Nobody had the right keys for the rotunda. They got mad and they hit Hardy with pipes on the hands and once on the shoulders, fairly hard, too.

The prisoners told Hardy to order the guard captain in the rotunda to open the door.

> Hardy asked them to open the door but the captain wouldn't do it. They were really mad.
>
> We went back through the block door...they had that gun against Hardy's head the whole time we were in that corridor. They took us back up to the second floor and lined us up against the wall.
>
> At one point, one of the prisoners with a pipe walked up to David R. Michelow, the only white guard hostage, and said 'What're you looking at, Whitey?' He said the prisoner then struck Michelow on the left side of his neck and face.
>
> They put us back in the cells again. I think that's when Shirley Chisholm came in. She talked to them. You know, the majority of the inmates were nice to us. Most of them were permitted to leave the area. I'd say only about 50 were what you call 'hard core.'
>
> Then they agreed that some of the prisoners would go to the courthouse and talk to Judge Bryant. The men who went were searched, but the guy who had the gun passed it to someone else who stayed behind to guard us just before he was searched.
>
> By this time, they had us stripped down to our underwear, but some of the prisoners found some old pants and gave them to us.
>
> But they did more than take our clothes. They took our wallets, all our money and our watches...they can't use regular money, so you know what they did? They took all of the paper money out and tore it up into little pieces and they laughed while they did it. But they did finally feed us.[4]

According to an article by Clare Crawford, Staff Writer for the Evening Star newspaper, dated October 12, 1972, Representative Shirley Chisholm (New York) went to the D.C. Jail about 10:30 a.m. on October 11, 1972, at the request of a prison psychologist who notified her that the prisoners had requested her. The article further reports:

> Mrs. Chisholm is a veteran of prison disturbances. Two years ago, she went into a similar situation in Queens, New York. She said she thought as she walked into the D.C. Jail courtyard yesterday, 'Here I go again.'
>
> Others involved in talks with the inmates credited her last night with being instrumental in persuading the prisoners to negotiate rather than to insist solely on being freed.
>
> One observer...said Mrs. Chisholm 'took charge.' She shouted, 'Listen, if you don't trust me, get a black you do trust!' Please God, let this be no Attica.
>
> * * *
>
> As the prisoners agreed to talk to her, Mrs. Chisholm immediately announced to them there would be no reprisals. Later when they demanded to go to U.S. District Court, she told them:
>
> 'We'll take you to court right now. And we'll guarantee your protection...I promised no reprisals.'
>
> * * *
>
> She said she cried when she listened to the inmates describing their objection to mixing young offenders with hardened convicts.
>
> 'The very touching thing was to have these men, inhumane as a lot of people might think they are, to have them be very concerned about their younger brothers in there with them. And hear them saying, 'We want these juveniles out of here...What are these babies doing in here?
>
> 'There must be some humanity in a man for him to even think about his younger brothers even in terms of his own very desperate plight.' she said.[5]

Six of the rioting inmates were permitted to appear before Judge William B. Bryant of U.S. District Court. An account of that meeting with Judge Bryant is reported by Mary Ann Kuhn,

Staff Writer for the Evening Star newspaper in the October 12, 1972 edition of that publication:

> One by one, the six inmates walked to the bench, some pleading with the Judge to order improvements at the century-old District Jail, others asking that he intervene in their individual court cases.
>
> * * *
>
> And so it went. Each inmate was permitted to talk as long as he wished. And to each one, presiding Judge William B. Bryant...said he could make no promises.
>
> Again and again he explained that he has jurisdiction only over a pending lawsuit filed last year by inmates charging that conditions at the Jail are cruel and inhumane.
>
> The suit, brought by the Public Defender Service on behalf of the inmates awaiting trials, has not had a full hearing. It charges that the overcrowded jail requires inmates to live in conditions worse than minimum housing standards and worse than those faced by convicted criminals.
>
> Bryant held an emergency hearing on allegations of guard brutality last May after a jail disturbance involving 40 prisoners protesting a lack of exercise.
>
> After hearing prisoner testimony that jail officials had failed to get legal and medical aid for some prisoners for as long as three days after the disturbance was quelled in May, Bryant said 'There is no excuse for the jailers' conduct.'
>
> He threatened to hold Jail Superintendent Anderson L. McGruder and others in contempt of court, but after a contempt hearing found them not guilty.
>
> His jurisdiction over that court case was apparently the reason the prisoners appeared before him yesterday outlining their grievances.

* * *

> 'You have made it known to every brother who came before you tonight that you can't do anything,' said Frank Gorham, the last of the six inmates to speak to the Judge. 'What we came for and what we're getting are two different things.'
>
> The Judge declared a recess. When he returned to the courtroom, he announced his decision to take immediate action on many of the inmates' demands. Then he ordered:
>
> Immediate segregation of 16 and 17 year old inmates from the adult jail population.
>
> Inspection of D.C. Jail by Public Defender Service lawyers, to be conducted before Saturday.
>
> Each of the inmates in Cell Block One where the disturbance occurred were to be interviewed by attorneys before midnight. The lawyers were instructed to take the inmates' complaints to court on an emergency basis, if necessary.
>
> * * *
>
> Judge Bryant accelerated disposition of the inmates' lawsuit against jail officials by ordering attorneys on both sides to file final papers in the case within a week or two.[6]

One of the most remarkable features of that explosive situation was the fact that there were no injuries or deaths as a result of the violence that marked the 22 hours the officers and Hardy were held hostage.

During the days immediately following the disturbance of October 11-12, 1972, the administration attempted to carry out the stipulations in Judge Bryant's order. There were allegations by some of the inmates of reprisals by the Jail administration, and tension among the inmate population was still running high, as reported by Michael Satchell, Staff Writer for the <u>Evening Star</u> newspaper, in an article dated October 15, 1972:

> The shock waves of Wednesday's trouble ripped through the Jail again Friday when 88 inmates barricaded themselves in a dormitory after a minor confrontation between an inmate and the Jail superintendent, Anderson McGruder.
>
> During yesterday's tour, numerous inmates stressed that it could happen again... and again.
>
> We took Hardy (D.C. Corrections head Kenneth Hardy) and the other hostages because we had to have the public's attention -- we had to make Congress listen...
>
> 'We're not concerned with minor things now, like the rats and the roaches. We got to have a new jail. Things are so bad here they can't get any worse.'
>
> McGruder, who led yesterday's tour, agreed. And R.B. Byard, senior captain of the corrections force and a 26 year veteran of the Jail, summed up the sentiments of other guards yesterday.
>
> 'Morale? It's as bad among officers as it is among the inmates,' Byard muttered.
>
> * * *
>
> To relieve the overcrowding in the jail, busloads of prisoners -- an exact count was not possible, McGruder said -- were continuing to be transferred to the Lorton Reformatory.
>
> McGruder and the inmates were in agreement on the often-voiced complaints about the length of time inmates spend in the prison while awaiting trial or sentencing, the confusion of many over their legal status, the lawyers who apparently ignore their clients for months at a time, and the living conditions.[7]

The article quoted one of the leaders of the revolt, who was awaiting sentencing on an armed robbery charge, as saying: "We never had any intention of hurting Hardy or those hacks (guards). We love Hardy. He's for us. We got confidence in the man because he's trying to help us. But we had to use him as a tool to focus attention to this place."[8]

Unfortunately, it was impossible to initiate any lasting reforms in the living conditions of the inmates because of the overcrowding and the physical condition of the 100 year old D.C. Jail. It would be four more years before the new detention facility would be ready for occupancy.

Correctional Officer Michael Roy Kirby was murdered in the Central Facility on November 30, 1973. On that day, when he did not report to his post at 3:15, his fellow officers began a search for him. His body was found hidden in a manhole and he had been stabbed numerous times. His murderers were never identified.

Kirby was the second correctional officer to lose his life at the hands of inmates in the 72 year history of the D.C. Penal Institution in Fairfax County, Virginia.

SOURCES

[1.] Editorial, "Lorton: New Dialogues and Directions, Washington Post Newspaper, September 30, 1972, Section B, p. 12.

[2.] Claiborne, William, "Dignity, Suffering and Kenneth Hardy," Potomac Magazine, Washington Post Newspaper, November 26, 1972, p. 11.

[3.] Ibid., p. 11.

[4.] Basham, William, Staff Writer, Evening Star Newspaper, October 2, 1972, Washington, D.C., Clipping file D.C. Department of Corrections Museum, Lorton, Virginia.

[5.] Crawford, Clare, Staff Writer, "Mrs. Chisholm Took Charge," Evening Star Newspaper, October 11, 1972, Section B, p. 1.

[6.] Kuhn, Mary Ann, "Plight of Jail Told Court," Evening Star Newspaper, October 12, 1972, Section 1, p. 1.

[7.] Satchell, Michael, "Inmates at Jail Tell of Reprisals; Officials Deny It," Evening Star Newspaper, October 15, 1972, Section D, pp. 1, 7.

[8.] Ibid., p. 7.

CHAPTER 34

THE FINAL DAYS OF THE OLD D.C. JAIL (1970-1980)

A century had passed since the D.C. Jail received its first occupants in late December 1875, and still it served as the city's holding facility. Over the years, the Jail had undergone several renovations that eventually upgraded its original capacity from 200 inmates to around 600. After its many years of operation, the physical plant was so antiquated that any further attempt to expand its walls would have been far too costly. Although the need for a larger and more modern building had long been apparent, it would not become a reality until 1976. In the meantime, the old jail was forced to accommodate the increase in population that began in 1970, and continued to rise throughout most of the decade. Overcrowded conditions was not a new experience for the Jail's administrators; it had reached that state many times during its years of operation. What was new, however, was the violence and notoriety that accompanied the increase in population during the 1970s.

When the decade of the 1970s began, the daily average population of the D.C. Jail was slightly over 1000. The increase continued, reaching 1122 by the end of 1972. Then in 1974, it declined to 823, which was still well above capacity. In 1975, it again took an upward trend and continued to increase at a steady pace throughout the remainder of the decade. As the inmate population increased, living conditions at the Jail worsened, causing unrest and violence among the inmates, which grew until it erupted in the uprising of October 11, 1972, noted in the previous Chapter. At the time of that uprising, the inmates had a lawsuit pending against the Department (Campbell vs McGruder) in which they alleged that conditions at the Jail constituted "cruel and unusual punishment," and Judge William B. Bryant had ordered the attorneys for each side to settle the issue as soon as possible. The Public Defender Service representing the inmates in the case, accused the city's corporation counsel of deliberately delaying the start of the trial. This was the beginning of litigation involving the inmates of the Jail, the U.S District Court, and the Department that continued over the following five years.

An editorial in the August 28, 1975 edition of the Washington Post noted:

> The city has just taken a few modest steps to relieve the disgraceful overcrowding at the D.C. Jail, a century-old facility. To generate these stirrings, it took, (1) some four years

> of litigation, (2) innumerable responses from city officials about the difficulties of doing much, (3) a court order - four months ago - to end the worst of the squalid conditions, (4) an eventual admission of a top jail official that he never intended to carry out one aspect of this court-required plan for relief, and (5) a renewed call by the judge for compliance. On August 15, assistant corporation counsel...noting that the 'crisis' atmosphere surrounding the lawsuit had brought direct intervention by the mayor's office to locate additional funds, finally informed the judge that the city government had discovered money and the space needed to bring the jail into compliance with the order.
>
> Given the shameful performance over the years, the city administration's latest response demands close monitoring before its effects can be properly assessed. The announced changes do not mean the end of intolerable conditions at the jail. The court order, issued by U.S. District Court Judge William B. Bryant, only requires a minimum of 48 square feet be provided for each inmate awaiting trial.
>
> These, mind you, are men entitled to a presumption of innocence until proven guilty. On August 7, assistant corrections department Director Charles M. Rodgers told the court that more than 150 of these inmates were doubled up in six-by-eight-feet cells. Now, according to city officials, each inmate awaiting trial is being given the minimum living space ordered.
>
> This, however, does not touch the problem of nearly half of the inmates in D.C. Jail who are already convicted or sentenced; many of them are still housed two to a tiny cell...[1]

Another editorial by the <u>Washington Post,</u> appearing Sunday, May 30, 1976, notes the following words by Judge William B. Bryant:

> ...The conditions in which inmates are housed at the D.C. Jail constitutes cruel and unusual punishment in the sense currently contemplated in American society...These are

conditions which turn men into animals...In some cases the punishment they inflict is more painful and enduring than the stocks or the rack, long since discarded as barbaric or primitive.

Imprisonment in conditions such as these absolutely guarantees that the inmates will never be able to return to civilized society, will never feel any stake in playing by its rules. For imprisonment under such conditons, where a man may be stuffed into a tiny cell with another, surrounded by the nocturnal moans or screams of mentally disturbed but untreated fellow inmates, plagued by rats and roaches, sweltering by summer and shivering by winter, unable to maintain significant contact with his family on the outside world, sometimes going for long periods without real exercise or recreation, can only have one message for him: Society does not acknowledge your existence as a fellow human being...

United States District Court Judge William B. Bryant, who wrote this chilling description of conditions at the D.C. Jail, is not known for hyperbole--nor is he given to impetuous outpourings from the bench. It is all the more significant, therefore, that he has run out of all patience with the city government's monumental failure to correct inhumane conditions at the jail. In two stern and well documented opinions issued on Monday--which is to say, after five years of litigaton, a series of clearcut court orders and an endless string of bureaucratic excuses for inaction--Judge Bryant has rightly concluded that nothing short of dramatic action by the court will force compliance by the city government.

The gist of his latest order is this: Either the city meets minimum, specific standards for humane treatment of inmates by dates certain, or it must start releasing some of the men being held on the lowest amounts of bail while awaiting trials. This does not mean that potentially dangerous criminals must be released. It does mean that continued failure of the city to relieve unconscionable and unconstitutional overcrowding will necessitate

> the release of selected inmates who have been locked up the longest simply because they are presumed to be innocent until proven guilty. If that happens, the city administration will have only itself to blame for having, once again, failed to fulfill its obligations.[2]

Throughout the controversy over the conditions in the Jail, the Department and city officials relied on the completion of the new Detention Center to solve the overcrowding in the Jail. However, when the Detention Center was finally ready for occupancy in April 1976, that was not the answer. The new facility's maximum capacity was 960 while the Jail's daily population averaged 1218 for the year 1976. The design of the Detention Center permitted the option of adding cell block modules that would increase its capacity to 1440. Construction of the additional modules would require several years to complete. It was decided that in the interim, the old jail would continue to serve as an annex to the new Detention Center to absorb the overflow of prisoners from that facility.

In 1978, an additional module was completed, and it was used to confine women. The women, who were housed in the Detention Center at 1010 North Capital Street, were transferred to the new module and the North Capital Street institution was closed temporarily until it could be renovated and reopened as a pre-release center.

Construction of the Metro subway in the area in 1978 weakened the foundation of the old jail, and the original building, along with an adjoining wing, had to be torn down. The remaining portion continued to serve as an annex to the new Detention Center until the summer of 1980 when the last inmates were removed and housed in a newly completed module of the Detention Center.

The remaining portion of the old jail stood vacant until 1982 when it was demolished to make way for a new wing to be added to the D.C. General Hospital. The salvageable Seneca sandstone that made up most of the exterior walls was preserved and donated to the Smithsonian Institution. The Castle, one of the Smithsonian's original buildings, was constructed with the same type of sandstone. This is a special stone that was quarried at Poolsville, Maryland around 1873, and is no longer available. The Smithsonian used the stones from the jail to complete a recent special project at the Castle.

In its 105 years of service, the old jail became a landmark in the southeast area of the District. Those of us who were part of the Department during the final years of the D.C. Jail had feelings of ambivalence at seeing the last remains of the old building crumble into rubble. LeRoy Anderson, the Department's Public Relations Officer, put our feelings into words: "It's like an ugly cousin,...In one way we're glad to see it go, but there is nostalgia."[3]

SOURCES

[1.] Washington Post, Editorial, August 28, 1975, "A Bit of Relief at D.C. Jail, Clipping File 1950-1975, D.C. Department of Corrections Museum, Lorton, Virginia.

[2.] Washington Post, Editorial, May 30, 1976, "D.C. Jail: An Intolerable Disgrace," Section B, p. 6.

[3.] Peck, Heather, "Relic of the Past, Old D.C. Jail Becomes Target for Wreckers," The Washington Times, November 9, 1982, Section B, p. 3.

CHAPTER 35

THE NEW DETENTION CENTER

The need for a new facility to replace the old D.C. Jail was apparent long before it was recommended by the President's Commission on Crime in the District of Columbia in its 1966 report to President Lyndon B. Johnson. Despite the urgent need to build a larger, more modern facility it was not until 1970 that funds were approved by Congress to start the planning for such a project, although requests for appropriations had been made in four successive budgets. With approval of funds, the initial planning got underway and groundbreaking ceremonies were held Sepember 6, 1973. Three years later, in April 1976, the first prisoners were transferred from the old D.C. Jail to the new facility, which was officially referred to as "The New Detention Center," or "The Central Detention Center." For the past several years, however, it has been referred to as simply "The Detention Center."

Completely modern in both design and function, the New Detention Center was built at a cost of approximately $30,050,000. The site chosen for the new facility was 19th and Massachusetts Avenue, S.E., adjacent to the D.C. General Hospital. The old D.C. Jail was also located within close proximity to the new facility, and, while the old building was still standing, it provided an opportunity to observe the difference between what is considered modern jail architectural design today with that of a century ago.

The following description of the layout of the Detention Center was taken from a leaflet that was prepared by the Department to be distributed at the official opening ceremonies in April 1976:

> General Layout: The three-story facility, which covers approximately 3.7 acres, is constructed of rose-colored, precast concrete. The building is designed to provide its own external security and has no perimeter fence. There are two wings, or cellblock modules, which extend from a corner of the administration-operations section and form a large outdoor recreation yard. All internal movement is electronically controlled at the central command station and the control rooms located on each floor at the juncture of the cellblock and the administration-operations modules. One security tower is located at the entrance sally-port. The entire building is

air conditioned, contains a central kitchen, laundry and is equipped with both elevators and escalators.

Capacity: Maximum capacity of 960 with the option to add cellblock modules which would bring the capacity to 1440.

Housing: There are 12 cellblocks; 2 per floor in each wing. Eighty individuals per cellblock are housed in 70 square-feet cells with built-in beds, desks and toilet facilities. Over 90% of the rooms have windows. There is a separate cellblock for women. On each floor, there are dining, recreation, and visiting facilities.

Visiting: Visiting is decentralized with facilities on each floor. There are 15 private visiting rooms for lawyers, clergy, etc. All other visiting is non-contact with plexiglass partitions and telephones.

Medical Facilities: There are 24 private rooms in the infirmary, and 6 treatment rooms: dental, minor surgery, radiology, laboratory, physical therapy, and pharmacy.

Education and Recreation: There are 12 classrooms; an inmate library, and 3 multi-purpose rooms, one on each floor. Men utilize the central courtyard for outdoor recreation, and the women have a separate outdoor facility, with areas of 12,100 and 5,300 square feet, respectively.[1]

As noted in the previous chapter, the Department's administrators had relied upon completion of the New Detention Center to relieve the severe overcrowding that existed in the old D.C. Jail. Its opening, however, did not solve the overcrowding problem as anticipated. It became necessary to begin construction of an additional module immediately, and continue the use of a portion of the old Jail in operation as an annex to the Detention Center in order to accommodate the ever increasing number of detainees being processed into the correctional system. When the new module was completed, late in 1978, it was used to house the inmates of the Women's Detention Center located at 1010 North Capital Street, N.W., which was then closed and reopened as a Community Corrections Center by the Department.

A second module was added to the Detention Center and was ready for occupancy in the summer of 1980. The addition of that module increased the capacity of the Detention Center to 1355 which was still not sufficient to meet the needs of the steadily increasing detention population. The daily average combined population (men and women) of the Detention Center for calendar year 1980, was 1377. By the end of 1982, however, the average daily population of the Detention Center had risen to 1903, an increase of twenty-seven percent over 1980, and the outlook for the remainder of the decade appeared to be further escalation of the inmate population of the Detention Center as well as the Department's other penal institutions.

Steps were taken to alleviate the overcrowding in the Detention Center by recovering a portion of the workhouse property from the Department of Human Services, which was still being utilized as an alcoholic rehabilitation center. The buildings were renovated and converted into housing for misdemeanant offenders. Named the Occoquan Facility, the newly converted institution opened in late March 1982, and by the end of that calendar year over 400 inmates were housed there. Plans to recover the remainder of the workhouse property were also underway by 1982 for conversion into housing for medium security inmates in an effort to reduce the severe overcrowding throughout the Department's penal institutions.

SOURCES

[1.] D.C. Department of Corrections, "New Detention Center," Leaflet, February 18, 1976, on file in the D.C. Department of Corrections Museum, Lorton, Virginia.

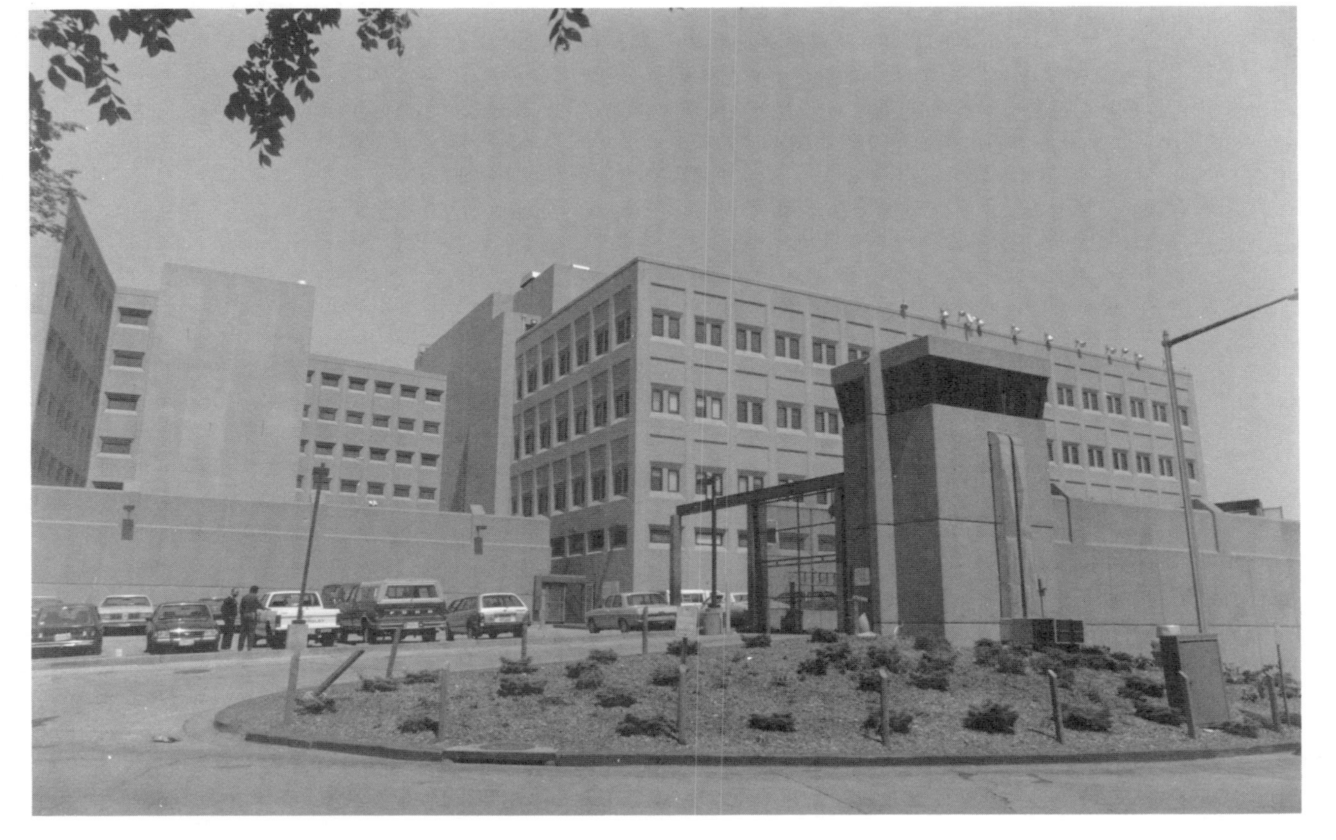

New Detention Center opened 1976. Photograph courtesy D.C. Department of Corrections.

CHAPTER 36

AUTHOR'S NOTE

The foregoing chapters record almost 200 years of the events and changes that have shaped the D.C. penal institutions into the Department of Corrections of today. The philosophies of the past have each contributed to the store of knowledge that will assist in molding the future. While each era reflected a different philosophy, significant events occurring in the past two decades have had great impact on the Department, and have left it in a state of crisis. While the approaches recently attempted as a result of the rehabilitation movement sounded plausible in theory, they did not work when put to practice. Thus, many of the problems the movement set out to solve are still present.

Howard B. Gill, one of America's pioneers in modern penology, has expressed his views on the future of corrections.

> Now we have reached 1970. And what is the wave of the future? Corrections is growing up - maturing - and the profession is seeking ego integrity and concentration. The need for a coordinated crime control is obvious, with its distinction, coordination, and centre of control. Lawyers, judges, law schools and the Bar Associations will increasingly take over at the helm of the correctional system. Prison personnel will be more highly trained.
>
> The community prison concept for treatable prisoners will become dominant. Work release, probation, parole, halfway houses, community sponsors, etc. will dominate—while the old bastiles will recede into the background and be used as reception centers for new and intractable prisoners. Knowledge, derived from the past, such as punishment, doing time, religion, education, industry, medicine, psychiatry and casework will continue to be used but with a new objective and emphasis - reduction of criminality, to be accomplished through selecting and refining these elements as they apply to the individual's criminality. Individual problem solving and acculturation to the community to which a criminal will return, combined with a coordinated crime control system is the wave of the future.[1]

Now that some observers in the field of corrections have denounced the rehabilitation movement as an unworkable failure, the Department, along with many other correctional systems throughout the country, is entering the final two decades of the 20th Century in a state of transition. Still faced with many problems that defy answers, correctional thinking is split on how to find a solution to the age-old problems of overcrowded institutions and recidivism. Those who have abandoned the rehabilitation movement have taken a hard line approach to find the solution by favoring stiffer sentences, abolishing parole, and reinstating the death penalty. While others, still willing to give rehabilatation another chance, would like to continue to explore community-corrections and other rehabilitative programs further. With no clear-cut philosophy to follow, the field of corrections is at a crossroads. With the turn of the 21st Century in sight, there is a need for a new movement; one that will meet the challenge of today's complex problems.

Whether Gill's prognosis will actually be the "wave of the future," or whether the "hard line approach" will prevail remain to be seen. One thing is certain, it will be interesting to see what new philosophy will emerge at the end of this transition period.

SOURCES

[1.] Virginia Caton, Notes from Lectures of Howard B. Gill, 1970. Unpublished. On file in the D.C. Department of Corrections Museum, Lorton, Virginia.

APPENDIX A

A BRIEF OVERVIEW OF THE ORIGIN OF THE FORMS OF GOVERNMENT IN THE DISTRICT OF COLUMBIA

The Act of 1802 that incorporated the City of Washington also provided for a Mayor and a 12-member City Council. The Mayor was appointed annually by the President of the United States, and the Council was originally elected by general ballot. The Act of 1812 amended the Charter of Washington and added an eight-member Board of Aldermen to be elected for a term of two years and permitted the City Council to elect the Mayor. A further reorganization of the government of the City of Washington in 1820 permitted the Mayor, the Board of Aldermen, and the City Council to be elected by ballot. This form of government continued until 1871.

An 1871 Act of Congress provided for a territorial form of government for the District of Columbia consisting of a Governor to be appointed by the President of the United States, with the "advice and consent of the Senate." Section Four of that Act provided for a Secretary of the District of Columbia.

> ...and in case of the death, removal, resignation, disability or absence of the governor from the District, the secretary shall be, and is hereby, authorized and required to execute and perform all the powers and duties of the governor during such vacancy, disability, or absence, or until another governor shall be duly appointed and qualified to fill such vacancy. And in case of offices of governor and secretary shall both become vacant, the powers, duties, and emoluments of the office of governor shall devolve upon the presiding officer of the council, and in case that office shall also be vacant, upon the presiding officer of the house of delegates, until the office shall be filled by a new appointment.[1]

In addition, the Act provided for a legislative assembly, consisting of 11 members, referred to as a council, and a 22-member house of delegates. Section 34 of the Act of 1871 provided for a delegate from the District of Columbia to the House of Representatives. The territorial form of government remained in operation until June 20, 1874, when it was repealed by Congress.

The Temporary Organic Act of 1874 created a new form of government for the District of Columbia which consisted of a three-man commission. The commissioner form of government was permanently adopted by the Organic Act of 1878, and continued to function until 1967.

No provision for franchise was made in the new government and residents of the District of Columbia did not exercise suffrage until 1961.

Reorganization Plan No. 3 (H. Doc. 132), effective August 11, 1967, "...abolished the existing three-commissioner form of government and established in its place a single commissioner and a nine-man council form of government."[2]

The 23rd Amendment to the Constitution, March 29, 1961, gave qualified voters in the District of Columbia the right to vote for electors for President and Vice President, and P.L. 90-292 approved April 22, 1968 provided for a non-voting delegate in the House of Representatives.

The District of Columbia Self-Government Reorganization Act of 1973, also known as "home rule legislation," gave the residents of the District of Columbia the right to manage local affairs and elect their own officials for the first time in 100 years.

SOURCES

[1.] D.C. Code, 1973 edition, Vol. 1, (Washington, D.C.: U.S. Government Printing Office, 1973), p. LIII.

[2.] *Ibid.,* p. LXIII.

APPENDIX B

AN OVERVIEW OF THE BOARD OF INDETERMINATE SENTENCES AND PAROLE

Although the Penal Commission, in 1909, viewed parole as a necessary step in the overall reform of the District's penal institutions, the Act creating the Board of Indeterminate Sentences and Parole was not passed until July 15, 1932. The long delay in carrying out the Penal Commission's recommendation was due in part to skepticism of the general public regarding the concept of parole, and the lack of uniformity of the parole laws in the states where such legislation had already been enacted. In his book, Parole With Honor, published in 1939, Wilbur LaRoe writes of the controversy that surrounded the issue in years between the Penal Commission's recommendation and the passage of the Board of Indeterminate Sentences and Parole legislation:

> That the public does not understand parole is the conviction of all students of the problem. The average layman is afraid of parole, looking upon it as a form of leniency based on sentimentalism. The penologist, on the other hand, regards it as a valuable, if not indispensable, part of our crime prevention machinery. Where there exists side-by-side such widely divergent opinions, there is obviously need for clarification.
>
> This need is created because of the lack of uniformity in parole laws and parole methods in the various jurisdictions. In many of our States, there is no parole system worthy of the name, and the several systems are so widely divergent that, as James V. Bennett well says they have nothing in common except the label 'parole.' In his recent and valuable Survey of Release Procedures, the Attorney General of the United States laments the fact that 'widely varying methods of administering these procedures prevail in the various jurisdictions, State and federal,' and that 'very little is known about them.' In his memorable work, Prisons and Beyond, Sanford Bates exclaims almost in despair: 'How difficult it is to analyze the public attitude toward the whole business of taking care of prisoners and how unreasonable it sometimes seems!'[1]

LaRoe further comments on the early attitudes regarding parole:

> In a metropolitan newspaper there appeared a cartoon picturing the law enforcement agencies sending criminals into the front door of a prison, while at the same time the board of parole opened the back door and let them out. The inference was plain: the realists were making a serious attempt to enforce the law, while the sentimental exponents of parole were nullifying their efforts by extending leniency to offenders. A humorous column in the Washington Times Herald suggests that all prisons be equipped with revolving doors, thus facilitating parole administration.[2]

In the absence of a parole system in the District of Columbia, the Attorney General, in 1918, organized a temporary board to serve the needs of prisoners being released from the Occoquan Workhouse and the Reformatory for Men at Lorton. The Board consisted of the General Superintendent of the District's penal institutions and the Assistant Superintendent of the Reformatory. This early Parole Board worked in conjunction with the Federal Parole Board.

An account of the operation of that temporary Parole Board in the District is detailed in an article appearing in the February 28, 1928 edition of the Star newspaper:

> The parole system--a salient feature of all Federal prisons--is in force at the District Reformatory and Workhouse. It provides that any prisoner who has a model-conduct record during the first one-third of his sentence is eligible for parole. He is summoned before a special parole board, and if all conditions are satisfactory for his release, he is liberated as a 'parole man' for the remainder of is term. In the case of a 10-year man this means that he can be released as a result of good behavior after he has served three years and four months.
>
> The former prisoner is given a good suit of clothes and $5 in cash, and a position is obtained for him. Subsequently he reports once a month to Supt. Tawse at the reformatory and tells how much money he is earning, how much he is saving, how he spends his spare time and so

> on. A visiting officer is apt to call at his place of employment or where he lives at any time, to check up on his statements.
>
> Even when the 'parolees' have served their full time, representatives of the reformatory and workhouse still keep tab on them to see that they follow the straight and narrow path of honesty and righteousness.
>
> As a rule from 40 to 50 men annually are paroled from the reformatory and a record of less than 10 percent violations of parole has been made since the inception of the honor system at Lorton. Several hundred skilled workmen are now earning monthly pay checks in various parts of the District from their labor as plumbers, masons, bricklayers, steamfitters, electricians, cooks, bakers, barbers, carpenters, foundrymen, tailors, gardners and farmers who learned their trades at Lorton.[3]

The Federal Parole Board had been established in 1910 by an Act that authorized parole of prisoners sentenced to terms of one year or more, after having served one third of their sentences, and originally functioned as follows:

> ...The power to grant and revoke parole was in the hands of boards of parole established at the several federal penitentiaries and prisons. The board of parole at each institution was composed of the superintendent of prisons in the Department of Justice and the warden and physician of the particular penitentiary. In each institution there was a parole officer whose duty it was to supervise parolees and to perform such other duties as the board might designate. No parole was effective until approved by the Attorney General. In 1913 the parole law was amended so as to make prisoners serving a life term eligible for parole after serving fifteen years.
>
> In 1930 a radical change was made whereby a single board of parole was established in the Department of Justice, to be composed of three members appointed by the Attorney General. This board was given power to grant paroles without approval by the Attorney General. In order to

> avoid employing a large number of parole officers in addition to the staff of probation officers already employed by the federal government, provision was made for supervision of parolee by the probation officers of the federal courts, who were required by the statute to 'perform such duties with respect to persons on parole as the Attorney General shall request.[4]

The Bill to establish a Board of Indeterminate Sentences and Parole for the District of Columbia was prepared by a special committee and written by Thomas P. Littlepage. Some of the local organizations and individuals behind the move to gain public support for the creation of the Board were the Department of Public Welfare, the Federation of Women's Clubs, Assistant U.S. Attorney M. Pearl McCall, Lieutenant Nina VanWinkle, head of the Women's Bureau of the Police Department, Michael M. Doyle, former judge of Police Court and M.M. Barnard of the D.C. Penal Institutions.

When the Act (P.L. 287, 72nd Congress) creating the Board of Indeterminate Sentences and Parole was finally passed in 1932, the indeterminate sentence system permitted the court to impose the maximum sentence for an offense with parole eligibility after one-fifth of the maximum time was served. In 1940, however, the law was amended to permit eligibility for parole after service of one-third of the maximum sentence.

The first Parole Board consisted of three members, appointed by the D.C. Commissioners, who served without compensation. They were: Isaac Gans, prominent Washington businessman who was appointed to a term of seven years; Dr. L.B.T. Johnson, psychiatrist, who specialized in troubled children appointed to a term of five years; and Dr. Emmett J. Scott, secretary-treasurer of Howard University, to a term of three years. Other early Parole Board members were Frank Jelliff, Leo Rover, and Wilber LaRoe, all of whom did much to shape Parole in the District of Columbia.

In the beginning the Parole Board had a number of obstacles to overcome. LaRoe writing in <u>Parole With Honor,</u> comments on the problems confronting the Board in the early years:

> The District of Columbia has almost an ideal parole system on paper, but its practical administration leaves much to be desired. Nearly half the prisoners fail to apply for parole, and less than 40 percent of the applications filed are granted. The board

members are busy men who can devote only a small portion of their time to parole work. The parole staff is on the Reformatory payroll. Thus the board is independent but it has no staff or budget of its own, a plainly undesireable situation. Rehabilatation is handicapped by unnecessary publicity given to parole applications.[5]

The Bureau of Rehabilitation, established in 1930, played a vital role in the early days of parole in the District. At the time the Parole Board was established, the District's penal institutions had no inmate classification system, "as the staff of the Parole Board in the early days was inadequate, the staff of the Bureau of Rehabilitation was asked by the Parole Board to give assistance in supplying social information for all persons in D.C. institutions eligible for parole consideration..." It is noted that a classification system was established in the District's institutions in 1937.

In addition to supervision of parolees, the Parole Board was responsible for the manditory good-time releasees who required supervision until their maximum terms expired. The good time releases posed a serious problem for the parole officers, since many times they were confirmed criminals who were poor risks and did not qualify for parole. Consequently, their recidivism rates were quite high. The staff of parole officers was not sufficient to give good time releasees adequate supervision and when employment was not immediately available, they would revert to crime soon after their release from the institution. The economic depression of the 1930's also contributed to unemployment for releasees.

Shortly after the Board of Indeterminate Sentences and Parole was established, an institutional parole office was placed in the Reformatory for Men, at Lorton, to counsel applicants for parole and to prepare hearing material for the Parole Board. It remained in operation until 1967. All parole hearings, including the Jail, Workhouse, and Women's Division, were held at the Reformatory for Men in a special board room. In 1937 Jacob B. Garrott was assigned as Institutional Parole Officer and served in that capacity until his retirement in 1967. During his thirty-year career as the Institutional Parole Officer, Garrott developed an efficient system of collecting and preparing hearing material for the Parole Board and devised a method of collecting statistics for use in reporting the incidence of recidivism. In the early years, inmates of the Men's Reformatory were employed to perform clerical duties in the Institutional Parole Office, including assisting prisoners with completing the necessary forms needed to apply for parole.

Eventually, the inmates were replaced by three paid Parole Officers and a clerical staff.

An amendment to the Parole Law in 1947 created a three-man Parole Board in which one member served on a full-time basis, with pay, and was designated by the Commissioners as Parole Executive. The other two members continued to serve without compensation, and one was chosen to function as Chairman of the Board.

From the time of its origin in 1932 until 1967, the District's Parole Board maintained a conservative level in granting parole. The percentage of grants per year averaged 30 to 40 percent of the applications. When an application for parole was denied the applicant could apply for a rehearing at some future date. In the beginning the Parole Board would determine the date of the rehearing. Later, however, this practice was discontinued and a rehearing date was set by law, based on the length of time the applicant was serving.

By 1950, the Parole Board's staff had increased, but it was still not large enough to be effective. The number of field officers had reached six and the caseload of each averaged 70 to 90 parolees and good time releasees, the latter comprising about 65 percent of the number under supervision.

The Karrick Committee (see Chapter 21) in 1957, investigating the District's prisons, probation, and parole made the following recommendations to improve the parole system in the District:

1. That a full-time three-member parole board be created and that salaries of $15,000 per year for the chairman and $14,000 for the other two members be provided.

2. That the law be amended to empower the parole board to discharge persons from parole prior to the expiration of their sentences.

3. That provision be made for additional staff as requested by the chairman of the parole board.

4. That to avoid any possible confusion in administrative responsibility that the title of parole executive be dropped from one of the members of the parole board and

> that the full-time board consist of a chairman and two members.[6]

In drawing its conclusions, the Karrick Committee stated:

> The Committee is convinced that while we have excellent probation and parole programs, a somewhat larger percentage of our crime offenders can be safely released into the community, if we provide adequate facilities for their selection and supervision. To be sure, both our overcrowded correctional institutions and conservative probation and parole rates may be traced in some degree to the inadequacy of existing supervision facilities.[7]

The only recommendation of the Karrick Committee that was carried out immediately was the provision for additional staff for the Parole Board. In 1959, the Board received authority to increase its staff, which in turn reduced the caseload of each parole officer to around 65 releasees.

It was not until 1967 that major changes occurred in the organizational structure of the Parole Board, as a result of recommendations made by the President's Commission on Crime in the District of Columbia. In that year, the Parole Officers were placed under the Department of Corrections, the Institutional Parole Office was abolished, and the Board was reorganized to include three full-time paid members.

Development of halfway houses and work release in the late 1960's and 1970's provided the Parole Board with additional resources. Now, while still under the jurisdiction of the Department of Corrections, the releasee could live and work in the community in a structured environment for a trial period of several months before his parole date. The trial period not only made transition to the community smoother for the releasee, but it also gave the Board an opportunity to observe his progress during that period and to use the information in its decision to grant or deny parole.

In 1975, Mayor Walter E. Washington named the first woman to the Board with the appointment of Joan A. Burt, a practicing attorney in the District, to a term of six years. At the same time, he appointed the Reverend H. Albion Ferrell as Chairman of the Board and Carl Coleman as the third member.

Since 1967, the Parole Board has been more liberal in granting parole. In contrast to the earlier days of the Parole

Board when the grants averaged about 30 or 40 percent of the applications, today's grants are about 50%. The number of Parole Officers has increased from six in 1950 to about 36 in 1982.

SOURCES

[1.] LaRoe, Wilbur, Jr. Parole With Honor. Copyright 1937, (Princeton, N.J.: Princeton University Press), excerpt reprinted with permission of Princeton University Press, p. Author's note.

[2.] Ibid.

[3.] Star Newspaper, February 28, 1928, Clipping File, Washingtoniana Room, Martin Luther King Library, Washington, D.C.

[4.] LaRoe, p. 58.

[5.] Ibid., p. 240.

[6.] Karrick, David B., Chairman, et. al., "Prisons, Probation and Parole in the District of Columbia," April 1957, Bureau of Rehabilitation, Washington, D.C., pp. 160-161.

[7.] Ibid., p. 164.

APPENDIX C

ACQUISITIONS OF LAND BY THE UNITED STATES GOVERNMENT KNOWN AS THE "LORTON RESERVATION"

1. Workhouse Tract
   Date Acquired: March 19, 1910
   Grantee: United States Government
   Grantor: George Selecman, et al.
   Date Recorded: April 1, 1910
   Deed Book: F-7, pages 212-218
   Appropriation Act Authorizing Purchase: Public Law 303
   Acreage Acquired: 1,154.70
   Consideration: $28,648.78
   Jurisdiction: Exclusive U.S.

2. Reformatory
   Date Acquired: April 10, 1913
   Grantee: United States Government
   Grantor: Jarvis, et al.
   Date Recorded: April 7, 1914
   Deed Book: S-7, pages 497-505
   Appropriation Act Authorizing Purchase: Act of Congress March 4, 1913
   Acreage Acquired: 1388.58
   Consideration: $29,203.90
   Jurisdiction: Joint U.S. and Fairfax County.

3. Reformatory
   Date Acquired: February 5, 1919
   Grantee: United States Government
   Grantor: Totten, et al.
   Date Recorded: March 28, 1921
   Deed Book: T-8, pages 410-414
   Appropriation Act Authorizing Purchase: Act of Congress March 4, 1913
   Acreage Acquired: 10.09
   Consideration: $490.05
   Jurisdiction: Joint U.S. and Fairfax County.

4. Reformatory
   Date Acquired: August 17, 1928
   Grantee: United States Government
   Grantor: Davis
   Date Recorded: August 21, 1928
   Deed Book: H-10, pages 569-570
   Acreage Acquired: 8.50
   Consideration: $2,500
   Jurisdiction: Joint U.S. and Fairfax County.

5. Reformatory
   Date Acquired: June 8, 1931
   Grantee: United States Government
   Grantor: Richmond Land Corporation
   Date Recorded: June 22, 1931
   Deed Book: X-10, pages 323-325
   Acreage Acquired: 1.5
   Consideration: $150.00
   Jurisdiction: Joint U.S. and Fairfax County.

6. Reformatory
   Date Acquired: August 22, 1934
   Grantee: United States Government
   Grantor: Wright
   Date Recorded: August 23, 1934
   Deed Book: O-11, page 482
   Acreage Acquired: 12.599
   Consideration: $2,200.00
   Jurisdiction: Joint U.S. and Fairfax County.

7. Lorton
   Date Acquired: August 3, 1944
   Grantee: United States Government
   Grantor: Myrtle V. Buckles (McElroy Tract) et al.
   Date Recorded: August 11, 1944
   Deed Book: Book 434, pages 36-40, Map 2926
   Appropriation Act Authorizing Purchase: (D.C. Appropriation Act 1943) amended July 1, 1943 (D.C. Appropriation Act 1944)
   Acreage: 401.79463
   Consideration: $24,910.98
   Jurisdiction: Exclusive Fairfax County

8. Lorton
   Date Acquired: July 11, 1951
   Grantee: United States Government
   Grantor: Violett Williamson (Violet Tract)
   Date Recorded: July 11, 1951
   Deed Book: Book 885, pages 302-303
   Appropriation Act Authorizing Purchase: Public Law 616, 81st Congress
   Acreage: 20.624
   Consideration: $3,350.00
   Jurisdiction: Exclusive Fairfax County

9. Reformatory
   Date Acquired: December 2, 1953
   Grantee: United States Government
   Grantor: Springman, Joseph M. & Annie O.
   Date Recorded: January 14, 1959

Deed Book: Book 1147, page 89-90
Appropriation Act Authorizing Purchase: Public Law 453
Acreage: 1.4753
Consideration: $1,420.00
Jurisdiction: Exclusive Fairfax County.

INDEX